APPLIED
IMPRESSION
MANAGEMENT

OTHER RECENT VOLUMES IN THE SAGE FOCUS EDITIONS

APPLIED IMPRESSION MANAGEMENT

How Image-Making Affects Managerial Decisions

Robert A. Giacalone
Paul Rosenfeld
editors

SAGE PUBLICATIONS
The International Professional Publishers
Newbury Park   London   New Delhi

For information address:

SAGE Publications, Inc.
2455 Teller Road
Newbury Park, California 91320

SAGE Publications Ltd.
6 Bonhill Street
London EC2A 4PU
United Kingdom

SAGE Publications India Pvt. Ltd.
M-32 Market
Greater Kailash I
New Delhi 110 048 India

Printed in the United States of America

Library of Congress Cataloging-in-Publication Data

Applied impression management : how image-making affects managerial
    decisions / Robert A. Giacalone, Paul Rosenfeld, editors.
        p. cm.—(Sage focus editions : 135)
    Includes bibliographical references and index.
    ISBN 0-8039-3994-9.—ISBN 0-8039-3995-7 (pbk.)
    1. Management—Psychological aspects. 2. Self-presentation.
3. Organizational behavior. 4. Psychology, Industrial.
I. Giacalone, Robert A. II. Rosenfeld, Paul.
HD38.A664 1991
658'.001'9—dc20   91-20160
                                                                  CIP

FIRST PRINTING, 1991

Sage Production Editor: Judith L. Hunter

Contents

Part VI. Impression Management: Looking to the Future

Acknowledgments

The publication of this volume represents for us the realization of another "impossible dream" that began as one of many "what if" sessions when we were graduate students at the State University of New York at Albany during the 1970s and early 1980s. In those days, the idea that the impression management theory we were investigating in the social psychology laboratory could be applied to organizational settings was met with skepticism, doubt, and, among the less sensitive, some snickers. Now, with the appearance of this our second book devoted to the subject, we have certainly convinced ourselves of the viability of organizational impression management; we hope we have convinced a few of the doubting Thomases as well.

Work on this book has allowed two old graduate school buddies to maintain their cross-country friendship and has given them a professional opportunity to nurture a close personal relationship. This project has been a success in no small part because we are also the best of friends.

As in past works, we wish to thank our families, friends, and colleagues for their love, support, encouragement, and tolerance. In particular, our sincerest thanks to our parents: Frank and Theresa Giacalone and Abraham and Judes Rosenfeld. We are also greatly indebted to Karen, Elizabeth, and Andrew Giacalone and a great librarian, Mary Sellen. Also, we wish to acknowledge the friendship and assistance of Steve Knouse, Catherine

Riordan, Marie Thomas, Kwok-Choi Wan, Patricia Thomas, Hinda G. Pollard, Jim Goodwin, Jack E. Edwards, David Alderton, Cliff Poole, John Rose, Edith Goldberg, Jim Mancuso, Jerry Suls, Brock Kilbourne, Dawn Storr, Farrell Scott Malkis, and the Shanske family.

It is impossible to imagine a book on impression management that does not acknowledge the contributions of Barry Schlenker's research and seminal book, *Impression Management*, as well as Mark Snyder's ground-breaking research on self-monitoring. Indeed, as graduate students we were greatly influenced by the work of these two "founding fathers" of impression management research, and we wish to thank them for empowering us with the theoretical and empirical foundations we needed for our work exploring impression management's application to organizational settings.

Finally, we are pleased to dedicate this, our second book, to those who first taught us to manage our impressions: our teachers, mentors (Dick T. for Bob, Jim T. for Paul), and colleagues at the State University of New York at Albany.

—Robert A. Giacalone, Ph.D.
Richmond, Virginia
—Paul Rosenfeld, Ph.D.
San Diego, California

PART I

Applying Impression Management to Organizations: An Orientation

1

From Extreme to Mainstream

Applied Impression Management in Organizations

PAUL ROSENFELD
ROBERT A. GIACALONE

The true test of a brilliant theory [is] what first is thought to be wrong is later shown to be obvious.

(Assar Lindbeck, Nobel Prize Committee)

Impression management phenomena . . . have passed from being artifactual contaminants to assuming independent status in the discipline.

(Alexander & Rudd, 1981, p. 83)

It is myopic to argue that self-presentation primarily involves pretense, deception, or illegitimacy. Self-presentation involves packaging desired self-identifications so that audiences draw a preferred conclusion. . . . There is nothing nefarious, superficial, or Machiavellian about packaging. Just as a textbook writer must edit information to present it in a readable, concise fashion, so must people edit information about themselves in everyday life to provide the "best" description possible.

(Schlenker & Weigold, 1990, p. 827)

AUTHORS' NOTE: The opinions expressed herein are those of the authors. They are not official and do not represent the views of the Navy Department.

Self-presentation is an ineluctable fact of modern life in general and of organizational life in particular, and often may be an excellent way for people to achieve their goals.

(Baumeister, 1989, p. 59)

A Tale of Two Students

Not long ago, two students gave class presentations on one of our favorite topics: impression management in the organization. After each had finished reviewing the key studies (taking care to emphasize our own work disproportionately), they were both required to indicate how they would use the research in their future careers as industrial/organizational psychologists. Their responses sounded as if they had been orchestrated by someone trying to market the current volume. One student described how he would attempt to train managers to recognize and react to the various impression management strategies that employees were using against them at work. The other student described how she planned to develop a training package to help employees become more skilled at impression management so that they might better succeed in the workplace.

Remarkably, no one in a graduate class of future psychologists thought either of the proposals outlandish, "Machiavellian," overly deceptive, unethical, or excessively cynical. They intuitively saw what organizational scientists and practitioners have increasingly recognized over the past decade: that "the maintenance of images and the control of outcomes are important matters in the world of organizations" (Higgins & Snyder, 1989, p. 73).

The Three Extremes of Impression Management Theory

That impression management (also referred to as *self-presentation*) is a ubiquitous feature of social and organizational life may seem obvious, but, as our opening quotes indicate, the obvious is not always considered correct. In fact, impression management has undergone a slow and at times painful transformation from being an "extreme" to its current status as a "mainstream" theory of organizational behavior and practice.

Chroniclers of impression management theory point to the work of sociologist Erving Goffman (1959) as stimulating modern-day interest in impression management (e.g., Leary & Kowalski, 1990; Tedeschi, Lindskold, & Rosenfeld, 1985, chap. 3). However, though Goffman's notion that concern for appearances is a vital component of social relations was path-breaking, its impact among empirically based social scientists was not at all immediate. Indeed, to many in experimental social psychology, where Goffman's theory was first popularized, impression management effects were in the "extreme"; they were artifacts, or instances of "evaluation apprehension" (Rosenberg, 1965) that threatened the validity of laboratory experiments. As Tedeschi and Rosenfeld (1981) note, "Evaluation apprehension was considered to be a contaminant that produced artifactual findings and as a factor that should be eliminated from the experimental setting" (p. 152).

A decade ago, while we were graduate students at the State University of New York at Albany, our colleague Jim Tedeschi (1981) edited a book that "mainstreamed" impression management theory as an explanatory mechanism for much of laboratory social psychology. Earlier, Tedeschi and Svenn Lindskold's (1976) graduate textbook had rather ambitiously attempted to reinterpret virtually the entire social psychological literature in terms of impression management. According to Baumeister (1986), the 1970s challenges by these and other impression management researchers to much of contemporary social psychology may explain why the mainstream was slow to accept the view from the impression management extreme:

> Many psychologists had spent their lives and staked their careers on theories about inner motives. They were less than delighted to be told that their theories were egregiously mistaken. . . . They could not dismiss self-presentation, but they did not have to like it. Self-presentation grew up as an all-purpose alternative explanation for many other theories. It was greeted and treated like a rude bastard relative at a family gathering. (p. vi)

Although later authors sought to limit the range of phenomena explained by impression management theory (e.g., Baumeister & Tice, 1984; Paulhus, 1982; Tetlock & Manstead, 1985), certainly (as the opening quote from Alexander and Rudd indicates) impression management theory had, by the early 1980s, become part of the mainstream social psychological establishment. Leary and Kowalski's (1990) recent authoritative integration of the impression management literature notes this movement from the sidelines to the establishment's playing field:

Despite a steady stream during the 1960s and 1970s, impression management remained a relatively peripheral topic in social and personality psychology, leading some to characterize the impression management approach as more of a guiding model than a theory of interpersonal behavior. . . . More recently, however, impression management has attracted increased attention as a fundamental interpersonal process. (p. 35)

Is It Real or Is It Memorex?

A man may not always be what he appears to be, but what he appears to be is always a significant part of what he is. (Dr. Willard Gaylin)

Although established, impression management theory still retained a sense of being "extreme" in another way. That is, impression management was, for many people, synonymous with insincere, deceptive, manipulative, Machiavellian actions. People engaged in impression management, but they didn't really believe it; they were simply saying and doing things to curry favor in the eyes of significant audiences. One of us expressed this view in describing attitude change that occurs in cognitive dissonance experiments: "Attitude change occurring in the forced compliance situation represents an uninternalized, temporary, feigned shift in attitudes that has the purpose of mending a spoiled identity" (Tedeschi & Rosenfeld, 1981, p. 158).

This "extreme" view of impression management has gradually been modified during the last decade, and, as Schlenker and Weigold's opening quote indicates, the current view among most theorists is that impression management behaviors are often sincere components of mainstream social behavior. Tetlock and Manstead (1985) describe this movement from fiction to fact:

Although some writers have used the term *impression management* to refer to the self-conscious deception of others (e.g., Gaes, Kalle, & Tedeschi, 1978) there is no compelling psychological reason why impression management must be either duplicitous or under conscious control. Impression management may be the product of highly overlearned habits or scripts, the original functions of which people have long forgotten. (pp. 61-62)

Organizational Impression Management:
Beyond Gordon Gecko

General Motors has no bad years, only good years and better years. (Harlow H. Curtice)

Even the frankest and bravest of subordinates do not talk with their boss the same way they talk with colleagues. (Robert Greenleaf)

If I thought the church was selling its soul to Madison Avenue, I'd be very upset. That is not the case. We're just trying to do a better job of getting our message out. (John W. Gouldrick, quoted in the *Los Angeles Times*, explaining the decision by the National Conference of Catholic Bishops to spend $5 million to publicize its antiabortion message; Horovitz & Biederman, 1990, p. A33)

Surely, one would think that with impression management becoming popular in the static environment of the social psychological laboratory, it would enjoy at least as much popularity in the organizational literature. However, in 1979, when, as graduate students, we first thought that impression management theory might be applicable to organizational settings ("impression management" and "management" did sound similar), most people we talked to felt the idea was not worth pursuing. Indeed, they might have had a point, because there were few organizational investigations of impression management before the early 1980s (e.g., Fletcher, 1979; Wortman & Linsenmeier, 1977). Not until the mid-1980s did the organizational impression management perspective begin to gain an identity theoretically distinct from the earlier literature on organizational politics (e.g., Mayes & Allen, 1977; Pettigrew, 1973; Schein, 1977; Tushman, 1977) and become conceptually entrenched in the organizational research arena (e.g., Giacalone, 1985; Giacalone & Rosenfeld, 1986, 1987; Ralston, 1985; Tedeschi & Melburg, 1984; Zerbe & Paulhus, 1987). It is only recently that the organizational impression management literature has expanded into the full range of organizational areas, including topics such as employment and selection interviews (Fletcher, 1990; Gilmore & Ferris, 1989), business ethics (Konovsky & Jaster, 1989; Payne & Giacalone, 1990), computer-based organizational surveys (Lautenschlager & Flaherty, 1990; Rosenfeld et al., in press), arbitration (Giacalone & Pollard, 1989), and marketing (Crane, 1989), to name just a few.

Part of the reason for this lack of interest in organizational applications of impression management is that until recently impression management has suffered from an "extreme" image among organizational behaviorists and practitioners. While few doubted that impression management was occurring all the time in organizations, there was scant interest in discussing it at the researcher or practitioner level, perhaps because it was considered too extreme to be respectable. Thus it remained the domain of the pop management literature (e.g., Korda, 1975; Molloy, 1978; Ringer, 1976) and of caricatures in popular culture such as the manipulative stock mogul Gordon Gecko in the movie *Wall Street* or Police Chief Daniels on TV's classic *Hill Street Blues.*

But while the caricatures of film and television often have limited impact on organizational reality, recent history has shown that disdain for the impact of impression management can have serious consequences. In October 1990, President George Bush was widely criticized for failing to show consistent leadership during a budget battle with the U.S. Congress. An article in the *New York Times* placed part of Bush's perceived failure on the president's dislike of his predecessor Ronald Reagan's excessive use of impression management techniques:

> But Mr. Bush also had secret disdain for Mr. Reagan's White House. He was appalled by the manner in which the men around the Gipper treated the President like a prop and the White House like a set at M-G-M. He was repelled by the way the Reagan handlers . . . turned politics into an extension of public relations, exercising iron control over the theme of the day, the definition of the story, the coordination of sound bites and pictures, the concentration on a few simple goals in speeches. As President, Mr. Bush rejected the public relations skills that Ronald Reagan had used so effectively, believing that it showed more integrity to run things in an ad hoc, definitely unvarnished way. But the chaos and confusion shrouding the White House during the budget debacle has raised questions . . . about the efficacy of the Bush style. . . . Is it smart to resist the notion—as President Bush does—that perception can quickly harden into reality? (Dowd, 1990, p. 1)

Given our previous experience with impression management theory, we had no disdain for its use or doubts about its viability in organizational research and practice. Having been weaned on laboratory social psychology, we had already seen impression management go from "the outhouse to the penthouse" and saw no reason we couldn't mainstream organizational impression management as well. Our initial attempt, now several years old (see Giacalone & Rosenfeld, 1989), established that impression management could be viewed as a "normal" part of doing organizational business, and the "extremists"—the Geckos and the Chief Danielses—were just that: a distortion of a universal characteristic of organizations rather than an extreme pattern of action.

The Present Volume

This book represents another push toward mainstreaming impression management. When we undertook compilation of the volume, it was our intention to apply impression management theory and research, for the first time, at the practitioner level. Indeed, if impression management is so ubiquitous in organizational life, management practitioners must certainly be in need of advice that organizational researchers can provide.

The results, contained in the chapters that follow, far exceeded even our usually overoptimistic expectations. The authors, many of them well known in the organizational behavior and management literature, attest that impression management is a normal and vital component of organizational functioning. Indeed, with coverage in the chapters that follow of subjects as diverse as organizational communication, conformity, justice, performance appraisal, culture, gender, conflict, and negotiation, it seems fair to say that impression management now provides explanatory power for a wide range of topics across the organizational sciences.

Coming Full Circle

Finally, this volume also affords an opportunity for impression management theory to come full circle—from the mainstream back to the extreme. In the next chapter, Dov Eden offers a brilliant analysis of how two former research "extremes"—impression management and self-fulfilling prophecy—can be utilized by managers to increase productivity:

> Both impression management and self-fulfilling prophecy were initially conceived as being triggered by something false: SFP by an incorrect expectation and IM by a distorted image an individual is trying to project in completing a test or questionnaire. . . . Both conceptualizations evolved into more generalized models of social influence involving both positive and negative, beneficial and harmful, productive and counterproductive outcomes.

It is our firm hope that the chapters contained in *Applied Impression Management* remove any lingering doubts about impression management as a viable, mainstream model for organizational researchers and practitioners. In fact, the wealth of anecdotal and research evidence in this volume suggests that it may be those who neglect the importance of impression management in the daily functioning of organizations who themselves may be in the extreme.

References

Alexander, C. N., & Rudd, J. (1981). Situated identities and response variables. In J. T. Tedeschi (Ed.), *Impression management theory and social psychological research* (pp. 83-103). New York: Academic Press.

Baumeister, R. F. (Ed.). (1986). *Public self and private self.* New York: Springer-Verlag.

Baumeister, R. F. (1989). Motives and costs of self-presentation in organizations. In R. A. Giacalone & P. Rosenfeld (Eds.), *Impression management in the organization* (pp. 57-71). Hillsdale, NJ: Lawrence Erlbaum.

Baumeister, R. F., & Tice, D. M. (1984). Role of self-presentation and choice in cognitive dissonance under forced compliance: Necessary or sufficient causes? *Journal of Personality and Social Psychology, 46,* 5-13.

Crane, F. G. (1989). A practical guide to professional services marketing. *Journal of Professional Services Marketing, 5,* 3-15.

Dowd, M. (1990, October 21). George Bush's communication breakdown on the budget. *New York Times,* sec. 4, pp. 1, 5.

Fletcher, C. (1979). Candidates' beliefs and self-presentation strategies in selection interviews. *Personnel Review, 10,* 14-17.

Fletcher, C. (1990). The relationship between candidate personality, self-presentation strategies, and interviewer assessments in selection interviews: An empirical study. *Human Relations, 43,* 739-749.

Gaes, G. G., Kalle, R. J., & Tedeschi, J. T. (1978). Impression management in the forced compliance paradigm: Two studies using the bogus pipeline. *Journal of Experimental Social Psychology, 14,* 493-510.

Giacalone, R. A. (1985). On slipping when you thought you had put your best foot forward: Self-promotion, self-destruction, and entitlements. *Group & Organization Studies, 10,* 61-80.

Giacalone, R. A., & Pollard, H. G. (1989). Comparative effectiveness of impression management tactics on the recommendation of grievant punishment: An exploratory investigation. *Forensic Reports, 2,* 147-160

Giacalone, R. A., & Rosenfeld, P. (1986). Self-presentation and self-promotion in an organizational setting. *Journal of Social Psychology, 126,* 321-326.

Giacalone, R. A., & Rosenfeld, P. (1987). Justifications and procedures for implementing institutional review boards in business organizations. *Journal of Business Ethics, 6,* 5-17.

Giacalone, R. A., & Rosenfeld, P. (Eds.). (1989). *Impression management in the organization.* Hillsdale, NJ: Lawrence Erlbaum.

Gilmore, D. C., & Ferris, G. R. (1989). The effects of applicant impression management tactics on interviewer judgments. *Journal of Management, 15,* 557-564.

Goffman, E. (1959). *The presentation of self in everyday life.* Garden City, NY: Doubleday.

Higgins, R. L., & Snyder, C. R. (1989). The business of excuses. In R. A. Giacalone Rosenfeld (Eds.), *Impression management in the organization* (pp. 73-85). Hillsdale, N Lawrence Erlbaum.

Horovitz, B., & Biederman, P. W. (1990, September 23). Personal PR: Newest "necessity." *Los Angeles Times*, pp. A1, A33.

Konovsky, M. A., & Jaster, F. (1989). "Blaming the victim" and other ways business men and women account for questionable behavior. *Journal of Business Ethics, 8*, 391-398.

Korda, M. (1975). *Power! How to get it, how to use it*. New York: Ballantine.

Lautenschlager, G. J., & Flaherty, V. L. (1990). Computer administration of questions: More desirable or more social desirability? *Journal of Applied Psychology, 75*, 310-314.

Leary, M. R., & Kowalski, R. M. (1990). Impression management: A literature review and two-component model. *Psychological Bulletin, 107*, 34-47.

Mayes, B. T., & Allen, R. W. (1977). Toward a definition of organizational politics. *Academy of Management Review, 2*, 672-678.

Molloy, J. T. (1978). *Dress for success*. New York: Warner.

Paulhus, D. (1982). Individual differences, self-presentation, and cognitive dissonance: Their concurrent operation in forced compliance. *Journal of Personality and Social Psychology, 43*, 838-852.

Payne, S. L., & Giacalone, R. A. (1990). Social psychological approaches to the perception of ethical dilemmas. *Human Relations, 43*, 649-665.

Pettigrew, A. (1973). *The politics of organizational decision making*. London: Tavistock.

Ralston, D. A. (1985). Employee ingratiation: The role of management. *Academy of Management Review, 10*, 477-487.

Ringer, R. J. (1976). *Winning through intimidation*. Greenwich, CT: Fawcett.

Rosenberg, M. J. (1965). When dissonance fails: On eliminating evaluation apprehension from attitude measurement. *Journal of Personality and Social Psychology, 1*, 28-42.

Rosenfeld, P., Giacalone, R. A., Knouse, S., Doherty, L., Vicino, S. M., Kantor, J., & Greaves, J. (in press). Impression management, candor, and microcomputer-based organizational surveys: An individual differences approach. *Computers in Human Behavior*.

Schein, V. (1977). Individual power and political behaviors in organizations: An inadequately explored reality. *Academy of Management Review, 2*, 64-72.

Schlenker, B. R., & Weigold, M. F. (1990). Self-consciousness and self-presentation: Being autonomous versus appearing autonomous. *Journal of Personality and Social Psychology, 59*, 820-828.

Tedeschi, J. T. (Ed.). (1981). *Impression management theory and social psychological research*. New York: Academic Press.

Tedeschi, J. T., & Lindskold, S. (1976). *Social psychology: Interdependence, interaction, and influence*. New York: John Wiley.

Tedeschi, J. T., Lindskold, S., & Rosenfeld, P. (1985). *Introduction to social psychology*. St. Paul, MN: West.

Tedeschi, J. T., & Melburg, V. (1984). Impression management and influence in the organization. In S. B. Bacharach & E. J. Lawler (Eds.), *Research in the sociology of organizations* (pp. 31-58). Greenwich, CT: JAI.

Tedeschi, J. T., & Rosenfeld, P. (1981). Impression management theory and the forced compliance situation. In J. T. Tedeschi (Ed.), *Impression management theory and social psychological research* (pp. 147-180). New York: Academic Press.

Tetlock, P. E., & Manstead, A. S. R. (1985). Impression management versus intrapsychic explanations in social psychology: A useful dichotomy? *Psychological Review, 92*, 59-77.

Tushman, M. (1977). A political approach to organizations: A review and rationale. *Academy of Management Review, 2*, 206-216.

Wortman, C., & Linsenmeier, J. (1977). Interpersonal attraction and techniques of ingratiation in organizations. In B. M. Staw & G. R. Salancik (Eds.), *New directions in organizational behavior* (pp. 133-178). Chicago: St. Clair.

Zerbe, W. J., & Paulhus, D. L. (1987). Socially desirable responding in organizational behavior: A reconception. *Academy of Management Review, 12*, 250-264.

2

Applying Impression Management to Create Productive Self-Fulfilling Prophecy at Work

Whenever I begin working in a new place, I spread the word informally among the big shots there that a highly talented guy is coming aboard. Then I get treated like an achiever already at the outset.
(a streetwise graduate student, upon hearing a lecture about SFP at work)

The young man quoted above exemplifies one way in which impression management (IM) can be used in order to create productive self-fulfilling prophecy (SFP). By bringing others to perceive him as competent, he gets them to expect much of him. Raising managers' expectations by this (or any other) means induces them to treat him accordingly, and this facilitates his performance. Expecting him to succeed, they unwittingly treat him in ways that increase the likelihood that he will succeed. This chapter explores the relationship between IM and SFP and presents examples from both micro- and macroorganizational behavior. Ways in which managers can use IM willfully to create productive SFP are proposed.

Self-Fulfilling Prophecy

SFP was originally defined by Merton (1948) as an expectation effect: The expectation that an event will occur leads people to act in ways that increase the likelihood that the event will occur. In his original conception, Merton thought of SFP as beginning with a *false* definition of some situation, such as when depositors incorrectly suspect that their bank is on the verge of bankruptcy and expect it to go under, taking their savings with it. Even though they are wrong, their expectations are false, and their bank is truly solvent and viable, they panic and withdraw their funds. Their precipitous action brings about the very outcome they foresaw: The bank fails, and their prophecy is fulfilled. The "prophets" play their role unintentionally, and even unknowingly.

Over the years, a less restrictive definition of SFP has revised Merton's focus on false expectations. True expectations, and expectations based on a kernel of truth, also fuel SFP processes by influencing expecters' behavior and making expected events more likely to occur. Examples of SFP abound in social life, as when the expectation that prices will rise sparks large and early purchases, increasing aggregate demand and fueling inflation; when expecting a boom attracts investors to buy stocks, thereby contributing to the bull market that they expected; when expecting an inert treatment to remedy an ailment speeds recovery in the placebo effect; and when expecting members of a stereotyped minority group to behave in certain ways leads members of the majority group to treat minority individuals in ways that mold their behavior to conform to the stereotype. SFP and interpersonal expectancy effects are common features of all our lives. Bringing them under rational control can help us to attain objectives, especially in organizations (Eden, 1990b).

Varieties of Interpersonal Expectancy Effects

Experimenter Effect

The first major focus on SFP in psychology concerned the "experimenter effect" (Rosenthal, 1976). Rosenthal discovered serendipitously that knowledge of the hypothesis could bring an honest scientist unwittingly to influence participants' responses. Expecting hypothesis-confirming behavior, experimenters unintentionally treat their subjects in subtle ways that are likely to evoke the expected behavior. In early studies, novice experimenters were led to believe that their rodent subjects were either "maze-bright" or "maze-dull," when in actuality the rats had been assigned randomly and therefore were equivalent in ability at the outset. Manipulating the experimenters' performance expectations in this way influenced them to produce the expected levels of performance even though they were instructed to be objective (e.g., Rosenthal & Fode, 1963).

Pygmalion Effect

SFP effects in laboratory research inspired the idea that, as experimenter expectations affect rat learning in the laboratory, teacher expectations may affect pupil learning in school (Rosenthal, 1985). This led to the landmark "Pygmalion in the Classroom" experiment by Rosenthal and Jacobson (1968), who showed that raising teacher expectations improved pupil achievement. They named the effect after George Bernard Shaw's *Pygmalion*, in which Professor Henry Higgins transforms an illiterate cockney lass, Eliza Doolittle, into a lady with exquisite mastery of the king's English.

From experimenter-subject and teacher-pupil expectation effects, the notion of "Pygmalion in management" soon surfaced. The Pygmalion effect in management is the boost in subordinates' performance resulting from raising their managers' expectations. Livingston (1969) wrote the first article titled "Pygmalion in Management," in which he developed the idea and presented illustrative case material. King (1971) published the first report of a controlled experiment demonstrating the Pygmalion effect among adults in a work organization. The Pygmalion notion has been researched and developed into a model of management integrating manager expectations and leadership and subordinate motivation and performance at both the one-on-one and macroorganizational levels (Eden, 1990a, 1990b; King, 1974). Stated in the most general terms, the practical implication of Pygmalion in management is that anything that raises managers' expectations concerning what subordinates are capable of achieving can lead to improvements in subordinates' performance.

Galatea Effect

Subordinate self-expectations mediate the Pygmalion effect. Field experimentation has shown that raising managers' expectations influences how they treat their subordinates (Eden & Shani, 1982), and that this "Pygmalion treatment" raises the subordinates' self-expectations (Eden & Ravid, 1982). In accordance with the expectancy theory of work motivation (Vroom, 1964), these high self-expectations motivate the subordinates to exert greater effort, culminating in improved job performance. However, the mediating role of employee self-expectations makes it feasible to create productive SFP at work bypassing the manager. The Galatea effect is the boost in subordinates' performance that results from directly raising their self-expectations. (Galatea is the name of the statue that the mythical Pygmalion sculpted and fell in love with, moving Venus to bring her to life.) Raising subordinates' self-expectations (by anyone, not necessarily the immediate supervisor) triggers an SFP process in which the subordinate takes on the role of the prophet who fulfills his or her own prophecy. Eden and Ravid (1982) produced a Galatea effect experimentally in an organizational setting and found it to be as potent as the Pygmalion effect, and Eden and Kinnar (in press) have replicated the Galatea effect.

Golem Effect

The Pygmalion and Galatea effects are productive outcomes of *raising* expectations. However, SFP is a double-edged sword, with negative as well as positive outcomes. The negative impact of *low* expectations on subordinate achievement is known as the Golem effect (Babad, Inbar, & Rosenthal, 1982). (*Golem* means dumbbell in Hebrew slang.) A manager who expects little of subordinates treats them as dumbbells. They "live down" to the low expectations, respond as dumbbells, and perform poorly, below their capabilities. All pay the price: manager, workers, and organization. We have no experimental data on the effects of lowering expectations, due to obvious ethical considerations. Through a combination of common sense, everyday observation, and extrapolation from experimental findings comparing the achievements of subordinates in Pygmalion and control conditions, we can conclude confidently that lowering expectations depresses performance.

The basic mechanism that creates SFP in management is the impact of manager expectations on manager behavior. When managers expect good performance on the part of subordinates, they unwittingly treat those subordinates better, with more effective leadership behavior, dubbed the "Pygmalion leadership style" (Eden, 1990b). Such leadership projects high performance expectations and facilitates subordinate achievement. As the field experimental research shows, when expectations are raised artificially, the performance gains are real. Anything that affects managers' or workers' expectations can trigger SFP. Sources of high expectations amenable to practical intervention in organizations include the immediate supervisor, consultants, goal setting and management by objectives (MBO), expectation training, organizational culture, and major organizational and technological changes. In this context, the images people project and the impressions they form can be crucial.

IM and SFP

IM is usually defined as the deliberate attempts individuals make to influence the images others form of them (e.g., Schlenker, 1980). IM has been shown to have implications for a wide variety of organizational phenomena (Giacalone & Rosenfeld, 1989). The conceptual framework of self-fulfilling prophecy in management is useful for innovating practical ways of employing IM in the service of organizational effectiveness. The parallel between SFP and IM is compelling. Both impression management and self-fulfilling prophecy were initially conceived as being triggered by something false: SFP by an incorrect expectation and IM by a distorted image an individual is trying to project in completing a test or questionnaire. IM and SFP are both processes of which the involved parties are often not fully aware. Both can be easily misconstrued as dishonest or unethical, sparking discussions of ethical considerations (Eden, 1984, 1986, 1990a, 1990b; Moberg, 1989). Both conceptualizations evolved into more generalized models of social influence involving both positive and negative, beneficial and harmful, productive and counterproductive outcomes.

The IM imperative to the manager who wants to get into the Pygmalion role is this: "Make people feel you expect a lot. If you harbor doubts about their potential, don't express them." The notion of applying IM to produce SFP implies that managers (and others) can exercise sufficient control over the impressions that they make to enable them to act out of concert with their true expectations. That is, even when actually expecting only mediocre performance of their subordinates, managers can convey confidence for success and thereby raise the subordinates' expectations in order to boost performance by producing SFP. IM can be a prime tool for shaping performance expectations, both those of managers and those of the subordinates themselves.

For managers knowledgeable about the theory and research concerning SFP, Pygmalion, and expectation effects, conveying high expectations via IM, even when in doubt, is not dishonest. Rather, it is a sensible application of scientific knowledge in the service of organizational effectiveness. Pygmalion-at-work research has shown that it is likely to succeed and prove that it was managers' doubts that were unfounded, not the high expectations they conveyed. Thus the "manager as Pygmalion" can stake out the high moral ground, free of any need to hide behind management's dubious prerogatives to do whatever it takes to get the job done (Mitchell & Scott, 1990).

The potential for IM to contribute to the SFP process has not been explored. This chapter describes the relationship between IM and SFP in management, and proposes practical means of using IM to trigger productive SFP for the benefit of individual employees, managers, and their organizations.

Using IM to Create Productive SFP

It is through managers' deliberate communication of high expectations, with the aim of putting themselves into the Pygmalion role, that IM has most potential to cash in on SFP. Managers can initiate productive SFP by projecting the image of a competent Pygmalion with high expectations, thereby encouraging their subordinates to take on the role of Galatea. The techniques proposed in the next section involve managers' use of IM in order to influence the impressions that their subordinates form of them, and consequently the subordinates' self-images. A later section of this chapter examines some IM techniques that subordinates can use to influence the impressions that their managers form of them.

"Let Me Be Your Pygmalion—You Be My Galatea"
Convey High Expectations

The central means for using IM to create SFP is the explicit and implicit communication of high performance expectations. Subordinates interpret many managerial acts as expressions of manager expectations and adjust their own self-expectations up or down accordingly. Projecting a Pygmalion image requires consistent encouraging, supporting, and reinforcing of *high* expectations regarding subordinates' potential to succeed. In the simplest and most straightforward instance, it is a manager reassuringly impressing upon a subordinate, "I know you can do this well." Pygmalions can transmit this message in an endless variety of ways. The point is to get this message across convincingly and to inspire high self-confidence among employees. Pygmalions constantly monitor their subordinates' performance expectations. When these expectations are high, the manager supports them. When they are low, the manager takes corrective action geared to persuading subordinates that they are capable of achieving success despite the self-doubts that they harbor.

Set Difficult Goals and Objectives

One of the clearest ways a manager can project high expectations is by demanding good performance. Difficult goals motivate greater effort and produce better performance than do easy goals or no goals (Locke & Latham, 1990). This is one reason MBO has been so popular. The role of goal setting and MBO in producing SFP in management has been described (Eden, 1984, 1988, 1990b). Moreover, Huber, Latham, and Locke (1989) have proposed using goal setting to manage impressions in organizations. The three perspectives on management effectiveness—IM, Pygmalion, and goal setting—converge on the common fulcrum of communicating high performance expectations. Setting challenging objectives is a down-to-earth way to impress upon subordinates that the manager is a Pygmalion. The motivational forces set in motion are the same whether there is a formal MBO program in force or not. Conversely, letting people know that little is expected of them projects low expectations and spawns Golem responses.

Too much of a good thing spoils it. Performance expectations and their operative cousins—goals and objectives—should be high, but not *too* high. The upper limit should be defined by worker ability. It is counterproductive to communicate unrealistically high expectations or to set unattainable goals. The image created is not one of a Pygmalion but of a fanatic boss who knows no reasonable limits. Only frustration results from leading workers to inescapable failure when herculean objectives are routinely set but not reached. Goals and objectives should be tailored individually to exceed each worker's current level of accomplishment by a moderate amount. By *emphasizing realistic goals* that can be attained by exerting somewhat greater effort, and by supplementing the goals with *support* and *work facilitation* behaviors, the manager manifests three of the four factors of effective leadership behavior found in Bowers and Seashore's (1966) landmark summary of leadership. The manager also projects the image of making tough but reasonable demands, and of owning up to his or her own responsibility to help subordinates accomplish them, and therefore is seen as a leader to be taken seriously.

Cultivate Subordinates' Self-Efficacy

Conveying high expectations raises subordinates' self-efficacy, which is the motivational crux of the Pygmalion effect. Bandura (1986) has defined self-efficacy as judgments people make of their capability to execute the behaviors required to perform successfully. High self-efficacy motivates people to exert effort and facilitates performance. Low self-efficacy stifles motivation and depresses performance. Pygmalions consistently bolster their subordinates' sense of self-efficacy by acting in a manner that expresses their belief in subordinates' ability to succeed. At the hands of a Pygmalion, workers' self-efficacy increases, motivating better performance. Managers have some control over sources of information that influence people's self-efficacy, particularly enactive attainment, vicarious experience, and verbal persuasion (Bandura, 1986). There are concrete behaviors that create the impression that Pygmalions believe in their subordinates, and hence enhance their sense of self-efficacy.

Enactive Attainment

Successful performance of a task strengthens one's sense of self-efficacy for that task and for similar activities. Failure has the opposite effect. Pygmalions provide subordinates with ample opportunity to "show their stuff." By giving people tough assignments and challenging goals, the manager expresses confidence in the subordinates' competence and impresses high expectations onto them. Countless Golems have been created by managers who never challenged their subordinates with hard tasks, thus depriving them of the opportunity to succeed.

The managerial imperative is clear: Prevent avoidable failure. Sequence assignments in ascending order of difficulty. Do not impose unattainable goals, and do not let overly ambitious subordinates bite off more than they can chew. Build self-efficacy gradually by assuring a long run of successes in ever more challenging tasks. Expose protégés to risk when you know they can bounce back from failure with their self-efficacy intact. Through these managerial behaviors subordinates perceive that their manager has well-founded confidence in their competence.

Vicarious Experience

Success and failure are contagious. Witnessing the success or failure of someone similar to us, we draw conclusions about our own self-efficacy. Pygmalions expose inexperienced employees to model veteran workers who assume mentoring responsibility in the anticipation that some of the seniors' prowess will "rub off" onto the juniors by imitation. The message "You can do it, too" is transmitted to novices. Their self-efficacy is nourished by an image of what they are assumed capable of accomplishing.

Pygmalions themselves constitute successful role models. In their review of IM, Leary and Kowalski (1990) cite the *publicity* of one's behavior, that is, the likelihood that others will observe one's actions, as central to the importance of IM for one's interpersonal relationships. Whether or not they know it, managers are always in the limelight, forever being watched by subordinates, and constantly making impressions. Confidence can be catching. The mere presence of a Pygmalion exuding optimism conveys an image to be imitated and increases worker self-confidence. However, this, too, is a double-edged sword. A cynical, defeatist, or otherwise discouraging attitude on the part of a manager projects the wrong image to impressionable subordinates. Managers who are unaware of their modeling role may unwittingly project the impression of not expecting much, thus inflicting damage without even realizing it. This can occur through what Babad, Bernieri, and Rosenthal (1989) have dubbed "expectancy leakage." One purpose of this chapter is to make managers and consultants cognizant of the manager's perennial, inescapable role as a model, and the ongoing IM that this role implies.

Verbal Persuasion

When successful performance and models are not feasible, Pygmalion can still boost subordinates' self-efficacy by verbal persuasion. A credible person can "talk someone into" higher self-efficacy. The best managers invest enormous effort in convincing employees they are capable of success. Such mentoring is effort well spent. This is especially true for workers who underestimate their abilities, such as underachievers who are unaccustomed to exerting effort and utilizing their capabilities.

Perceiving the series of ever more demanding tasks, observing the positive models made available by the manager, and listening to the manager telling them that they have what it takes, subordinates perceive their managers in the image of Pygmalion and get the message that they are going to make it. They develop an enhanced sense of their own capability to succeed on the job. Managers' use of these self-efficacy-building behaviors transforms workers' self-images regarding what they are capable of accomplishing. The result is performance "beyond (previous) expectations" (Bass, 1985), as their prophecy of success is fulfilled with the aid of IM.

Manage Subordinates' Attributions of Success and Failure

Fostering success and preventing avoidable failure are not enough. Every instance of success or failure is an opportunity to manage impressions. This is illustrated marvelously by a story retold by McCall, Lombardo, and Morrison (1988) about the reaction of an executive to a manager who, feeling contrite after having made a mistake that cost the company $100,000, was suggesting that he be fired: "Why should I fire you when I've just invested $100,000 in your development?" (p. 154). What an impression that must have made!

Pygmalions use such opportunities to influence how subordinates *evaluate* their experiences of success and failure, and to ensure that they form the "right" self-conceptions. In the wake of success and failure, both workers and managers contrive explanations for what happened and attribute it to a variety of causes (Weiner, 1974). The cause chosen in turn influences self-conceptions of (in)competence and expectations for future performance, setting the stage for a new round of SFP. It is most conducive to positive SFP when people attribute success to ability. When workers attribute success to their own ability, they consider themselves competent and expect future success: "I did it once, so I'm pretty good, and I'll be able to do it again."

However, attributing failure to inability arouses feelings of incompetence, *decreases* self-efficacy, and leads to negative SFP. Attributing failure to inability begets further failure as negative SFP takes over. Conversely, when workers think they have failed due to lack of effort, bad luck, or other temporary causes not indicative of their ability, their self-image of competence remains intact, and they can still reasonably expect to succeed in the future if they try harder or if their luck changes. Therefore, productive SFP is best served by attributing failure to lack of effort, bad luck, or unique circumstances that are likely to change for the better.

Thus the impact of achievement on self-concept is tempered by the individual's attributions. Making the "right" attributions fosters a self-image of competence, bolsters high expectations for future achievements, and promotes positive SFP. Making the "wrong" attributions damages people's image of competence, results in low expectations, and facilitates the Golem effect.

Left to their own devices, workers often make attributions that weaken their image of self-competence and dampen their expectations, bringing on self-inflicted Golem effects. Moreover, the impression made by the reactions of managers to subordinate success and failure can be crucial for the self-attributions that subordinates make. When managers give the impression of blaming subordinates for their failure, or of taking credit for their success, as they are wont to do given what we know about attribution biases, misattributions on the part of the subordinates are more likely.

Attribution research has revealed several types of errors, distortions, and biases that lead people to make misattributions. One type of misattribution results from self-serving bias. This is the tendency to attribute success internally, to oneself, and to attribute failure to external causes (Bradley, 1978; Miller & Ross, 1975). Self-serving bias is likely to lead managers to credit their own prowess for their subordinates' successes. Such internal attribution on the part of managers, if believed and internalized by the subordinates, leaves the latter with the impression that their success sprang from an outside source, their omnipotent manager. In such a case, the subordinates' self-efficacy does not get the boost it deserves, and their success is in this sense "wasted."

Another type of distortion is the tendency of "actors," such as employees, and "observers," such as managers, to make different attributions for the same behavior (Jones & Nisbett, 1972). In particular, subordinates are apt to attribute the cause of their performance to situational conditions, whereas managers are more likely to attribute the same performance to factors internal to the subordinates. Gioia and Sims (1985) found evidence for both of these types of attribution distortion in a well-controlled experimental simulation. The tendency for managers to distort their cognitions in a way that leads them to attribute subordinate failure to sources internal to the subordinates can be highly dysfunctional and can trigger negative SFP, particularly among subordinates who are vulnerable to images projected from above. By blaming subordinates for failure, managers not only exonerate themselves from responsibility, they also impress upon the subordinates the added burden of an internal attribution and its concomitant low expectations. If the manager so dominates the subordinates psychologically that his or her attributions overpower theirs, and his or her self-serving, internal-to-the-subordinate attribution overshadows or supplants their external attributions, they get the impression that they are at fault. Consequently, they lower their expectations concerning their future performance, and a Golem effect is in the making. Thus, through the impression it makes on subordinates, the supervisor's tendency to misattribute failure to internal causes in the subordinates constitutes a risk factor in the Golem effect.

When the attribution process is mismanaged, success is lost to misattribution instead of being experienced as efficacy-enhancing mastery. Therefore,

Pygmalions actively foster self-efficacy among workers by guiding their attributions. In the wake of every significant success or failure, Pygmalion is on the scene, making sure that subordinates attribute success to their own competence and failure to insufficient effort or to factors that are either temporary or beyond their control.

Create a Supportive Socioemotional Climate

Managers who expect more show it by being more supportive (Eden & Shani, 1982). Support is a dimension of leadership that, when combined with a strong task orientation, improves performance (Bowers & Seashore, 1966). Support can be expressed in simple words as well as nonverbally via body language. Supportive behaviors create a warm interpersonal climate between Pygmalions and their subordinates. In lay parlance this is dubbed "good chemistry." Specific nonverbal behaviors that build a supportive socio-emotional climate include making eye contact, nodding approvingly, smiling, drawing near to the subordinate physically, voicing warm intonation, and holding one's body in an erect, attentive posture during conversation. These subconscious manager behaviors naturally accompany high expectations. Through them Pygmalions give subtle, but concrete, expression of support for their subordinates. Through appropriate training, these behaviors can be added to managers' repertory of controlled acts used for managing subordinates' impressions of their managers as Pygmalions who believe in them.

Facilitate Subordinates' Work

"Work facilitation" is a central feature of effective leadership (Bowers & Seashore, 1966). Eden and Shani (1982) found that work facilitation is characteristic of Pygmalion leadership. Pygmalions work hard. They invest considerable time and effort in informing, instructing, coaching, and otherwise facilitating subordinates' performance. Their high expectations are derived from their belief in their subordinates' ability to succeed, *provided that they exert the requisite effort*. They monitor their subordinates' performance (Komaki, 1986) and intervene when necessary with corrective action. Many of the Pygmalion leadership behaviors have a training flavor. These include such acts as staying with subordinates the extra hour, giving the additional explanation, providing know-how, demonstrating again how to do it right, and challenging subordinates to expand their current abilities by getting involved in more demanding work. These behaviors convey the message that the manager believes in the subordinates' capacity to gain from all the input being invested in them. Thus the very instrumental managerial acts that facilitate work performance also strengthen the manager's Pygmalion image.

Provide Feedback

Pygmalions provide more feedback to their subordinates than do managers who expect little. Pygmalions do not wait for the annual performance review to let people know where they stand. Withholding feedback is not a neutral act; it is overt neglect. Evaluating subordinates' performance and informing them how they are doing are management acts that make subordinates aware that someone who cares is watching and keeping accounts (Komaki, 1986). Giving positive feedback affords the manager opportunities to communicate confidence that the good work will go on. Negative feedback should be supplemented with encouragement that subordinates are capable of improving their performance and expression of confidence that they will do so.

Giving feedback is a constructive manager behavior in the wake of either success or failure. Feedback involves the transmission of valid information about performance, with no negative evaluation of the recipient's inherent worth. Making people feel incompetent after they have failed is not negative feedback; it is destructive criticism. Baron (1988) has shown that destructive criticism depresses both expectations and performance. It damages the recipient's ego and decreases the likelihood of improved performance in the future. Moreover, it destroys the manager's Pygmalion image. Destructive criticism creates Golems.

SFP Through IM Initiated by the Subordinate

The classical Pygmalion paradigm casts the manager's expectations as the independent variable, the manager's leadership as an intervening variable, and the subordinate's motivation and performance as the dependent variables. One way of integrating SFP and IM is to extend the SFP model by the addition of antecedent behaviors on the part of the subordinate that influence the manager's expectations. This addition puts the subordinate in control of SFP, rendering him or her the initiator, as well as the beneficiary, of the process. The causal chain in the integrated IM-SFP model takes on the following form: subordinate IM behavior → manager expectations → manager behavior → subordinate performance. Inducing positive SFP by getting subordinates to influence their managers' expectations toward them has hardly been considered. Discussing the role of social and material outcomes in motivating self-presentation behavior, Leary and Kowalski (1990) suggest that "being viewed as competent may result in a raise in salary or in better working conditions" (p. 37). These authors state also that "employers, teachers, supervisors, and other authorities are likely to bestow positive outcomes on those who suitably impress them and negative outcomes on those who do not" (p. 39). Leary and Kowalski view employees' motivation for impressing their superiors in terms of the high power and status of the latter and the resulting dispensing of rewards or punishments. The present perspective adds evoking productive leadership behavior from superiors as a potential outcome.

"Let Me Be Your Golem"

Examples of counterproductive SFP caused by willful projection of a nerdish image abound in nature. Everyone is familiar with the child who willfully projects an image of a dumbbell in order to stave off pressure to study hard in school. In the world of work, the Hawthorne studies made "restriction of output" famous. Workers who produce at a level appreciably below their capacity while feigning supreme effort are using IM in order to convince managers and time-and-motion engineers that that is the upper limit of their ability, hoping to win loose standards and generous premium payments. Much ingenuity is invested by both sides in this game of using a negative impression as an excuse for poor performance and in debunking the game. (See Higgins & Snyder, 1989, for a more generalized treatment of excuses as a type of IM in organizations.) It is a game in which both sides lose. Fortunately, it is not the only game in town.

"I'm Not Going to Be Your Golem Anymore"

IM can be used to reduce or eradicate negative SFP by countering low expectations on the part of one's managers. Individuals who perform far below their ability due to the negative influence of their superiors' low expectations on their own self-expectations may be unaware of the process, and therefore defenseless. Such Golems can improve their lot using IM. Special training or counseling could make underachievers conscious of the debilitating SFP process, immunize them against it, and avert its recurrence. Immunization should focus on helping victims of negative SFP become aware of the process and showing them how use IM to raise the expectations of their supervisors in order to prevent their supervisors from treating them as Golems. When potential Golems engage less in the kinds of actions that project a dumbbell image, and more in actions that make them look competent and raise their supervisors' expectations, they are using IM to mitigate negative expectation effects. Knowing this empowers potential victims to disrupt the negative SFP process by not succumbing to their supervisors' low expectations.

Applying IM in this manner entails conveying to potential Golems the message that it is to their advantage to maintain their own high expectations of themselves, to act and "look" like achievers, and to do the best job they can. By presenting an image of competence, they may break the vicious SFP cycle and actually raise their supervisors' expectations. By refusing to become the manager's Golem and persisting in projecting a Galatea image, they may eventually draw the manager into the Pygmalion role. This way they stand a good chance of mastering SFP and making it work for them instead of against them.

Use of IM to counter negative SFP can be taught one on one by mentors in a coaching role or via specialized group training, as in the U.S. Navy's Pygmalion-at-Sea workshop training for low-performing sailors (Crawford, Thomas, & Fink, 1980). The Pygmalion-at-Sea project was a concerted training and coaching effort designed to improve the sailors' image in their own eyes as well as in their supervisors' eyes in order to raise performance expectations and create productive SFP. The populations that stand to benefit most from IM immunization training are those that are most at risk for Golem effects, including known low performers, those stigmatized by blemishes on their records, and persons readily stereotyped as likely to fail.

Besides chronic low performers, individuals who have respectable records of past achievements may need immunization against imminent Golem effects as they naturally advance through stages in their careers and lives that arouse expectations that can precipitate negative SFP. Multitudes of capable workers suffer performance debilitation due to widespread beliefs that decline comes "naturally" to certain situations that arise in life. For example, the general public has been bombarded with information, much of it exaggerated, about burnout and about aging. Consequently, (mis)informed workers may come to expect personal and career crises as they approach mid-life and performance decrements as they approach retirement age. Through SFP, such expectations may precipitate difficulties that would not have been experienced had they not been anticipated. Immunization through IM workshop training, counseling, or coaching could mitigate these types of harmful

SFP. For example, training aging persons to be aware of the kinds of behaviors that project an "old" impression and practicing "acting young" can help them to counteract the otherwise natural expectations on the part of others (and themselves) that the aging individual inevitably declines. Some relevant behaviors are keeping physically active, being cheerful, moving briskly, not dwelling on the past, and not complaining about (or even revealing) little aches and pains. Such behaviors project a youthful image and decrease the likelihood that others will expect performance decrements and then act in ways that precipitate such decrements. We know that most dimensions of job performance do not decline with age (McEvoy & Casio, 1989; Waldman & Avolio, 1986), and that some improve. However, due to the strong age stereotype, the objective facts are no safeguard against negative SFP. It is one's youthful or aged image that counts. IM training can help preserve the image.

"Be My Pygmalion, and Let Me Be Your Galatea"

Preventing negative SFP to avoid Golem effects is only one practical implication of subordinates' use of IM to create SFP. Another direction is for workers themselves to create positive SFP effects where they do not yet exist and intensify them where they do exist. Workers seem to understand this when they try to project an image of success. Employees, particularly young novices, often realize that first impressions are important. We are taught to cultivate the outward appearance and mannerisms that make us look successful (Schlenker, 1980). The considerable effort invested in grooming, speech, posture, poise, and image projection primes us to trigger positive SFP. Impressing upon our supervisors that we are capable leads them expect more of us. This puts them in the role of Pygmalion, and induces them to treat us as Galateas, increasing our likelihood of achieving success. The streetwise student spreading the word in new organizational settings that he is exceptionally capable, described in the opening of this chapter, exemplifies this type of IM application.

As in other applications of SFP and IM, creation and dissemination of positive images have their practical and ethical limits. Projecting so high a level of competence that one will not be able to meet the expectations engendered is counterproductive and foolish, as well as dishonest. The upper bound of the competency image one can reasonably project without crossing the line to dishonesty and ultimate exposure and failure is demarcated by the upper bound of one's true ability. There is a consensus among authors that manager expectations, like goals, should be high and challenging, moderately exceeding previous levels of attainment (Eden, 1990b). Therefore, the target level of others' expectations aimed for by the image projected should be high, but not much beyond potential attainment. Obviously, integrity is not universal, and not every savvy individual is honest. Mitchell and Scott's (1990) exposé of the ethic of personal advantage, and their call for confronting this ethic, applies here. We need to be alert to misuses of IM, no less than any other tool that may be corrupted to gain an unfair advantage. Both extremes are unacceptable: Acquiescing to an image that underrepresents one's true competence squanders productive potential, and projecting a superstar image not supported by substance is doomed to bring on failure, derision, and the accusation of foul play.

Using IM to Create Organizationwide SFP

Some forms of SFP go beyond superior-subordinate relations and occur on a grander scale. Most of the theory and research on IM concerns how people use self-presentation to manage the impressions of others. Most of the varieties and examples of IM discussed above are of this genre. However, as Leary and Kowalski (1990) have pointed out, self-presentation is not the only means to manage others' impressions. This section discusses ways of applying IM to produce organizationwide SFP that are not based on how managers present themselves, but rather on other changes they make in their employees' organizational environment that influence impressions and expectations.

Constructively Labeling

Labeling people creates powerful impression effects that are commonly ignored by personnel experts and practitioners. We can use labeling to promote positive SFP in organizations. Pygmalion effects have been produced using labels such as "super staff," "HAP" (high aptitude personnel), "handpicked," and "high command potential." Such labels are easily generated in everyday situations. Much inventiveness is invested in devising appropriate names for important projects and campaigns in organizations, such as "Operation Blastoff," "Zero Defects," and "Project Rainbow." Similarly, job titles are carefully chosen to bestow upon incumbents a sense of dignity, status, and significance, as when a data entry clerk is dubbed an "information systems technician" or when employees who manage no one are given the title "assistant manager" or "management associate." Properly chosen labels create positive images, convey high expectations, and nourish positive SFP.

Derogatory and demeaning labels should not be tolerated. It is management's responsibility to inhibit Golem effects and to foster positive SFP by supplanting negative labels with positive ones. Providing an officially sanctioned label for an identifiable target group likely to be negatively stereotyped or stigmatized will reduce the tendency to invent sarcastic labels. For example, chronically low performers could be relabeled "upward bound," "high potential," or at least something neutral.

Clear the Record of Information That Makes a Bad Impression

Labels, as well as other types of image-provoking information, are registered in employee records and stored in personnel files. A manager often sees a new employee's file before he or she ever sees the employee. The manager's impressions are set before he or she even lays eyes on the person. Individuals who got off to a bad start in school or in a job get locked in to their ignominious pasts by unforgetting—and unforgiving—records. Worse than the living memory of teachers, managers, and peers who witnessed past failure, the written record remains as an indelible reminder that creates, renews, and reinforces bad impressions, even among persons who had no involvement in the original disgrace. A record rife with failure creates expectations for "more of the same." The permanence of the record makes it impossible to shake off the negative impression. The record accompanies the individual throughout the organization and throughout his or her career. Many individuals never realize their potential because they are forever victimized by the impressions formed by their records.

We can free individuals from the shackles of their past by clearing records of entries that are likely to arouse bad impressions and negative expectations in new managers. Stigmatizing labels and codes, if they must be used at all, should be expunged after a reasonable period of time. Like moving-violation points on a driving record, a diagnostic, disciplinary, or rating entry in an employee's record should include an expiration date. Furthermore, a company could withhold the record of a new hire or a new transfer from the manager for an initial period of several months. During this time expectations would be formed on the basis of supervisor-subordinate interaction and observation of the subordinate's work rather than on the basis of the past preserved in the record. This is not feasible in companies in which a manager can phone a new transfer's previous supervisor and obtain a quick evaluation. It is certainly applicable to new hires.

Organizations need "worker protection programs" akin to the witness protection programs used by the FBI to preserve the lives of criminals who turn state's evidence and need to be hidden from the long arm of mob revenge. Promising workers with bad performance records should be relocated in the same company or elsewhere, given new employee identities, and afforded "another chance" at a job free of the impressions aroused by their work histories and the inevitable Golem effect that they trigger each time anew. This way the recurrence of destructive SFP would be blocked. Once the record has been erased, a potentially irrelevant source of bad impressions is eliminated, and what counts is what one does "from now on." A well-known advantage of migrating to a new social environment for many individuals is that they get off to a new start, leaving their past failures behind. Managers should enable capable workers with unproductive records to become "organizational immigrants" with clean expectation slates and a chance to begin anew without having to fight negative impressions held over as relics of past folly.

Piggybacking on Changes in Personnel and Organization

The endless changes in organizational structure, personnel assignments, product lines, work methods, and operating procedures provide virtually unlimited opportunities for altering members' impressions. The unfreezing of images, conceptions, and expectations wrought by organizational changes, whether "natural" or planned, can be made more worthwhile through judicious use of IM. Managers often either present the change or are on hand to render an interpretation of it. Therefore, they can determine whether a change is perceived as a threat or as an opportunity by managing employees' impressions of the change. Any nontrivial change brings members to anticipate the repercussions that might have positive or negative impacts on their work and careers. These are moments during which a "window of impressionability" opens. During such moments, alert managers interject timely words of assurance, encouragement, confidence, and optimism, giving the change a positive "face." By creating a positive image for the anticipated change, the manager creates high expectations, initiates positive SFP, and increases the change's likelihood of succeeding. When members are apprehensive due to their anticipation of an imminent turn for the worse in their situation, the optimistic words and deeds of a sanguine executive can reduce the suspense and avert a potential Golem effect as negative impressions are replaced by positive ones.

There are countless examples of organizational changes for which success was augmented by positive images and impressions and changes that failed at least in part due to a negative view on the part of those concerned. Even the classical Hawthorne experiments may have succeeded in boosting productivity by unwittingly creating the impression of a successful project, raising workers' expectations (Eden, 1986). Conversely, ruinous debilitating effects can be wrought on any innovative program by individuals who harbor a negative view of it. A strategically placed skeptic can doom a program by smearing it: "Those Whiz Kids up there have cooked up another one of their ingenious inventions for us; personally, I don't think it has a chance."

In piggybacking, managers seize upon changes, even those undertaken for extraneous reasons and those initiated by *force majeure*, as opportunities for the deliberate creation of productive SFP by molding positive impressions of these changes. Telling people that the new computer system, the redesigned office layout, the revised procedures, the improved routing, the replacement engineer, the changes in the sources of raw material, the new software, the new warehouse forms, the weekend retreat, the divisional reorganization, the new chief of accounting, or any other change in how things are done is a beneficial change that should be expected to improve productivity may make such changes more productive than otherwise. The cost of piggybacking is nil, and the potential payoff is appreciable.

Foster High-Expectation Culture

Culture is intimately involved in SFP at work because it is a rich source of collective competence images. "Productivity is a cultural phenomenon par excellence, both at the small-work-group level and at the level of the total organization" (Schein, 1985, pp. 43-44). Mythmaking is a promising way to project images and affect organizational culture. Boje, Fedor, and Rowland (1982) have proposed using mythmaking in the interests of organizational effectiveness. Their approach can be used to enrich the stock of myths that portray images of success, accomplishment, and effectiveness, and to uproot negative myths that imply organizational impotence or helplessness. Consider the positive SFP that flows from the widely accepted images "We're Number One," "We are a can-do organization," or "We're lean and mean" compared with the collective Golem effect generated by myths such as "Nothing ever gets done right around here" or "We live by Murphy's Law and the Peter Principle."

Mastery of mythmaking requires macro-level leverage over pervasive, systemwide sources of images. Changing organizational culture and replacing pernicious myths with positive ones is a task for top managers with high visibility and credibility, for "*the unique and essential function of leadership is the manipulation of culture*" (Schein, 1985, p. 317). Myths and images concerning the organization's competence or incompetence are the stuff of organizational culture. Top executives have unique leverage over organizational culture through the medium of systemwide IM and organizational mythmaking. Properly used, IM fosters productive systemwide SFP. An example is in order.

An Organization Designed to Shape Expectations

Noy, Solomon, and Benbenishti (1983) compared the effectiveness of forward- versus rear-echelon treatment centers to which Israel Defense Forces (IDF) combat psychiatric casualties were evacuated during the 1982 conflict in Lebanon. Noy et al. tested the applicability of treatment principles learned from earlier experience of the British, French, and American armies. The key elements in the treatment of combat reactions are "immediacy, proximity, and expectancy," according to which treatment should begin immediately, in close geographical proximity to the battlefield, and should foster and maintain expectations of a quick return to the front. The criterion of success in treating combat reaction is the proportion of evacuees that return to their units to resume combat duties. In the Lebanon conflict, IDF casualties of equivalent severity were evacuated to forward or rear centers solely on the basis of "local tactical and technical conditions," not medical considerations. Therefore, the effectiveness of the two types of treatment centers could be compared.

The difference was dramatic. The forward treatment centers returned 59% of those treated to their units, compared with only 39% in the rear treatment centers. As the authors note: "Proximity is not merely geographic. It is also a state of mind, a part of the expectancy set" (p. 7). IM is used to make sure the evacuees know that they are still "in it." The expectancy that the soldiers will return to their units is maintained for both professional staff and evacuees by their proximity to the battlefield and by props that keep their minds near the front. The forward treatment centers are army compounds in which all personnel wear uniforms, have reveille at dawn, bear arms, guard the perimeter of the base, maintain military discipline respecting the chain of command, and carry on daily activities in accordance with the familiar accoutrements of military routine. In contrast, the atmosphere in the rear treatment centers resembles that of a civilian medical facility and is more conducive to the maintenance of illness behavior. Personnel wear civilian clothes, use no military ranks, and have little to remind them of their actual status as soldiers. The impression is one of being "out of it."

Noy et al. provide an especially dramatic example of how a "culture" of expectancy can form images and influence success. Two treatment units in northern Israel were located only 200 meters apart geographically, but very far apart psychologically. One was a rear-echelon treatment center and the other was hastily established next to the first as a makeshift forward treatment center for casualties airlifted from the front. Though the soldiers sent to both centers had comparable symptoms, the one defined as a forward treatment center returned a much higher percentage of evacuees to their units. The geographical propinquity of the two centers and their equal distance from the front could not account for the difference in success rates. The inescapable conclusion is that the impressions conveyed by the staff and the various symbolic arrangements in the organizational environment profoundly influenced the ultimate success of the treatment center in accomplishing its mission. The IDF forward treatment center is an exquisite example of macroorganizational design that creates the image desired by management, fosters desirable SFP, and promotes attainment of the organization's goals.

When staff, style, symbols, and routine all mesh in creating an atmosphere that conveys a particular expectancy image, the effect can be overpowering. Peters (1978) describes the manager's job in terms of the manipulation of symbols to create images by use of "mundane tools." These tools are nothing more than the everyday, nitty-gritty behaviors that constitute the manager's job and how he or she "frames" them, including how, where, and with whom the manager spends time, what gets onto his or her agenda, and the settings he or she chooses or creates as a symbolic backdrop for actions. "Calendar behavior" involves the use of agenda-setting and wording of minutes of meetings to shape images and expectations. Peters explains the impact of the mundane tools that create and manipulate symbols over time in terms of the extent to which they reshape beliefs and expectations. Consistent reinforcement of images shapes expectations and induces change consistent with those images. We all know some managers who are masters at manipulating furnishings, visual aids, schedules, and other environmental cues in ways that create and sustain an image of achievement and high expectations.

Cooke and Rousseau (1988) have constructed the Organizational Culture Survey for assessing culture in terms of the dominant norms and expectations in organizations and in their subunits. One of the 12 dimensions measured by their survey is "achievement culture," which is a feature of high-expectancy culture. Using such instruments, it is possible to diagnose an organization's culture in terms of its potential for SFP and to spell out in more operational terms just how to alter the images in order to create organization-wide SFP applications.

IM and the Consultant as Messiah

Consultant and Client as Pygmalion and Galatea

Managers are not the only ones who can increase their effectiveness by using IM to enact the prophet role in organizations. SFP operates in managerial consultation as well as in management (Eden, in press). As the manager is a prophet vis-à-vis subordinates, so the consultant is a prophet vis-à-vis clients. Consulting works best when the consultant takes the role of Pygmalion and the clients take the role of Galatea. The consultant must believe, or at least appear to believe, in the client's capacity to improve in order for the consultation to succeed. SFP is the key to this fact of life in consulting. In order to gain the most from SFP in the consultant-client relationship, it is essential that the consultant convey high expectations of the client's likelihood of improving. Therefore, consultants must use IM judiciously to arouse in their clients confidence both in the consultant as a competent professional who can help them and in themselves as clients experiencing temporary difficulties that they are capable of overcoming. Consultants must project an inspiring image of professional competence. Once clients have formed a favorable impression of their consultant as an expert who can give them the insights and tools they need to overcome their difficulties, they expect success, and the positive SFP process is initiated.

In the recursive relationships between consultants and clients, IM and SFP are two-way processes. Clients, as subordinates vis-à-vis their managers, gain from the consulting relationship by being good Galateas. In order to maximize their benefits from consultants, clients should convey the impression of being capable of overcoming their present difficulties. When clients project an image of intractability, it demoralizes consultants, dampens their expectations, and dilutes or prevents any positive SFP effects that might have resulted. Appearing basically competent and likely to succeed, clients ease their consultants into the Pygmalion role. Thus IM is important for managers who want to be successful clients.

"And a Savior Is Come Unto Zion"

Some consultants are natural Pygmalions who believe in both clients' capacities to excel and their own capacity to help clients overcome the obstacles that block utilization of their potential. Dubbed "Messiahs" (Eden, 1990b, in press), these consultants project a moving image, appear perfectly fit for their role, and spark hope of deliverance among their clients. The consultant as Messiah shares with charismatic leaders the ability to inspire people to believe in their own capacity to achieve levels of performance previously considered unattainable. As despair gives way to optimism and self-confidence among their clients, the basic ingredients for beneficial SFP are in place. The Messiah's very arrival boosts expectations and triggers positive SFP as members throughout the client organization believe "Now we're really doing something about our problems!" At the same time, the clients' high expectations of the Messiah reinforce the Messiah's efforts in consulting with the client. The Messiah's arrival is energizing, for people are motivated to invest their efforts in programs that they expect to succeed. The client-beneficiaries may not later realize that the immediate cause of improvement was their own effort at solving their own problems.

A reputation of past success helps consultants create the impression they need in order for clients to let them enact the Messiah role. When the consultant's prowess is legendary, the impression of his or her competence begins operating even before he or she arrives. The Messiah's power to deliver clients from what is ailing them is magnified by the anticipation aroused waiting for him or her to come, and by a craftily staged arrival. Thus consultants of high repute use IM as a tool to generate high expectations that help mobilize client energy for productive ends. Conversely, a consultant who thinks the client has dim prospects of improving unwittingly conveys that impression to the client and triggers a Golem effect. It is doubtful that consultants can use IM successfully to overcome the nonverbal "leakage" (Babad et al., 1989) of low expectations in interaction with clients for whom they have no respect. Once the client senses the consultant's low opinion and poor prognosis, negative SFP is likely. Clients can ill afford the negative SFP produced by prophets of doom. The best way for consultants to serve clients toward whom they harbor low expectations is to disengage.

The Messiah role involves high risk for the consultant. It may not be easy to live up to the client's high expectations. Sky-high expectations engendered by a wildly exaggerated impression should be discouraged. High—but realistic—expectations on the part of all involved contribute to positive SFP.

The likelihood that a consulting intervention will succeed is improved when the consultant expects much both of self and of clients and when clients expect much both of the consultant and of themselves. The consultant bears the responsibility for ensuring a high level of all these expectations, and using IM to get into the role of Messiah is the way to do it. Therefore, the consultant should act to create an impression that ensures a high level of confidence on the part of the client regarding the consultant's capacity to contribute to the organization. The consultant's image, poise, reputation, bearing, and dress are important in making this impression. The consultant must both maintain his or her own high expectations and manage the impressions of the clients regarding the consultant's ability to help the organization.

As with other applications of IM, there is a fine line between legitimate use of IM to raise the client's expectations in the client's interests and self-serving oversell of an inflated image of the consultant designed to promote the consultant's own interests at the client's expense. Crossing that line leads to unrealistic expectations, failure, and a tarnished reputation for the consultant in the long run. Moreover, it gives IM a bad name. The consultant should avoid crossing that line lest the Messiah become a false prophet.

Conclusions

SFP is too often regarded as a natural phenomenon with which we must live, for better or for worse, but over which we can exert little influence. Once we realize that SFP begins with expectations, and that we can influence these expectations, it becomes apparent that we can gain at least some control over the SFP process. IM is one of the handiest tools available for influencing other persons' expectations. Therefore, employing IM in the ways proposed in this chapter promises to help make SFP operate more often in our favor. Linking up the concepts of IM and SFP enriches both approaches. IM adds to previous discussions of SFP in management and suggests new dimensions of theory and application not fully explored in this chapter. SFP adds to IM deeper understanding of some of the interpersonal and organizational processes put into motion by the different styles of self-presentation, and by other means adopted by managers and consultants to influence the impressions of others. Now that IM has come out of the closet of its prior arcane scientific treatment and into the live arena of management applications, other researchers and practitioners will undoubtedly uncover more ways of using IM to create productive SFP.

References

Babad, E. Y., Bernieri, F., & Rosenthal, R. (1989). Nonverbal communication and leakage in the behavior of biased and unbiased teachers. *Journal of Personality and Social Psychology, 56*, 89-94.

Babad, E. Y., Inbar, J., & Rosenthal, R. (1982). Pygmalion, Galatea, and the Golem: Investigations of biased and unbiased teachers. *Journal of Educational Psychology, 74*, 459-474.

Bandura, A. (1986). *Social foundations of thought and action: A social/cognitive view.* Englewood Cliffs, NJ: Prentice-Hall.

Baron, R. (1988). Negative effects of destructive criticism: Impact on conflict, self-efficacy, and task performance. *Journal of Applied Psychology, 73*, 199-207.

Bass, B. M. (1985). *Leadership and performance beyond expectations.* New York: Free Press.

Boje, D. M., Fedor, D. B., & Rowland, K. M. (1982). Myth making: A qualitative step in OD interventions. *Journal of Applied Behavioral Science, 18*, 17-28.

Bowers, D. G., & Seashore, S. E. (1966). Predicting organizational effectiveness with a four-factor theory of leadership. *Administrative Science Quarterly, 11*, 238-263.

Bradley, G. W. (1978). Self-serving bias in the attribution process: A reexamination of the fact or fiction question. *Journal of Personality and Social Psychology, 36*, 56-71.

Cooke, R. A., & Rousseau, D. M. (1988). Behavioral norms and expectations: A quantitative approach to the assessment of organizational culture. *Group & Organizational Studies, 13*, 245-273.

Crawford, K. S., Thomas, E. D., & Fink, J. J. (1980). Pygmalion at sea: Improving the work of effectiveness of low performers. *Journal of Applied Behavioral Science, 16*, 482-505.

Eden, D. (1984). Self-fulfilling prophecy as a management tool: Harnessing Pygmalion. *Academy of Management Review, 9*, 64-73.

Eden, D. (1986). OD and self-fulfilling prophecy: Boosting productivity by raising expectations. *Journal of Applied Behavioral Science, 22*, 1-13.

Eden, D. (1988). Pygmalion, goal setting, and expectancy: Compatible ways to raise productivity. *Academy of Management Review, 13*, 639-652.

Eden, D. (1990a). Pygmalion controlling interpersonal contrast effects: Whole groups gain from raising expectations. *Journal of Applied Psychology, 76*, 394-398.

Eden, D. (1990b). *Pygmalion in management: Productivity as a self-fulfilling prophecy.* Lexington, MA: Lexington.

Eden, D. (in press). Consultant as Messiah: Applying expectation effects in managerial consultation. *Consultation.*

Eden, D., & Kinnar, J. (in press). Modeling Galatea: Boosting self-efficacy to increase volunteering. *Journal of Applied Psychology.*

Eden, D., & Ravid, G. (1982). Pygmalion vs. self-expectancy: Effects of instructor- and self-expectancy on trainee performance. *Organizational Behavior and Human Performance, 30*, 351-364.

Eden, D., & Shani, A. B. (1982). Pygmalion goes to boot camp: Expectancy, leadership, and trainee performance. *Journal of Applied Psychology, 67*, 194-199.

Giacalone, R. A., & Rosenfeld, P. (Eds.). (1989). *Impression management in the organization.* Hillsdale, NJ: Lawrence Erlbaum.

Gioia, D. A., & Sims, H. P., Jr. (1985). Self-serving bias and actor-observer differences in organizations: An empirical analysis. *Journal of Applied Social Psychology, 15*, 547-563.

Higgins, R. L., & Snyder, C. R. (1989). The business of excuses. In R. A. Giacalone & P. Rosenfeld (Eds.), *Impression management in the organization.* Hillsdale, NJ: Lawrence Erlbaum.

Huber, V. L., Latham, G. P., & Locke, E. A. (1989). The management of impressions through goal setting. In R. A. Giacalone & P. Rosenfeld (Eds.), *Impression management in the organization.* Hillsdale, NJ: Lawrence Erlbaum.

Jones, E. E., & Nisbett, R. E. (1972). *The actor and the observer: Divergent perceptions of the causes of behavior.* New York: General Learning Press.

King, A. S. (1971). Self-fulfilling prophecies in training the hard-core: Supervisors' expectations and the underprivileged workers' performance. *Social Science Quarterly, 52*, 369-378.

King, A. S. (1974). Expectation effects in organizational change. *Administrative Science Quarterly, 19*, 221-230.

Komaki, J. L. (1986). Toward effective supervision. *Journal of Applied Psychology, 71*, 270-279.

Leary, M. R., & Kowalski, R. M. (1990). Impression management: A literature review and two-component model. *Psychological Bulletin, 107*, 34-47.

Livingston, J. S. (1969). Pygmalion in management. *Harvard Business Review, 47*(4), 81-89.

Locke, E. A., & Latham, G. P. (1990). *A theory of goal setting and task performance.* Englewood Cliffs, NJ: Prentice-Hall.

McCall, M. W., Jr., Lombardo, M. M., & Morrison, A. M. (1988). *The lessons of experience.* Lexington, MA: Lexington.

McEvoy, G. M., & Casio, W. F. (1989). Cumulative evidence of the relationship between employee age and job performance. *Journal of Applied Psychology, 74*, 11-17.

Merton, R. K. (1948). The self-fulfilling prophecy. *Antioch Review, 8*, 193-210.

Miller, D. T., & Ross, M. (1975). Self-serving biases in the attribution of causality: Fact or fiction? *Psychological Bulletin, 82*, 213-225.

Mitchell, T. R., & Scott, W. G. (1990). America's problems and needed reforms: Confronting the ethic of personal advantage. *Academy of Management Executive, 4*(3), 23-35.

Moberg, D. J. (1989). The ethics of impression management. In R. A. Giacalone & P. Rosenfeld (Eds.), *Impression management in the organization.* Hillsdale, NJ: Lawrence Erlbaum.

Noy, S., Solomon, Z., & Benbenishti, R. (1983). *The forward treatment of combat reactions: A testcase in the 1982 conflict in Lebanon.* Tel Hashomer, Israel: Israel Defense Forces, Medical Corps, Mental Health Department, Research Branch.

Peters, T. J. (1978). Symbols, patterns, and settings: An optimistic case for getting things done. *Organizational Dynamics, 7*, 3-23.

Rosenthal, R. (1976). *Experimenter effects in behavioral research* (enlarged ed.). New York: Irvington.

Rosenthal, R. (1985). From unconscious experimenter bias to teacher expectancy effects. In J. B. Dusek, V. C. Hall, & W. J. Meyer (Eds.), *Teacher expectations* (pp. 37-65). Hillsdale, NJ: Lawrence Erlbaum.

Rosenthal, R., & Fode, K. L. (1963). The effect of experimenter bias on the performance of the albino rat. *Behavioral Science, 8*, 183-189.

Rosenthal, R., & Jacobson, L. (1968). *Pygmalion in the classroom: Teacher expectation and pupils' intellectual development.* New York: Holt, Rinehart & Winston.

Schein, E. H. (1985). *Organizational culture and leadership: A dynamic view.* San Francisco: Jossey-Bass.

Schlenker, B. R. (1980). *Impression management: The self-concept, social identity, and interpersonal relationships.* Monterey, CA: Brooks/Cole.

Vroom, V. H. (1964). *Work and motivation.* New York: John Wiley.

Waldman, D. A., & Avolio, B. J. (1986). A meta-analysis of age differences in job performance. *Journal of Applied Psychology, 71,* 33-38.

Weiner, B. (1974). *Achievement motivation and attribution theory.* Morristown, NJ: General Learning Press.

3

The Management of
Shared Meaning in Organizations

Opportunism in the Reflection of
Attitudes, Beliefs, and Values

GERALD R. FERRIS
THOMAS R. KING
TIMOTHY A. JUDGE
K. MICHELE KACMAR

It has been said that politics in organizations is simply a fact of life, but there continues to be a lack of clarity and precision in our understanding of political behavior. There seem to be several reasons for this state of confusion concerning the nature of politics in organizations. One is that, for many, politics represents the "dark side" of organizational life, and thus is relegated to nothing more than hushed conversations and hallway gossip. Another is that theory and systematic empirical research on organizational politics have lagged far behind intuition and anecdotal evidence. Indeed, this phenomenon is so pervasive in organizations that it is time to develop a more informed understanding of its dynamics.

In this chapter, we characterize the management of shared meaning as providing the context or background for organizational politics, and then demonstrate how people in organizations can use the manipulation of shared meaning, in the form of perceived similarity and "fit," to influence important human resources decisions and actions. The nature and consequences of such

behavior are critical because they influence work environments and the "cas
of characters" we might find in organizations in the future.

The Management of Shared Meaning

One of the most curious aspects of organizational politics is that, on the
one hand, it has been linked to nearly every major area of study in manage
ment and organizations, yet, on the other hand, the concept itself is virtuall;
impossible to pin down. It is a fact of life in organizations (Ferris, Russ, &
Fandt, 1989), yet it rarely appears in management textbooks. At least part o
the political process is perpetually in the background; attempts to isolate .
specific behavior and bring it into the foreground often result in analyzin;
some related concept, or analyses of related concepts end up dealing with th
political process. This argues for an approach that begins by looking at thos
aspects of the political process that exist in the background, then move
forward and considers specific influence tactics and how they are related t
the background. This is the approach we take in this chapter.

In large part, organizational politics exists in the shadows. The term
politics is most often associated with the activities of government; indeed
politics is the way things get done in the affairs of the state. Much of th
public's knowledge of politics comes from its highly visible ceremonial o
symbolic aspects. Most of the true work of politics, the "way things ge
done," however, takes place in the shadows. The funding of the Nicaragua
Contras, which was directed out of the public eye in the basement of th
White House, is an infamous example. Weatherford (1985) argues that mos
of the real work of government takes place beneath the stately surface o
Washington, in the miles of unnamed catacombs populated by shops and
restaurants under the Capitol building. The fact that these corridors have n
formal names is significant; it allows the real work of politics to remain i
the shadows.

Smircich and Morgan (1982) have conducted an analysis that attempts t
explain one concept, leadership, while implicitly dealing with organizationa
politics. Leadership is understood as a process in which individuals attemp
to define reality for others by managing the meaning of events. In genera
this refers to interpreting situations "in such a way that individuals orien
themselves to the achievement of desirable ends" (p. 262). If those led accep
the leader's interpretation, their subsequent actions will follow as a natura

onsequence of the situation. Smircich and Morgan's argument is a compel-
ing one, yet it seems to generalize far beyond the phenomenon of leadership.

Ritti and Funkhouser (1987) argue that, while there does seem to be a
elationship between the actions of leaders and organizational results, partic-
pants selectively interpret events in ways that support a belief in the efficacy
f management. Thus the "myth of leadership" is enacted by all organiza-
ional participants, and leaders merely follow the guidelines set up for them
vithin a particular organization. So do leaders create reality for others or do
hose others have control in the enactment process? Most likely, both are
rue. If so, it puts the focus directly on the process of enactment or reality
reation. In general, this is one of the aspects of the political process that
xists in the background of organizational life.

According to Sederberg (1984), politics consists of any deliberate attempt
o "create, maintain, modify, or abandon shared meanings" (p. 7) among
articipants in a social setting. Rather than being inherent properties of
ituations, meanings are the result of our responses to those situations and
ur subsequent interpretations. Whether more or less, we all have a say in
he interpretations of those events and some consensus forms, usually legit-
mated by organizational symbols and myths. These "shared meanings" then
rovide guidelines for future interpretations and organizational behavior.
The idea is to manage the meaning of the situation to produce the outcomes
esired.

Sederberg (1984) asserts that all behavior is not political, since the empha-
is is on deliberate attempts to control the meanings shared by all. This omits
ondeliberate behavior such as routine or mindless activity and types of
eliberate behavior that are not specifically geared toward creating, main-
aining, or altering shared meanings. This provides a way out of the dilemma
osed by some theories in which politics is synonymous with virtually all
uman behavior. Recently, Langer (1989) outlined the severely dysfunc-
ional consequences to organizations of mindless behavior, implying that,
ounterintuitively, nonpolitical behavior is much more destructive to organ-
zational functioning than is political behavior. In this view, politics "be-
omes an arena of ceaseless conflict in which the contenders struggle to
mpose their respective meanings upon one another" (Sederberg, 1984, p.
6). This is consistent with what we believe exists in the background, setting
he stage for influence processes.

Additionally, there is another very interesting implication of this under-
tanding of politics. According to Sederberg (1984), the ultimate goal of
olitics is to end politics. If political behavior succeeds in establishing a set

of shared meanings once and for all, politics becomes unnecessary. This
combined with the implications stemming from Langer's (1989) work
suggests that, while political behavior is necessary, it is not a necessary evi
Indeed, the only system that is truly devoid of political behavior is th
totalitarian. On a smaller scale, the lack of politics from this perspectiv
accounts for such dysfunctional behavior as groupthink. We believe thi
more positive side of politics is necessary to provide a balance in the wa
organizational politics is viewed. This will allow us to develop a mor
complete understanding of the influence process and, more important, wi
serve as the basis for the creation of cooperative, win-win situations amon
organizational participants.

Characterizing organizational politics as deliberate attempts to manage c
control the meanings shared by others provides an interesting opportunity t
examine how employees in organizations, as well as job applicants, use thi
process to influence key human resources decisions. This characterization i
similar to the "managed thought" notion proposed by Chatman, Bell, an
Staw (1986) in their discussion of the role of impression management i
organizations. But before getting to that, we must develop further the contex
or background within which political behavior takes place.

Setting the Stage:
How Work Environments Allow Political Behavior

In Goffman's (1959) classic work on interpersonal interactions, he use
the metaphor of a stage with actors playing roles to portray the way peopl
interact in various spheres of everyday life. Such a metaphor is also a usefu
one for our purposes in examining the nature of political behavior in organi
zations, because people act, play roles, or otherwise attempt to manag
meanings that will lead to some positive outcome. But before we mor
carefully examine the "performances" that our organizational actors enac
we need to understand other characteristics of the work environment, c
"stage," that serves as the backdrop or context that allows the emergence an
successful execution of political behavior.

Perhaps the most central characteristic of our organizational environmer
(or stage) that feeds the struggle to manage shared meanings is ambiguity
The ambiguous nature of work environments tends to provide fertile groun
for this struggle to flourish in a number of respects. March (1984) notes tha
as one moves up the organizational hierarchy, objectives become mor

ambiguous and conflicting, as do the work and performance expectations of employees. Nemeth and Staw (1989) concur; they expand on March's observations by focusing specifically on how performance is measured and defined. As one progresses upward in organizations, the nature of work and its outcomes become increasingly nebulous and evaluation criteria become unclear. As such lack of clarity occurs with regard to evaluation criteria, organizations tend to rely more on personal characteristics, demeanor, and "potential" in performance evaluations, all of which would seem to be quite amenable to deliberate manipulation. Kanter (1977) reinforces this point in suggesting that as uncertainty increases (with rank), interpersonal factors affect performance evaluations to a greater degree.

Ambiguity emerges not simply as a function of how job performance is measured and evaluated, but in the personnel selection process as well. Gilmore and Ferris (1989a, 1989b) characterize many employment interview situations as being conducted by interviewers with little experience and limited information about the job for which they are evaluating candidates. Such situations, they argue, provide increased opportunities for political behavior of applicants to be effective.

The very nature of work environments, then, seems to be characterized by a considerable degree of ambiguity, uncertainty, and unclear meanings of requisite employee characteristics, performance, and beliefs/values. Ambiguity, along with the variance often seen in accountability, has been found to stimulate increased political behavior (Fandt & Ferris, 1990). Such a "stage" seems to provide a perfect opportunity for the effective manipulation or management of shared meaning, which can take place through several important human resources practices.

The actor-on-stage metaphor can be misleading, however, in one respect. Rather than polished performances that have been memorized from scripts and rehearsed endlessly with direction from others, the portrayals of political actors in organizations are more like improvisations drawn from their experiences to play to the audience. Using situations, techniques, and their own talents, these actors are continually attempting to manage the experience for others, whether it is an entertainment experience or one directed at accomplishing organizational tasks. In both cases, ambiguity provides the richness that the skilled performer uses to manage situations.

For those who must control situations and achieve specific outcomes, improvisational players can be exceedingly problematic, a factor that, no doubt, has led to the negative view of organizational politics. The notion of improvisation, however, has another side, as suggested by Mangham (1986):

"Each actor, however, has scope for invention and a freedom which allows all concerned the thrill of participation" (p. 65). This supports our contention that politics has a positive side.

Playing the Part:
Managing Shared Meaning in Human Resources Practices

With the stage constructed, we can now sit back and enjoy the performance. But perhaps a bit more information about the work environment and what it does to decision makers will help us to cast the upcoming performances in a more well-defined context.

The above section depicted the work environment as characterized by a considerable degree of ambiguity, particularly as one ascends the organizational hierarchy. What was not discussed, but is absolutely critical to the performances of our actors in this context, is how the ambiguity affects decision makers, thus further facilitating the demonstration and effective execution of political behavior.

Nemeth and Staw (1989) suggest that ambiguity in the work environment contributes to uniformity in beliefs, and that individuals tend to seek consensus in their opinions of ambiguous stimuli. Thus decision makers in such contexts may be particularly susceptible to influence by others in creating the impression of shared meaning. Furthermore, Nemeth and Staw argue that under such ambiguous conditions, adherence to organizational norms and conforming to the particular tastes or preferences of supervisors become surrogates for promotion criteria. Kanter (1977) notes that in order to reduce uncertainty or ambiguity in the hiring process, managers tend to "reproduce themselves," relying on similarity in personal characteristics and attitudes as selection criteria. All of these factors (organizational norm adherence, conformity to preferences of supervisor, similarity in attitudes, and the like) seem to be easily manipulated by experienced actors (perhaps even by understudies), and thus more clearly set the stage for the upcoming performances.

Act I: Personnel Selection

It is argued here that one of the more important goals of those managing shared meanings in the personnel selection process is to increase the evaluator's perception of the fit between the applicant and the organization. It may be that the specific behaviors and tactics vary depending on the situation, but the overall objective of enhancing the perception of congruence between the characteristics one has to offer the organization and what the organization wants remains the same. Therefore, the notion of "fit" may hold great promise for explaining how and why individuals seek to manage impressions in the interview.

Most writings on fit seem to emphasize "chemistry" (Ricklefs, 1979) or "right types" (Klimoski & Strickland, 1977). Rynes and Gerhart (1990) have argued that such notions add little to the understanding of fit. An explicit definition of fit is needed to clear the conceptual ambiguity in the construct. Fit is understood here as an issue of how closely the goals, values, and characteristics or traits of the applicant match those of employees considered successful in the hiring organization. Because most interviewers probably consider themselves successful employees, this may actually translate into how closely applicants resemble the interviewers. They simply use the ambiguity inherent in any notion of a "successful employee" to come up with an understanding that they themselves fit.

This helps explain why fit is an important criterion in selection decisions. Another reason is that by selecting individuals consistent with overall business strategies, decision makers may enhance organizational performance. Writers in the strategy literature have argued this to be the case (Gupta, 1986; Hambrick & Mason, 1984; Szilagyi & Schweiger, 1984). A way to implement strategy is by designing an organization's culture to enhance strategic objectives (Butler, Ferris, & Napier, 1991). Firms may select employees who expressly fit the culture. Schein (1990) contends that culture is perpetuated by the selection of new employees who already have the "right" set of beliefs and values. Similarly, others have contended that in order for a corporate culture to flourish, it is important that applicants fit into the existing value system of the organization (Fombrun, 1983). Also, managers may seek to hire individuals similar to themselves who think like they do in order to form a homogeneous constituency and thus build their own power bases (Beer, Spector, Lawrence, Mills, & Walton, 1984; Gilmore & Ferris, 1989a, 1989b). A final understanding of fit (perhaps more appropriately "fitting in") alludes to a person's ability to be a team player, to pull his or her own weight, and to act according to expectations; in our terms, to act less improvisationally and more according to script.

Research has demonstrated that the greater the extent to which an applicant is perceived to fit the job, culture, or organization, the greater the applicant's likelihood of receiving a job offer (e.g., Rynes & Gerhart, 1990). Fit seems to be a rather vague and largely undefined concept, which allows it to take a number of forms and permits applicants to play upon this ambiguity and exercise a great degree of influence over the selection process and outcomes. For example, fit has been viewed as attitude similarity between applicant and interviewer/evaluator, and such perceived similarity in attitudes has been associated with favorable evaluations (e.g., decisions to hire) of job applicants (e.g., Peters & Terborg, 1975; Schmitt, 1976).

Fit also has been interpreted with respect to appearance, personality, and values, and the extent to which each of these is consistent with some expected or desired level. Molloy (1975) has elevated appearance and dress to a high level in the role it is believed to play in interpersonal evaluations, including personnel selection decisions. Other prescriptive, anecdotal sources list proper dress as a highly ranked consideration in securing a job offer (Allen, 1983). And on a less anecdotal note, recent research has shown that appearance does affect interviewer judgments (Rynes & Gerhart, 1990).

The research on fit reviewed earlier suggests that assessments of fit typically have focused on the personality of the applicant. Organizations certainly differ in their strategic missions, and since differing strategic missions may require individuals possessing particular personality traits, it seems reasonable to expect that the overall personality composition of employees differs significantly by organization. As mentioned earlier, several writers in the strategy literature have emphasized that the match between the characteristics of the individual and the strategic characteristics of the organization is of central importance in determining organizational success.

For example, an organization that has typically pursued an aggressive business strategy may be more likely to have aggressive employees. If so, the organization may desire to hire aggressive employees in the future. If the applicant perceives the personality desired, he or she might seek to manage the way in which his or her personality is perceived. If the interviewer, for example, presents the impression that cohesiveness and cooperation are very important to the organization, the applicant may take particular care not to appear aggressive or stubborn.

It may be that the personality of the interviewer alone is the dominant effect. The applicant may not be aware of the personalities of other organization members; he or she may be exposed only to the interviewer's personality. If the interviewer displays certain attributes, the applicant may seek to show actions that manifest those traits. The interviewer displaying certain actions makes it more likely that the applicant will act in reciprocal fashion. Thus, in such cases, the applicant has effectively managed the shared meaning of personality similarity and the interviewer may well recommend hiring due to perceived fit to the job (when it is actually perceived similarity to him- or herself). Research on personality and fit has shown that job applicants who possess personality characteristics congruent with the job for which they are being evaluated tend to be judged as more suitable for that job (Paunonen, Jackson, & Oberman, 1987).

Act II: Performance Evaluation

Another very important human resources management activity is performance evaluation. Despite the traditional assumption that performance evaluation operates in a quite systematic and rational way, leading to accurate and valid assessments of "true" performance, we suggest that this process and its corresponding outcomes are susceptible to considerable influence from nonperformance factors and deliberate manipulation by both evaluators and evaluatees.

As noted earlier, the ambiguous nature of work performance as one moves upward in the organization's hierarchy provides the opportunity for the management of meaning to be effective. As Nemeth and Staw (1989) note, where performance evaluation and promotion criteria are vague and ambiguous, surrogate criteria emerge in the form of conformity to organization norms and the particular tastes and preferences of one's supervisor. Thus, according to Nemeth and Staw, those seeking favorable performance reviews and upward advancement in such ambiguous circumstances can be expected to monitor their environments carefully and attend to any salient cues regarding supervisor expectations, preferences, and social approval. Ferris, Russ, and Fandt (1989) suggest that when performance outcomes are less easily measured objectively, we tend to focus on employees' behavior rather than their actual results. Pfeffer (1981a) even argues that in such ambiguous situations, we tend to evaluate people on the basis of beliefs, values, and effort. The performance evaluation and promotion system, according to March (1984), then becomes essentially a filter that screens people on the basis of similar attributes (i.e., perceived similarity to some stereotype, to existing managers, or to the person making the evaluation), thus serving to reduce variation and increase homogeneity among managers in the firm.

It seems, then, that like the improvisational actor, organizational actors have considerable opportunity in the performance evaluation process to manage shared meaning and influence the evaluations they receive. March (1984) and Ferris, Russ, and Fandt (1989) suggest that employees will often attempt to manage their reputations by substituting measures of process (e.g., effort, behaviors) for measures of outcomes (e.g., actual results), particularly in bad times, when outcome measures might suggest poor performance. In good times, managers would likely prefer to be evaluated on actual outcomes, since those outcomes would be favorable and would lead to positive evaluations of performance.

Consistent with this tendency to evaluate employees on the basis of attitudes, beliefs, values, and effort, we might suggest that the goals one states could become a surrogate measure of one's performance. In fact, Ferris and Porac (1984) have shown that goal setting can be used as a strategy for managing impressions and shared meaning. Research by Dossett and Greenberg (1981) further clarifies this process by showing that regardless of later performance level, individuals who set the highest goals were given the highest performance evaluations by their supervisors. People who set high goals thus seem to set the initial impression that they are doing the right things, that they are ambitious, hardworking, and energetic, and certainly must be effective performers. Therefore, with such meaning managed, effort as reflected in the goals set becomes a substitute or surrogate for performance outcomes, and the actual level of subsequent performance (even if poor) becomes irrelevant.

Because the evaluation of performance in many jobs is not amenable to objective assessment and quantification, we find that subjective performance ratings by supervisors typically incorporate a variety of nonperformance factors, thus leading to a violation of the most sacred principle of performance evaluation: that *performance* alone, and not the person in the abstract, is being evaluated. The violation of this fundamental principle suggests that factors such as liking, perceived similarity in values, beliefs, and attitudes, and fit may well explain much of the content of performance ratings in organizations. Wayne and Ferris (1990), for example, found that impression management tactics of subordinates contributed to increased liking by the supervisor, which led the supervisor to rate the subordinate's job performance more favorably. Graen (1989) suggests that perhaps the most important characteristic bosses look for in subordinates, which leads to these subordinates being evaluated more positively and achieving in-group status, is the extent to which the subordinates think like the boss, make similar decisions, and support the boss on matters of importance to him or her. Furthermore, attitudinal similarity was found by Ross and Ferris (1981) to be associated with higher performance evaluations and salary increases. These all appear to be characteristics or behaviors that are easily manipulated.

A final area of performance evaluation systems where meanings and the interpretation of outcomes can be manipulated concerns the sources of evaluation, and the increased use of subordinate self-evaluations used in conjunction with supervisor evaluations of the subordinate's performance. The primary focus of both research and practice on self-evaluation has been the extent to which employees are accurate self-assessors (Ashford, 1989). A basic assumption about self-evaluation, which has probably slowed progress in this area, has been that if employees are allowed to evaluate themselves, they will inflate their ratings. In fact, existing research has shown some tendency on the part of subordinates to rate themselves lower than their supervisors rate them. Such findings can be interpreted in several ways. One interpretation is that when subordinates are given this responsibility they take it seriously and carry it out conscientiously in an effort to provide the most accurate evaluation possible. An alternative interpretation is that subordinates use self-evaluation as an impression management strategy to create a particular impression of themselves for the supervisor. In fact, Teel (1978) argues that subordinates may consciously rate their performance lower in order to gain the praise of the supervisor. Subordinates who convey the impression of being unduly self-critical likely find this strategy to be more effective and instrumental in achieving positive evaluations from the supervisor than employing a strategy of inflated ratings. We would likely impute the characteristic of humility to the former and egoism to the latter, and we are socialized to react more favorably to a humble person than to an arrogant one.

In summary, it appears that the intentional management of shared meaning can be played out quite effectively in organizations through both personnel selection and performance evaluation processes. The ambiguous work environmental context regarding both requisite selection criteria and performance indicators provides substantial opportunity for the management of impressions and shared meaning by organizational actors. But these improvisational performances rely upon a basic principle of social behavior for their effective execution. That principle is that similarity (perceived or actual) leads to attraction. Byrne (1969) suggests that agreement or perceived similarity leads to attraction because it increases the individual's confidence that his or her opinions or beliefs are correct. Furthermore, as noted by Nemeth and Staw (1989), ambiguity contributes to uniformity or consensus in beliefs because individuals actively seek consensus in their opinions of ambiguous events.

Command Performance: The Management of Shared Values

Values represent a particularly important part of organizational life (e.g., Peters & Waterman, 1982), and play a critical role in the political process, particularly in the management of meaning. Values tend to be seen as a critical component of organization culture (Schein, 1990) embodied in the language, rituals, and ceremonies of leaders (Clancy, 1989; Peters & Waterman, 1982). The notion of shared values is considered quite important in organizations today (e.g., Posner, Kouzes, & Schmidt, 1985), and we tend to reward employees who share similar value orientations with more favorable evaluations and upward mobility (Enz, 1988; Senger, 1971). Values have perhaps never been seen as more critical in organizations than they are today; increased reports of unethical and self-interest-maximizing behavior have stimulated such interest. The communication of and shared orientations toward certain values are seen as helping to shape the behavior of employees and to direct the course of the firm (Schein, 1985). Although there is no dispute as to the importance that values are believed to hold in organizations, what needs to be examined is the extent to which shared values necessarily represent true similarity or merely managed meaning. This necessitates a closer examination of the assumptions made concerning the value-behavior linkage, and the degree of specificity with which values are typically articulated in organizations.

Value-Behavior Assumptions

At least three primary positions that characterize the relationships among attitudes, beliefs, values, and behavior can be delineated. Perhaps the most traditional position is that values, which are internal beliefs built up over time through early socialization, serve to structure or direct behavior. Thus one typically makes the inference that observable behavior is the overt manifestation of internally held values, beliefs, and attitudes. This position would suggest a strong linkage or relationship between values and behavior.

A second position, popularized by Weick (1979), dates back to psychologist/philosopher William James (1950). This position recognizes a strong linkage among values, attitudes, and behavior, but one that emerges in a manner different from that suggested by the first position. This position would suggest that retrospective sense-making is what establishes the attitude-behavior relationship. That is, one exhibits a particular behavior and then, retrospectively, attempts to make sense of why one did so. Weick's phrase, "How can I know what I think until I see what I say?" seems to reflect this position. Also, this position is not dissimilar from the dynamics of cognitive dissonance theory as presented by Festinger (1957), in which individuals are forced to behave in a certain manner and then must attach internal meaning to that behavior through attitudes, beliefs, or value-related attributions. Thus the second position, like the first position, would suggest a strong linkage among values, beliefs, attitudes, and behavior. It simply differs in that the linkage is formed retrospectively rather than prospectively.

The third position is a new one and quite different in nature from the other two. This position is generated by the opportunistic or self-interest-maximizing nature of political behavior, and it suggests no necessary relationship between, or a decoupling of, values and behaviors. This position argues that no direct inferences can be made that a particular observed behavior is the overt manifestation of a related value, belief, or attitude, as noted in the first two positions. The underlying motive serving to structure or direct overt behavior is constant, although the specific behaviors may differ. Thus the behaviors become decoupled, so that they no longer reflect the social value, belief, or attitude one might normally infer. As with the "destructive achiever" personality, values are not integrated with actions (Kelly, 1987, 1988); instead, the self-serving or political motive would suggest that socially approved or desirable behaviors can be exhibited in certain situations where they are rewarded.

Several examples might illustrate more clearly the nature of this third position. Some research recently has demonstrated that the expression of particular types of attitudes or moral judgments can be viewed as conscious self-presentations in which people align themselves with a specific social identity or value system (Reicher & Emler, 1984). Also adopting a self-presentational interpretation of moral judgments, Johnson and Hogan (1981) suggest that attitudes, personality, and moral judgments can represent mechanisms for communicating to relevant others one's self-image, or at least the image with which one wants to be credited.

Fairness, equity, and justice are quite important concepts involved in organizational life (e.g., Folger & Greenberg, 1985; Greenberg, 1987). Interestingly, Greenberg (1988) recently reported evidence to suggest that managers view fairness and the appearance of being fair quite differently. It was more important for managers to *appear to be fair* than it was for them actually to be fair.

Still others have discussed the opportunistic use of cooperation, citizenship, and commitment behaviors in organizations. Frost (1987) suggests that by simply appearing to be cooperative, individuals may effectively disarm their opponents while undermining their efforts behind the scenes.

Finally, Enz (1988) has conducted some interesting research on the nature of value congruity in organizations, and has found that expressing certain values that are espoused by top management can be a manipulative strategy to gain power. She found that *believing in* value similarity was more critical in power attainment than actual similarity, thus characterizing power as a social definition of perceived value similarity.

Specificity in Value Articulation

We have discussed throughout this chapter the important role played by ambiguity in the work environment as providing fertile ground and essentially creating the stage on which managed meaning performances take place. Up to this point, however, ambiguity has been viewed as a natural, unintended consequence of organizational complexity. We might complicate things a bit at this juncture by suggesting that ambiguity may be created and/or maintained intentionally in organizations in an instrumental manner to achieve certain objectives. If this is so, we might make better sense of how the managed meaning of shared values is facilitated.

Eisenberg (1984) argues that ambiguity is a conscious strategy in organizational communication, and he makes reference to the nature of organizational values. He argues that values tend not to be precisely articulated; rather, they remain implicit in myths, stories, and sagas and are thus expressed equivocally. Such ambiguous expression of core values allows for multiple individual interpretations, yet it permits people genuinely to believe they are in agreement. Ambiguity is thus used strategically to foster agreement and diversity at the same time. We might extend this perspective to the personnel selection and performance evaluation processes mentioned earlier in this chapter and argue that hiring standards and performance criteria may be intentionally kept ambiguous in order to provide the organization maximum flexibility in interpretation and action. Other research has suggested that powerful executives often attempt to protect their privileged positions through intentional equivocation and vagueness, thus using ambiguity strategically (Williams & Goss, 1975).

The Cast of Characters:
Political Behaviors of Actors and Their Consequences

We have spent some time now discussing organizational politics as grounded in the conscious and intentional management of shared meaning, and we have demonstrated how these dynamics unfold in some important human resources management processes. Our discussion would not be complete, however, if we failed to consider the negative or dark side of organizational politics. First, we will discuss how political environments emerge and are maintained; we then move to a more specific examination of the particular types of political characters that roam the corridors of organizational society. We make the point that these political characters both help shape the political environment and are shaped by that environment.

Traditional assumptions concerning behavior suggest that values that have been learned throughout life drive behavior. That is, we have been socialized and taught to value one thing or another and therefore our actions will reflect this predisposition. Thus people who have strong moral convictions, as those are defined within a specific culture, will not act unethically, politically, or illegally because these behaviors can be considered immoral in that culture and are thus inconsistent with the value system adopted, which drives behavior. Similarly, there are people who hold values outside that culture. When acting consistently with their own set of values, we see these individuals as maximizing their own positive outcomes, that is, behaving politically in this negative sense (e.g., Lerner, 1990).

Others have argued that situations, not values, influence people to act politically, and that it is individuals who possess the ability to monitor their environments and discern desired behaviors or responses (i.e., high self-monitors) who are in the best position to exhibit and capitalize on opportunistic or political behavior (Snyder, 1987).

It is clear that some work environments lend themselves to more political behavior than others (Baum, 1989; Ferris, Fedor, Chachere, & Pondy, 1989; Riley, 1983). But, paradoxically, these are often environments that mirror our society as a whole, made up of people from various subcultures and diverse backgrounds with different values and resulting high levels of ambiguity. This does not necessarily have to result in negative, self-maximizing behavior, but it often does because organizations find it difficult to tolerate such diversity and thus engage in politics that result in negative organizational practices. These are often labeled as political when, in fact, they are *in response* to the lack of true political environments (i.e., those characterized by diversity, ambiguity, and a tolerance for multiple values). Thus, rather than being seen as an innocent bystander in this process, organizations need to accept some responsibility for the type of politics encountered in the workplace. Let's examine this notion more closely.

Schneider (1987) has argued recently that "the people make the place," suggesting that the personalities, value systems, and behaviors of incumbent employees in organizations shape the psychological environment. This perspective has interesting implications for the emergence and maintenance of opportunistic political behavior and the development of negative political environments. Beer et al. (1984) suggest that managers like to select people in their own image, possibly for power-enhancing and political reasons. To the extent that those managers having input are opportunistically inclined, they might perpetuate and even add to the negatively charged political environment by selecting people who think and behave like they do. Furthermore, there is evidence to suggest that job candidates seek out organizational environments on the basis of the match they perceive between their own personalities, values, and so forth, and those reflected by the organization (Tom, 1971). Thus the personnel selection process, from the standpoints of both decisions made by the organization and the job search process of potential candidates, can serve to influence the nature and degree of opportunism that exists in organizations. The message communicated is, "There is simply no tolerance for any behavior other than that sanctioned by the organization, consistent with its central values." But what happens when individuals get caught between the officially required response and what threatens the individual, as in a case of whistle-blowing, for example? No matter how clear the expression and acceptance of organizational values, certain of those values will always come into conflict. If there is little tolerance for diversity and ambiguity, any deviations will be viewed as opportunistic or political in the most insidious sense.

The socialization of new employees into the organization also may create negative political situations. To a degree, socialization can be construed as simply social learning theory (Bandura, 1977) in action. Weiss (1977) has demonstrated not only the social learning of supervisory style, but also social learning of work values (Weiss, 1978). New employees watch incumbent employees and model or imitate their behavior. If the behaviors being modeled are opportunistic in nature, and the new employees are being rewarded (or at least not punished) for behaving in this way, these types of actions in the organization should increase. As part of the socialization process, of course, these behaviors are not defined as "political" for the newcomer, but rather simply "the way things are done around here."

A more formalized socialization process, mentoring, also may cause negative political activities in the organization. Kram (1985) suggests that in the mentoring process, both the protégé and the sponsor have goals. Protégés seek to gain exposure, upward mobility, and so forth, while mentors seek to gain respect by developing young talent, but also to contribute to their own power or influence bases by fostering protégé commitment and support for mentors' interests. Obviously, both perspectives can be considered political in the negative sense, and can contribute to the opportunistic nature of the work environment through coalition building and power-base enhancement.

Other organizational situations also can contribute to negative political behavior. Janson and Von Glinow (1985) suggest that organizational reward systems might actually reinforce employees for acting unethically and op- portunistically. They suggest that the behaviors, attitudes, and norms that are created and maintained by the organizational reward system may conflict with the behaviors and attitudes stakeholders expect to see, thus perhaps quite unintentionally reinforcing negative political behavior.

Similarly, Hirsch (1987) has suggested that managers may become "free agents" due to the lack of commitment organizations show their employees (i.e., terminations, layoffs, concessions). A free-agent manager would be a self-interest-maximizing individual who comes to view this route as the only one that will lead to survival given the circumstances. Also, given such circumstances, managers would perceive the greatest return not from com- mitment and personal investment in the well-being of the organization, but rather from decisions and actions that increase their "personal stock value" to the external market, even if it is at the expense of the organization. The implicit message from the organization is construed as "You had better take care of yourself because we aren't going to take care of you." Such environ- ments thus serve to punish employees for not behaving opportunistically. Similarly, Jackall (1988) suggests that the managers who succeed are those who view themselves and all other employees as replaceable objects or commodities and whose actions reflect this viewpoint.

By examining some of the explanations for the development and mainte- nance of negative political behaviors in this section, one could argue that the actions of the organization are in fact encouraging such behavior. Through selection, socialization, and reward systems in organizations, unethical or negative political behaviors may be perpetuated.

We have begun to identify some of these negative political characters that emerge or are created in work environments, but let's look at a few more and also at some additional consequences of such negatively oriented political environments.

Kanter and Mirvis (1989) recently reported on a rather disturbing phenomenon occurring in organizations: the increased *cynicism* among American workers. They found, in a national survey, that about 43% of the respondents fit the profile of the cynic, who sees selfishness, favoritism, and exploitation as characteristic of workplaces, and reflects a fundamental lack of trust and commitment. Like Hirsch (1987), Kanter and Mirvis use the free-agent metaphor to characterize cynical managers and professionals who market their services to the "highest bidder" and reflect no commitment to any single organization. Thus it seems that negative organizational politics can be both a cause of cynicism and a consequence. That is, cynicism may well emerge as a reaction to increased opportunistic behavior, but cynics may then select negative political behaviors as their reaction in turn to this state of affairs.

A quite interesting type of cynic or opportunistic character identified by Kanter and Mirvis (1989) is the "Articulate Player." This individual is the classic organizational politician, who prides him- or herself on being "in the know" and understands the negative side of politics very well. Articulate Players, like Maccoby's (1978) "Gamesman," are willing to do whatever it takes to get ahead and are concerned with the power of appearances. They feel "It's not what you are, it's what you appear to be" (Kanter & Mirvis, 1989, p. 34). The Articulate Player is particularly relevant to our earlier discussion of the management of shared meaning concerning beliefs and values, and to this discussion of the opportunistic reflection of social values. This political character, according to Kanter and Mirvis, is particularly adept at faking expected emotions, attitudes, and values.

The feigning of emotions, attitudes, and values presents a very complex picture of organizational life, where one cannot distinguish the genuine from the superficial. This can be seen a little more clearly with regard to the true feelings of altruism and commitment versus their opportunistic reflection. Fandt and Ferris (1990) argue that at a very surface level, there appears to be a fundamental incompatibility between prosocial or citizenship behavior (e.g., Brief & Motowidlo, 1986; Organ, 1988) and political/opportunistic behavior. Yet, the extent to which such an incompatibility exists remains unclear at present. It is quite possible, for example, that what appear to be prosocial behaviors on the surface are actually intended to promote an individual's self-interest, not the interests of others (e.g., the mere appearance of being altruistic can be quite self-serving).

An implication that can be drawn from Hirsch's (1987) work is that the strong commitment and dedication of the "organization man" (Whyte, 1956) has been replaced by the self-interest-maximizing orientation of the opportunistic organizational free agent. One might suggest that if this new breed of employee exhibits any type of behavior that might be defined as commitment, he or she does so only in a calculating manner, with the action specifically designed to achieve a desired response or outcome. In fact, Penley and Gould (1988) discuss a dimension of the organizational commitment construct referred to as "calculative commitment," which represents an instrumental approach not unlike that just suggested and is characterized by items such as "I will give my best effort when I know it will be seen by the 'right' people in the organization" (p. 59).

In summary, it seems that organizational policies and activities may be encouraging the development of a skilled opportunistic manager of the future. Because there is little tolerance for ambiguity and diversity in the environment, this type of manager is forced to "read" situations and to seek out and anticipate the proper responses in given situations in order to reap rewards. Such opportunistic behavior can result in value systems that might be viewed as becoming disconnected or decoupled from behavior. Thus, for example, one does not espouse a philosophy or value because one necessarily believes it, but rather because it is instrumental to one's attaining rewards and approval from, or fitting in with, influential others who value such a philosophy.

Thus one might dub the clever and skillful opportunistic politician an "organizational chameleon" of sorts, effectively managing impressions of relevant others essentially to "become" exactly what the situation dictates. But while chameleons change so as to fit in unobtrusively, this individual makes sure that the changes in behavior are such that fitting in becomes a quite visible, public, and attention-attracting process, a staged performance, designed to achieve some personally beneficial result.

Conclusion

Organizational politics is a fact of life, and one would be hard-pressed to argue it is not. But such a statement in itself does not take us far in developing a more informed understanding of political dynamics in organizations. We have characterized organizational politics as the intentional management or manipulation of shared meaning, and we have demonstrated how this phenomenon is played out through two important human resources management processes. The natural and strategically manipulated ambiguity in both personnel selection and performance evaluation makes these important processes vulnerable to managed meanings of similarity, agreement, and fit. Finally, we have provided some thoughts on how such behavior influences and is influenced by the nature of work environments; specifically, how behavior can be turned toward the opportunistic and potentially destructive when organizational environments will not tolerate diversity, ambiguity, and alternative shared meanings and values.

As we have seen, organizational politics is a complex, multidimensional construct, and one that is in desperate need of more precise insight and articulation. We have provided an analysis of how shared meaning is manipulated as providing the background in which politics are played out in organizations in an effort to add to our understanding of this complex process. It seems that a number of important questions remain in this area, but a critical one seems to be how politics, both positive and negative, affects the performance and effectiveness of organizations. To date, there has been some disagreement on this issue, with Pfeffer (1981b) arguing that politics should be viewed as functional and some recent empirical data showing that political behavior tends to be associated with poorly performing firms (Eisenhardt & Bourgeois, 1988).

Clearly, to begin to understand a phenomenon one must accept that it exists. To a certain extent, political behavior still suffers from a lack of acceptance as a natural, constant aspect of organizational life. However, it is one thing to accept that political behavior exists; it is another thing entirely to acknowledge that it has a positive side. One of our goals has been to highlight this more complete view of organizational politics.

A final thought concerns the general perspective we have taken in our discussion of organizational politics. The reader may feel that our fascination with appearances, images, and impressions is misguided and cynical, and that our analysis begs (no, screams!) the question, "Where's the beef?" We think not, and we conclude with a quote from Tom Peters: "Perception is all there is. There ain't no such thing as steak, sad to say, just the sizzle" (Kanter & Mirvis, 1989, p. 130).

References

Allen, J. G. (1983). *How to turn an interview into a job.* New York: Simon & Schuster.

Ashford, S. J. (1989). Self-assessments in organizations: A literature review and integrative model. In L. L. Cummings & B. M. Staw (Eds.), *Research in organizational behavior* (Vol. 11, pp. 133-174). Greenwich, CT: JAI.

Bandura, A. (1977). *Social learning theory.* Englewood Cliffs, NJ: Prentice-Hall.

Baum, H. S. (1989). Organizational politics against organizational culture: A psychoanalytic perspective. *Human Resource Management, 28,* 191-206.

Beer, M., Spector, B., Lawrence, P. R., Mills, D. Q., & Walton, R. E. (1984). *Managing human assets.* New York: Free Press.

Brief, A. P., & Motowidlo, S. J. (1986). Prosocial organizational behavior. *Academy of Management Review, 11,* 710-725.

Butler, J. E., Ferris, G. R., & Napier, N. K. (1991). *Strategy and human resources management.* Cincinnati: South-Western.

Byrne, D. (1969). Attitudes and attraction. In L. Berkowitz (Ed.), *Advances in experimental social psychology* (Vol. 4, pp. 35-90). New York: Academic Press.

Chatman, J. A., Bell, N. E., & Staw, B. M. (1986). The managed thought: The role of self-justification and impression management in organizational settings. In H. P. Sims, Jr., & D. A. Gioria (Eds.), *The thinking organization: Dynamics of organizational social cognition* (pp. 191-214). San Francisco: Jossey-Bass.

Clancy, J. J. (1989). *The invisible powers.* Lexington, MA: Lexington.

Dossett, D. L., & Greenberg, C. I. (1981). Goal setting and performance evaluation: An attributional analysis. *Academy of Management Journal, 24,* 767-779.

Eisenberg, E. M. (1984). Ambiguity as strategy in organizational communication. *Communication Monographs, 51,* 227-242.

Eisenhardt, K. M., & Bourgeois, L. J. (1988). Politics of strategic decision making in high velocity environments: Toward a midrange theory. *Academy of Management Journal, 31,* 737-770.

Enz, C. A. (1988). The role of value congruity in intraorganizational power. *Administrative Science Quarterly, 33,* 284-304.

Fandt, P. M., & Ferris, G. R. (1990). The management of information and impressions: When employees behave opportunistically. *Organizational Behavior and Human Decision Processes, 45,* 140-158.

Ferris, G. R., Fedor, D. B., Chachere, J. G., & Pondy, L. R. (1989). Myths and politics in organizational contexts. *Group & Organization Studies, 14,* 83-103.

Ferris, G. R., & Porac, J. F. (1984). Goal setting as impression management. *Journal of Psychology, 117,* 33-36.

Ferris, G. R., Russ, G. S., & Fandt, P. M. (1989). Politics in organizations. In R. A. Giacalone & P. Rosenfeld (Eds.), *Impression management in the organization* (pp. 143-170). Hillsdale, NJ: Lawrence Erlbaum.

Festinger, L. (1957). *A theory of cognitive dissonance.* Stanford, CA: Stanford University Press.

Folger, R., & Greenberg, J. (1985). Procedural justice: An integrative analysis of personnel systems. In K. M. Rowland & G. R. Ferris (Eds.), *Research in personnel and human resources management* (Vol. 3, pp. 141-183). Greenwich, CT: JAI.

Fombrun, C. J. (1983). Corporate culture, environment, and strategy. *Human Resource Management, 22,* 139-152.

Frost, P. J. (1987). Power, politics, and influence. In F. M. Jablin, L. L. Putnam, K. H. Roberts, & L. W. Porter (Eds.), *Handbook of organizational communication* (pp. 503-548). Newbury Park, CA: Sage.

Gilmore, D. C., & Ferris, G. R. (1989a). The effects of applicant impression management tactics on interviewer judgments. *Journal of Management, 15,* 557-564.

Gilmore, D. C., & Ferris, G. R. (1989b). The politics of the employment interview. In R. W. Eder & G. R. Ferris (Eds.), *The employment interview: Theory, research, and practice* (pp. 195-203). Newbury Park, CA: Sage.

Goffman, E. (1959). *The presentation of self in everyday life.* Garden City, NY: Doubleday.

Graen, G. B. (1989). *Unwritten rules for your career.* New York: John Wiley.

Greenberg, J. (1987). A taxonomy of organizational justice theories. *Academy of Management Review, 12,* 9-22.

Greenberg, J. (1988). Cultivating an image of justice: Looking fair on the job. *Academy of Management Executive, 2,* 155-157.

Gupta, A. K. (1986). Matching managers to strategies: Point and counterpoint. *Human Resource Management, 25,* 215-234.

Hambrick, D. C., & Mason, P. D. (1984). Upper echelons: The organization as a reflection of its top managers. *Academy of Management Review, 9,* 193-206.

Hirsch, P. (1987). *Pack your own parachute.* Reading, MA: Addison-Wesley.

Jackall, R. (1988). *Moral mazes: The world of corporate managers.* New York: Oxford University Press.

James, W. (1950). *The principles of psychology.* New York: Dover.

Janson, E., & Von Glinow, M. A. (1985). Ethical ambivalence and organizational reward systems. *Academy of Management Review, 10,* 814-822.

Johnson, J. A., & Hogan, R. (1981). Moral judgments and self-presentations. *Journal of Research in Personality, 15,* 57-63.

Kanter, D. L., & Mirvis, P. H. (1989). *The cynical Americans: Living and working in an age of discontent and disillusion.* San Francisco: Jossey-Bass.

Kanter, R. M. (1977). *Men and women of the corporation.* New York: Basic Books.

Kelly, C. M. (1987). The interrelationship of ethics and power in today's organizations. *Organizational Dynamics, 14,* 5-18.

Kelly, C. M. (1988). *The destructive achiever: Power and ethics in the American corporation.* Reading, MA: Addison-Wesley.

Klimoski, R. J., & Strickland, W. J. (1977). Assessment centers: Valid or merely prescient? *Personnel Psychology, 30,* 353-361.

Kram, K. E. (1985). *Mentoring at work: Developmental relationships in organizational life.* Glenview, IL: Scott, Foresman.

Langer, E. J. (1989). *Mindfulness.* Reading, MA: Addison-Wesley.

Lerner, A. W., (1990). *The manipulators: Personality and politics in multiple perspectives.* Hillsdale, NJ: Lawrence Erlbaum.

Maccoby, M. (1978). *The gamesman.* New York: Bantam.

Mangham, I. L. (1986). *Power and performance in organizations.* Oxford: Basil Blackwell.

March, J. G. (1984, August). Notes on ambiguity and executive compensation. *Journal of Management Studies,* pp. 53-64.

Molloy, J. T. (1975). *Dress for success.* New York: Warner.

Nemeth, C. J., & Staw, B. M. (1989). The tradeoffs of social control and innovation in groups and organizations. In L. Berkowitz (Ed.), *Advances in experimental social psychology* (Vol. 12, pp. 175-210). New York: Academic Press.

Organ, D. W. (1988). *Organizational citizenship behavior.* Lexington, MA: Lexington.

Paunonen, S. V., Jackson, D. N., & Oberman, S. M. (1987). Personnel selection decisions: Effects of applicant personality and the letter of reference. *Organizational Behavior and Human Decision Processes, 40*, 96-114.

Penley, L. E., & Gould, S. (1988). Etzioni's model of organizational involvement: A perspective for understanding commitment to organizations. *Journal of Organizational Behavior, 9*, 43-59.

Peters, L. H., & Terborg, J. R. (1975). The effects of temporal placement and attitude similarity on personnel selection. *Organizational Behavior and Human Performance, 13*, 279-293.

Peters, T. J., & Waterman, R. H., Jr. (1982). *In search of excellence: Lessons from America's best run companies.* New York: Harper & Row.

Pfeffer, J. (1981a). Management as symbolic action: The creation and maintenance of organizational paradigms. In L. L. Cummings & B. M. Staw (Eds.), *Research in organizational behavior* (Vol. 3, pp. 1-52). Greenwich, CT: JAI.

Pfeffer, J. (1981b). *Power in organizations.* Marshfield, MA: Pitman.

Posner, B. Z., Kouzes, J. M., & Schmidt, W. H. (1985). Shared values make a difference: An empirical test of corporate culture. *Human Resource Management, 24*, 293-310.

Reicher, S., & Emler, N. (1984). Moral orientation as a cue to political identity. *Political Psychology, 5*, 543-551.

Ricklefs, R. (1979, September 19). The hidden hurdle: Executive recruiters say firms tend to hire "our kind of person." *Wall Street Journal*, p. 1.

Riley, P. (1983). A structurationist account of political culture. *Administrative Science Quarterly, 28*, 414-437.

Ritti, R. R., & Funkhouser, G. R. (1987). The ropes to skip and the ropes to know (3rd ed.). New York: John Wiley.

Ross, J., & Ferris, K. R. (1981). Interpersonal attraction and organizational outcomes: A field examination. *Administrative Science Quarterly, 26*, 617-632.

Rynes, S., & Gerhart, B. (1990). Interviewer assessments of applicant "fit": An exploratory investigation. *Personnel Psychology, 43*, 13-35.

Schein, E. H. (1985). *Organizational culture and leadership: A dynamic view.* San Francisco: Jossey-Bass.

Schein, E. H. (1990). Organizational culture. *American Psychologist, 45*, 109-119.

Schmitt, N. (1976). Social and situational determinants of interview decisions: Implications for the employment interview. *Personnel Psychology, 29*, 79-101.

Schneider, B. (1987). The people make the place. *Personnel Psychology, 40*, 437-453.

Sederberg, P. C. (1984). *The politics of meaning: Power and explanation in the construction of social reality.* Tucson: University of Arizona Press.

Senger, J. (1971). Managers' perceptions of subordinates' competence as a function of personal value orientation. *Academy of Management Journal, 14*, 415-423.

Smircich, L., & Morgan, G. (1982). Leadership: The management of meaning. *Journal of Applied Behavioral Science, 18*, 257-273.

Snyder, M. (1987). *Public appearance, private realities: The psychology of self-monitoring.* New York: W. H. Freeman.

Szilagyi, A. D., & Schweiger, D. M. (1984). Matching managers to strategies: A review and suggested framework. *Academy of Management Review, 9*, 626-637.

Teel, K. S. (1978, July). Self appraisal revisited. *Personnel Journal*, pp. 364-367.

Tom, V. R. (1971). The role of personality and organizational images in the recruiting process. *Organizational Behavior and Human Performance, 6*, 573-592.

Wayne, S. J., & Ferris, G. R. (1990). Influence tactics, affect, and exchange quality in supervisor-subordinate interactions: A laboratory experiment and field study. *Journal of Applied Psychology, 75,* 487-499.

Weatherford, J. M. (1985). *Tribes on the hill.* South Hadley, MA: Bergin & Garvey.

Weick, K. E. (1979). *The social psychology of organizing* (2nd ed.). Reading, MA: Addison-Wesley.

Weiss, H. M. (1977). Subordinate initiation of supervisor behavior: The role of modeling in organizational socialization. *Organizational Behavior and Human Performance, 19,* 89-105.

Weiss, H. M. (1978). Social learning of work values in organizations. *Journal of Applied Psychology, 63,* 711-718.

Whyte, W. H., Jr. (1956). *The organization man.* New York: Simon & Schuster.

Williams, M. L., & Goss, B. (1975). Equivocation: Character insurance. *Human Communication Research, 1,* 265-270.

PART II

Human Resources and Careers

4

Impression Management and
Career Strategies

DANIEL C. FELDMAN
NANCY R. KLICH

Foxiness should be well concealed: one must be a great feigner and dissembler. And men are so naive . . . that a skillful deceiver always finds plenty of people who will let themselves be deceived.

(Machiavelli, 1513/1988)

Experience shows that . . . those who have done great things are those who have set little store by keeping their word, being skillful rather in cunningly confusing men.

(Machiavelli, 1513/1988)

There has been a fundamental shift in the strategies people are using to advance their careers in organizations. David Riesman (1950) has called it the transition "from the era of the invisible hand to the era of the glad hand." Amitai Etzioni (1989) has called it the transition from the "I and we" model of organizational life to the "me first" model. In a recent *U.S. News & World Report* study titled "The New Organization Man," Buckley (1989) found that 56% of the respondents surveyed felt that "managers try too hard to look like stars when what is really needed is old-fashioned competence and hard work."

Whatever it has been labeled, however, the common thread to all these cultural critiques of changes in organizational life is the observation that individuals are pursuing career advancement more and more through non performance-based means (Feldman, 1985, 1988). Feldman and Weitz (1990) have called this propensity to pursue career growth through non-performance-based means a "careerist orientation to work," and note that this orientation to work incorporates six key beliefs:

(1) Merit alone is insufficient for advancement in organizations. Creating the appearance of being a winner, or looking "promotable," is as important.

(2) In order to advance, it is critical to pursue social relationships with superior and coworkers. On the surface these relationships should appear to be social in nature, but in reality they are to be used instrumentally for job contacts and insider organizational information.

(3) Looking like a "team player" is central to career advancement. However individuals should still pursue self-interest at work through what Christophe Lasch (1979) calls "antagonistic cooperation," that is, appearing cooperative and helpful on the surface while simultaneously seeking information about how to overcome one's competition.

(4) In the long run, an individual's career goals will be inconsistent with the interests of any one organization. Therefore, in order to advance, individual must appear to be loyal and committed to their current employers, while at the same time keeping their résumés circulating and otherwise "keeping their options open."

(5) Dishonest or unethical behaviors are sometimes necessary in order to get promotions to which one feels entitled. However, it is important not to advocate dishonest or unethical behavior or even acknowledge the existence of such behaviors. Instead, individuals should become adept at inconsistency (Jackall, 1983), and develop the ability to hold public positions that are either mutually inconsistent or inconsistent with past public positions.

(6) Much of the "real work" of many jobs cannot be tangibly assessed, nor can relative success on those jobs be easily validated. Thus it is important to construct the illusion of success and power socially through symbols such as dress and office design. These props might include locks on file drawers positioning visitors so the sun is in their eyes, and having visitors' chairs lower than the office occupant's desk.

Organizational researchers have long been interested in impression management, or the ways in which individuals create and maintain their image with people of power or influence in their lives (Schlenker, 1985; Snyder 1985; Tetlock & Manstead, 1985). Impression management behaviors may be used to elicit attributions of likability and/or competence from influential people. In organizational settings, six impression management techniques seem to be used most frequently in creating the illusion one is competent, successful, and worthy of additional rewards and promotions (Duarte, 1987; Jones & Pittman, 1982; Schlenker, 1980):

(1) *Ingratiation:* Individuals use flattery, agreeing with others' opinions, and doing favors to get people with influence and power to like them. For instance, in his successful book, *How to Win Friends and Influence People,* Dale Carnegie (1973) identifies figuring out a client's good points and playing them to the hilt as the critical ingredient in getting ahead.

(2) *Intimidation:* Individuals convey the image of being potentially dangerous to those who might stand in the way of their advancement. Managers, for example, might use veiled threats of exposure of organizational problems with supervisors who are trying to block their promotions.

(3) *Self-promotion:* Individuals embellish their accomplishments or make overstated claims about their abilities in order to win the respect and admiration of their supervisors. Individuals may self-promote by strategically displaying certificates or awards, claiming they have outside job offers, and puffing up reports of their accomplishments.

(4) *Exemplification:* Individuals create the impression of being selflessly dedicated or self-sacrificing, so that people in positions of influence will feel guilty about not giving them desired rewards or promotions. For example, an individual might always arrive at work early or leave late in order to create the image of dedication to his or her job.

(5) *Accounting:* Individuals attempt to distance themselves from negative events in which they have been involved. Among other ways, they may do this by denying personal responsibility for the problem (making excuses such as "I was merely following orders") or by diminishing the dimensions of the problem (making justifications such as "It's really not so bad").

(6) *Supplication:* Individuals try to get people in positions of influence to be sympathetic or nurturant toward them. Employees might bolster the allegiance their bosses have to them by asking to be mentored or "taken under their wings."

In this chapter, we will examine in more detail five areas where impression management tactics are being used as major means to career advancement. In addition, we will consider the long-term consequences of a careerist orientation to work for the individuals who pursue advancement through non-performance-based means, and for the organizations in which they are employed. Indeed, at a time when there is daily clamor about the lack of

America's competitiveness in international markets and the cannibalization of corporations on the domestic front, this decoupling of competence and career advancement has fundamental implications for the culture and quality of American business into the twenty-first century (Feldman, 1990).

Impression Management and Career Strategies: Examples From Organizational Life

There are five ways, in particular, in which impression management techniques are utilized extensively to pursue career advancement:

(1) using dress, office design, and other symbols to create the illusion of power
(2) generating outside offers or external evidence to demonstrate "market value"
(3) changing techniques for writing résumés and preparing for job interviews
(4) finessing ethical issues and moral dilemmas at work
(5) using "networking" and inauthentic interpersonal relationships with superiors and colleagues to gain advantage on the job

Each of these areas is considered in turn below.

Dress, Office Design, and Other Power Symbols

Since the publication of John Molloy's (1975) *Dress for Success*, more and more managers are falling into what Meg Greenfield calls "the trappings trap." They believe it is central to their career advancement to look and play the role of a person in power, and are very attuned to the expanding list of stratagems that are proliferating in self-help books and columns. Image consultants persuade individuals to communicate what they are like, how they are likely to behave, and how they should be treated by adept use of personal appearance, props, and scenery. Indeed, the latest *Directory of Personal Image Consultants* lists almost 300 firms, with annual sales in excess of $20 million.

For example, in *The Winning Image*, James Gray (1982) argues that color affects the impressions managers make, and that managers should be very sensitive to the signals they are sending with their clothing. He notes, for instance:

> Blue is the color of conservatism, accomplishment, devotion, deliberation, introspection. It therefore goes with people who succeed through application, those who

know how to earn money, make the right connections in life, and seldom do anything impulsive. They make able executives and golfers, and they usually dwell in neighborhoods where other lovers of blue are to be found.

Betty Lehan Harrigan (1977) takes these general observations to their logical conclusion in her book *Games Mother Never Taught You*. She notes that "today's business is a tangible game board" and that "neophytes must grasp the design of the game board and learn the initial placement of the pieces before making any irreversible move." Among her specific hints: Try to have your pay directly deposited to your bank; woo the secretaries who deposit checks for their bosses to collect salary data; don't eat in dining halls at work you don't need special ID badges to get into; get the *Wall Street Journal* delivered at work because it is a "distinctive emblem"; and network with others while in the bathroom.

Michael Korda (1975), in *Power! How to Get It, How to Use It*, takes on the task of discussing the more intangible symbols of space and time. He notes, for example, that "a large office is pointless unless it is arranged so that a visitor has to walk the length of it before getting to your desk, and it is valuable to put as many objects in his path . . . to hinder his progress." Korda recommends using a small calendar, "which is easily filled up, and which gives the impression of frenetic activity, particularly if one's writing is fairly large." He also suggests intimidating one's visitors by keeping them waiting, sitting them with the sun glaring in their eyes, and facing them toward large, ticking clocks.

All of these self-help books that guide managers to power share the common attribute of being divorced from concerns about performance and competence. They encourage individuals to look like team players while pursuing distinctively uncollaborative behavior; they teach individuals much more about how to look like they have power than about how to exercise power constructively.

Testing the Waters and Getting Market Value

Robert Jackall (1983), in "Moral Mazes: Bureaucracy and Managerial Work," notes that performance in organizations today is "socially defined." Making a profit matters, but it is much more important in the long run to be perceived as "promotable" and "valuable to the corporation." Moreover, because much of the work managers do is intangible, and because it is hard to attribute the success of a group to any one particular individual, managers turn to self-promotion techniques to create the perception that they are both promotable and valuable.

There are several specific strategies individuals use to assert their value to their company. One stratagem managers use is joining many professional organizations, civic groups, and social clubs. In this way, managers meet, and get known by, an ever-widening circle of people. If the network gets wide enough, sooner or later colleagues in the home institution get the impression that the individual is "well known"—forgetting for the moment that he or she is well known for activities not related to work.

Another strategy individuals use, related to the first, is pursuing formal leadership roles in these professional organizations, civic groups, and social clubs. Attributes such as "leadership" are very hard to define tangibly in organizational life. Consequently, organizations often look externally to help them define and evaluate the everyday behavior they regularly see. By serving as officers or board members of external organizations, individuals create the impression that they have the leadership attributes to be promoted. This strategy also has the side benefit, in terms of impression management, of facilitating the use of social relationships for business purposes and for subsequent job hunting.

A third strategy individuals use in self-promotion is regularly job hunting and generating outside job offers. Most organizations, despite protestations to the contrary, really do not distribute much merit pay. The difference in pay between "average" and "outstanding" is often quite small because top management does not want the hassle of defending pay decisions based on largely unobservable criteria. To get a real bump in pay, many managers realize they need to generate outside offers. They job search and job hunt to obtain more lucrative offers (which they really do not want) to provide external evidence of their "market value" to top management (who can use the external evidence as justification for internal salary "adjustments").

What is interesting about all these strategies is that top management is reluctant to use its own internal judgment and standards about people they observe on a day-to-day basis 40 to 50 hours per week. Instead, unsure about its own ability to make tough calls, top management relies on external cues. As a result, ambitious managers realize how important it is to create the illusion of being promotable and valuable to the corporation. External visibility replaces internal competence as the criterion for career advancement and reward system decisions.

Résumé Construction and Interviewing Behavior

One of the fastest growing areas of the image management industry is the publication of self-help books on writing résumés and preparing for job interviews. The point of both types of manuals is selling oneself to key decision makers by using self-promotion and ingratiation tactics. Interestingly enough, the jargon of this industry is replete with marketing terms, such as "product differentiation" and "knowing your market." Ultimately, job seekers are coached on how to "package" and "price" themselves in the "market."

In terms of résumé construction, one of the impressions individuals try to create is the illusion of linearity. The résumé is to be constructed so that the current job goal is not only consonant with past educational and work experiences, but is also seen as the logical next step in the individual's career. Thus we see former teachers of high school Spanish who are currently getting their MBAs describing their teaching jobs in terms of "organizational and presentational skills," and their initial choice of foreign-language teaching as an early outcropping of their burgeoning interest in international business. The reality of careers—that people's needs and abilities change, that people tire of jobs and bosses and want to move on—is carefully suppressed.

Another impression that résumés try to generate is that their authors know how to play the job-hunting game. Often it is not the content of the résumé but its style that matters—knowing what items should be included (e.g., number of people supervised) and what items should not (e.g., anything from high school). Presumably, the ability to play the game and conform on the résumé foreshadows the ability to learn a new game and conform if hired.

Résumé services and self-help books proclaim that a successful job search depends on enhanced descriptions of previous jobs. Applicants are encouraged to reframe their previous jobs, stressing such attributes as responsibility, leadership, cooperation, and communication skills. Moreover, some résumé advisers go so far as to suggest that applicants should tailor their résumés for each job to which they are applying, to create the impression that they are uniquely qualified for that specific job.

There are two key impressions applicants try to convey in the interview: First, they truly desire this job, and, second, they are circumspect and can behave in ways that embarrass neither themselves nor their employers. Interviewees create these impressions by using both ingratiation and self-promotion tactics (Baron, 1986). They make self-enhancing statements designed to draw attention to their competence and likability; they try to conform to the interviewer's opinion on various job-related issues; they glorify their past accomplishments and take credit for visible successful projects; they overstate their desire and willingness to work for every potential employer. Moreover, the careful manipulation of personal appearance and nonverbal communication adds credibility to these verbally created impressions.

Literally hundreds of specific tips have been published along these lines to help applicants land jobs in the interview. For instance, in *The Landau Strategy: How Working Women Win Top Jobs* (Landau & Bailey, 1980), job seekers are told: (a) "This is very important—they [successful interviewees] take the trouble to give the impression that their job moves follow some kind of logic, that there's some kind of rhyme and reason to what they want to do"; (b) when the interview occurs over dinner, "choose forkable foods" and "don't equivocate when the time comes to order, execute the task swiftly and surely, stay away from the 'shall I have this or shall I have that' syndrome."

With both résumé construction and interviewing behavior tactics, the goal is to discover what it is the potential employer wants, and then package oneself as exactly what the organization is looking for. What is especially ironic about this *pas de deux* is that both the interviewer and the interviewee know that the other is being occasionally deceptive—and in what ways—and yet the selection process is viewed so seriously and self-righteously anyway. In many cases, the endgame of the selection process is not to demonstrate strength, but to fail to demonstrate weakness.

Ethical Behavior and Impression Management

On the way up the corporate hierarchy, managers often run into the following dilemma: Acting ethically will not be rewarded by one's superiors and can knock one off the fast track to the top. Moreover, apologizing for past indiscretions is also often frequently prohibited because it implies that the organization has been wrong or unethical—and this would entail more investigations and the uncontrollable laying of blame. As a result, one of the abilities that upwardly mobile managers use to advance their careers is an adeptness at inconsistency, at creating the illusion that wrong is right and that new positions are consistent with old positions, even when the empirical evidence supports the opposite point of view.

Jackall (1983) notes that the first part of this adeptness is flexibility, or not taking "giving one's word" too seriously. For example, we see frequent examples of top managers saying they "fully support" a subordinate, and then firing that person within days. When the issue is pushed, some press release about "new evidence" or "new circumstances" may be issued, with no details, so that specific inconsistencies and the nature of past commitments cannot be highlighted or pursued. The goal is to lessen the negative implications of the transgression not only by "pinning the blame" on the now-absent subordinate (excuses), but also by implying that any indiscretion was unintentional or unforeseen (justifications).

Another element of this adeptness at inconsistency is the coining of new terms and doublespeak (Schlenker, 1980; Snyder, 1985; Tetlock & Manstead, 1985). These new terms either obfuscate reality or transform something negative into something positive. There will be no new taxes, but there will be "revenue enhancements" and "user fees." No one was fired, but people were "outplaced," "dehired," "reduced in force," or "permanently separated." New words are used to manage impressions; where previously managers were valued for their ability to present ideas clearly and concisely, now they are valued much more for their ability to temporize and equivocate.

A third element of this adeptness at inconsistency is moral relativism or justification, the notion that there are no absolute standards of right and wrong and that ethical behavior can be judged only in context. Taking this view of ethical behavior, many actions that previously had been considered unprofessional now become acceptable. For instance, we are informed by authors such as Michael Korda on getting power that (a) it's okay to recognize that honesty is not always the best policy (provided you don't go around saying so), (b) it's okay to be Machiavellian (provided you can get away with it), and (c) it's okay to undermine your boss and replace him or her (provided you never express anything but respect and loyalty for him or her while you're doing it).

We see the paradoxes of ethical behavior and impression management when organizations face some type of visible crisis—product failure, financial reverses, or an accident such as the *Exxon Valdez* oil spill. The organization first states that it was blameless. Then it states that all its procedures were appropriate and working effectively. Then it states that it will conduct a full-scale investigation and correct any deficiencies so the public will never have to worry again. However, the thoughtful observer might ask: How can an organization assert that it is blameless before it investigates? If the procedures were working effectively, then how could the disaster have happened? If changes are made, then does that not imply the previous administrative procedures were indeed deficient?

Upwardly mobile managers must learn how to create the impression of ethical behavior by mitigating the negative nature of their behavior if they are to advance up the corporate ladder. They do this first by manipulation of words and symbols, and then later and more permanently by walling off fixed internal standards from external reality.

Inauthentic Interpersonal Relationships

The final example of impression management in career advancement concerns the use of inauthentic interpersonal relationships. In order to advance their careers, many individuals try to manage impressions so that they appear friendly and supportive, while more covertly they are pursuing self-interested or even competitive aims.

In terms of dealing with colleagues, it is very important in the corporate world today to be considered a "team player." However, being viewed as only a team player can be the kiss of death for an upwardly mobile manager. Therefore, he or she uses a technique called "antagonistic cooperation" (Lasch, 1979). In antagonistic cooperation, an individual is unfailingly friendly to coworkers and collaborates smoothly on joint projects, while simultaneously garnering negative information about colleagues' personal lives or professional competence to be used for the individual's own career purposes at some later date.

In terms of dealing with superiors, perhaps no impression management techniques are more frequently used than ingratiation and exemplification. Granted, ambitious managers are learning to be more subtle than those of the past—no more *What Makes Sammy Run*—but nonetheless they are willing to create the impression they both like and respect their superiors (while all the while complaining about these superiors' incompetence and insensitivity to friends). In addition, upwardly mobile managers often seek out opportunities to be ingratiating to their superiors without an audience of peers, so they come early, stay late, or take up the same sports as their bosses. The goal is not to develop genuine friendships outside of the office, but to develop a source of inside information to be used on the job.

In terms of relationships with subordinates, managers often engage in a process called "organizational seduction" (Lewicki, 1981). Employees are encouraged to make career decisions that are against their true best interests, especially when they are considering leaving the organization for greener pastures. First, the supervisor tries to make the employee doubt his or her own feelings about the job ("Things aren't as bad here as you think"). Then the supervisor may try guilt ("You owe us after all we have done for you" or

"How can we get along without you?"). Third, the supervisor might appeal to an employee's pride ("You are an incredibly value asset"). Fourth, the seducing organization tries to keep the employee in line through fear ("Because your stay in the organization has rendered you unique, you would be unlikely to succeed anywhere else"). The impression to be created is that of benevolent and omniscient paternalism, while the reality is somewhat more self-serving.

These issues of inauthentic interpersonal relationships among coworkers are not new, but they have become more salient as the lines between work lives and personal lives have become fuzzier. As upwardly mobile managers increasingly use their coworkers as friends and their friends to build business contacts, the dangers of being hurt by falsely created impressions multiply.

Conclusions and Implications

While some have argued that impression management is ill intentioned (e.g., Jones, 1964; Tedeschi, 1981), most researchers have pointed out that not all impression management is devious (Liden & Mitchell, 1988; Schlenker, 1985). Some people use impression management tactics simply to be liked; many people who use impression management techniques may even do so unconsciously or unknowingly. What we have argued here, however, is that impression management strategies are being used more frequently and assertively to achieve career success, and that in some cases impression management is supplanting competence and integrity as a criterion for promotion and advancement.

However, not all impression management is career enhancing. When an individual uses impression management, he or she not only reaps career-enhancing benefits, but also runs the risk of appearing deceptive or manipulative. People are sensitive to overdone images or ones that appear feigned and inconsistent with reality; impression management that appears inauthentic can sidetrack the careerist. The real dilemma facing the upwardly mobile individual, then, is not whether to use impression management at all, but rather how much to use it and how often. Most typically, this dilemma is resolved by, on the one hand, using self-aggrandizement on the qualities that are most critical to the job, and, on the other, feigning modesty and making self-demeaning statements on the qualities that count the least (Schlenker, 1980).

In the long run, however, the new careerism may indeed lower the standards of excellence in organizations (Feldman, 1985, 1988). In part, this is because careerist professionals may be spending too much time searching for other jobs or too much energy creating the images of success. Second, implicit in the new careerism is the "home-run strategy": Make the big play, and move on. Too often, both attention to long-term goals and day-to-day conscientiousness are ignored or undervalued as a result. Third, careerist managers and professionals are much less likely to be job involved and committed to their organizations. After all, why make investments in the current job or organization when the name of the game is to keep moving?

The new careerism has a downside even for the managers who practice it successfully. First, it often creates "anticipatory dissatisfaction" (Staw & Feldman, 1979). Even when all the typically important aspects of a job are satisfactory, managers may be disgruntled because their jobs may not be optimal for launching their next career moves. Indeed, in a recent *Fortune* interview, a new MBA noted about his career plans: "I'm not going to stay with this job just because I like it." Second, a careerist approach to work can lead to self-absorption and, in some cases, to lowered self-esteem. Thinking of oneself as a consumable commodity to be bought or sold is at best disconcerting and at worst self-alienating. It puts the bidding price of one's self-esteem in the hands of others whom one cannot control.

The solutions to the problem of overreliance on impression management for career advancement are neither obvious nor easy to accomplish in the short run. First, performance must become the primary criterion for career advancement. This means that managers' jobs need to be more clearly defined in terms of results and desired methods used to achieve results; rewards must be based on performance, not politicking. Second, organizational selection and promotion systems must become more skill-based. Less emphasis should be given to information obtained from interviews and "grateful testimonial letters," and much more given to actual skills, abilities, and knowledge. Third, organizations need to be more concerned with how and by whom employees are socialized. Newcomers need to interact and work with supervisors and coworkers who are competent and have achieved success through tangible merit rather than through impression management. Finally, organizations need to be more active in managing their employees' careers so that employees believe their chances for advancement are based more on job accomplishments than on networking. At the very least this involves better career information systems, human resources planning and forecasting, periodic skills assessment and training, and realistic information about career opportunities and progress.

Certainly, upwardly mobile managers will turn to impression management techniques to advance their careers, and many of those efforts will be neither malevolent nor hurtful. Nonetheless, it is crucial to keep in mind the important ethical distinction between climbing the ladder of success and wielding a machete to make a path to the top (Goodman, 1979). Being good in the inside world should be as important as looking good to the outside world; "value added" should be appreciated as much as, if not more than, "market value."

References

Baron, R. A. (1986). Self-presentation in job interviews: When there can be "too much of a good thing." *Journal of Applied Psychology, 16*, 16-28.

Buckley, J. (1989). The new organization man. *U.S. News & World Report, 106*, 40-51.

Carnegie, D. (1973). *How to win friends and influence people.* New York: Pocket Books.

Duarte, N. T. (1987). *The effect of subordinates' assertive self-presentation behavior on performance appraisal.* Unpublished doctoral dissertation, University of Florida Graduate School of Business.

Etzioni, A. (1989, February 1). The "me first" model in the social sciences is too narrow. *Chronicle of Higher Education*, p. 144.

Feldman, D. C. (1985). The new careerism: Origins, tenets, and consequences. *Industrial-Organizational Psychologist, 22*, 39-44.

Feldman, D. C. (1988). *Managing careers in organizations.* Glenview, IL: Scott, Foresman.

Feldman, D. C. (1990). Risky business: The recruitment, selection, and socialization of new managers in the twenty-first century. *Journal of Organizational Change Management, 2*, 16-29.

Feldman, D. C., & Weitz, B. A. (1990). *From the invisible hand to the glad hand: Understanding the antecedents and consequences of a careerist orientation to work.* Manuscript submitted for publication.

Goodman, E. (1979). *Close to home.* New York: Fawcett Crest.

Gray, J., Jr. (1982). *The winning image.* New York: AMACOM.

Harrigan, B. L. (1977). *Games mother never taught you.* New York: Rawson, Wade.

Jackall, R. R. (1983). Moral mazes: Bureaucracy and managerial work. *Harvard Business Review, 61*, 118-130.

Jones, E. E. (1964). *Ingratiation.* New York: Appleton-Century-Crofts.

Jones, E. E., & Pittman, T. (1982). Toward a general theory of strategic self-presentation. In J. Suls (Ed.), *Psychological perspectives on the self* (pp. 231-262). Hillsdale, NJ: Lawrence Erlbaum.

Korda, M. (1975). *Power! How to get it, how to use it.* New York: Random House.

Landau, S., & Bailey, G. (1980). *The Landau strategy: How working women win top jobs.* New York: Lester & Orpen Dennys.

Lasch, C. (1979). *The culture of narcissism.* New York: Warner.

Lewicki, R. J. (1981). Organizational seduction: Building commitment to organizations. *Organizational Dynamics, 10*, 5-22.

Liden, R. C., & Mitchell, T. R. (1988). Ingratiatory behaviors in organizational settings. *Academy of Management Review, 13*, 572-587.

Machiavelli, N. (1988). *The prince* (Q. Skinner & R. Price, Eds.). Cambridge: Cambridge University Press. (Original work published 1513)

Molloy, J. T. (1975). *Dress for success.* New York: P. H. Wyden.

Riesman, D. (1950). *The lonely crowd: A study of the changing American character.* New Haven, CT: Yale University Press.

Schlenker, B. R. (1980). *Impression management: The self-concept, social identity, and interpersonal relations.* Monterey, CA: Brooks/Cole.

Schlenker, B. R. (Ed.). (1985). *The self and social life.* New York: McGraw-Hill.

Snyder, C. R. (1985). The excuse: An amazing grace? In B. R. Schlenker (Ed.), *The self and social life* (pp. 235-260). New York: McGraw-Hill.

Staw, B. M., & Feldman, D. C. (1979). *Thinking of jobs as careers* (working paper). Evanston, IL: Northwestern University Graduate School of Management.

Tedeschi, J. T. (1981). *Impression management theory and social psychological research.* New York: Academic Press.

Tetlock, P. E., & Manstead, A. S. R. (1985). Impression management versus intrapsychic explanations in social psychology: A useful dichotomy? *Psychological Review, 92*, 59-77.

5

Performance Appraisal

The Means, Motive, and Opportunity
to Manage Impressions

PETER VILLANOVA
H. JOHN BERNARDIN

A common and essential feature of organizations is the requirement for members to subordinate personal interests when they conflict with the generalized obligations prescribed by the organization (Katz & Kahn, 1978). However, organizations are never completely successful in persuading employees to subordinate their own personal aspirations when they conflict with organizational goals. The inevitable disagreement between personal and organizational goals contributes to the political drama of organizational life and makes organizations fertile settings for the exercise of social influence (Ferris & Mitchell, 1987; Ferris, Russ, & Fandt, 1989).

An organizational event that is replete with opportunities for the exercise of social influence is the annual performance appraisal (Fandt & Ferris, 1987). Unfortunately, while the performance appraisal has received considerable research attention (Bernardin & Beatty, 1984), surprisingly little work has been done to investigate the effects of impression management (IM) in this context. As a result, much of the discussion that follows draws from research on the performance appraisal that only indirectly addresses the role of IM in this area. However, recent signs of scholarly activity are encouraging. For example, several conceptual models expressly addressing the role of IM in the context of the performance appraisal have been proposed (e.g.,

Villanova & Bernardin, 1989; Wayne, 1987), and a number of empirical studies purposely designed to test social influence hypotheses in the context of appraisals have been conducted (e.g., Wayne & Ferris, 1990; Wayne & Rubenstein, 1987; Zalesny, 1990).

In an earlier paper, we proposed a four-stage model of ratee IM effects on performance appraisal ratings (Villanova & Bernardin, 1989). Also in that paper, we provided numerous examples of how raters could purposely manipulate ratings in order to serve specific motives (e.g., purposely deflate ratings in order to keep valuable employees who might otherwise be promoted or transferred versus purposely inflate ratings so that subordinates might reciprocate with higher ratings of leadership or supervisory competence). There has also been considerable discussion of individual, job, and organizational factors that promote the use of social influence tactics in organizations (e.g., Fandt & Ferris, 1987; Gardner & Martinko, 1988; Liden & Mitchell, 1988; Ralston, 1985). Thus employee motivations for engaging in impression management (e.g., Ferris et al., 1989), their selection of IM strategies (e.g., Kipnis, Schmidt, & Wilkinson, 1980), the variable success of these strategies under different situational conditions (e.g., Giacalone, 1985; Mitchell & Liden, 1982), and the rating behaviors that raters employ in order to manage impressions (e.g., Greenberg, 1990) have received some attention as of late.

Notwithstanding this progress, there remains a need to address more specifically what rater motives and what appraisal system characteristics contribute to rating biases. Therefore, our purpose in this chapter is partially to fill this gap in two ways. First, we offer observations of contemporary performance appraisal practices in organizations that promote rating distortion. Second, we review some rater motives that contribute to the occurrence of rating bias. Finally, when possible, we offer some prescriptions for reducing the occurrence of rating bias stemming from the IM concerns of raters.

Features of Appraisal Systems That Promote Rating Distortion

As depicted in the title of this chapter, performance appraisals provide means, motive, and opportunity for the exercise of social influence. The means aspect of the title explicitly recognizes that performance appraisals

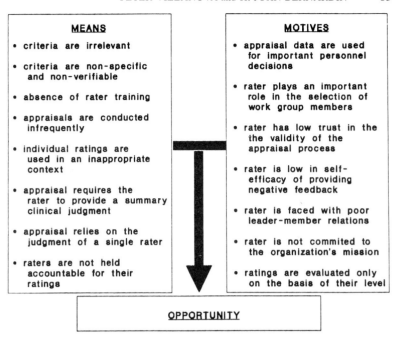

Figure 5.1. Means, Motive, and Opportunity to Distort Ratings

serve as tools for influencing the behavior of organizational members (Austin, Villanova, Kane, & Bernardin, in press; Cummings, 1983). *Motive* refers to the increased desire to act in a self-interested fashion when appraisal results are perceived to have personal consequences (see Greenberg, 1984; Stires & Jones, 1969). Finally, when features of the appraisal system are considered favorable to the pursuit of rater personal motives, the appraisal situation may be perceived by raters as an organizationally sanctioned *opportunity* to behave in a self-interested manner.

Figure 5.1 outlines characteristics of appraisal systems that serve as means for rater impression management by facilitating the manipulation of performance ratings. As shown in the figure, the means of appraisal and rater motives combine to produce perceptions of opportunity to distort ratings purposely in order to serve raters' personal goals. When raters are *motivated* to distort ratings and they perceive that the *means* to do so exist, they will take advantage of the perceived *opportunity* and purposely distort their ratings. In this section we explain the various means (i.e., features of appraisal

Table 5.1 Appraisal Characteristics That Inhibit IM Behaviors

---

(1) Criteria for appraisal are relevant to the job.

(2) Criteria for appraisal are clearly defined.

(3) Raters are trained on the appraisal process and IM behaviors.

(4) Performance appraisals are conducted more frequently than once a year and/or a performance diary is maintained.

(5) Performance appraisals are targeted at the appropriate level of ratee aggregation.

(6) Performance judgments are made on specific dimensions and are then combined statistically to arrive at an overall rating.

(7) Multiple rater systems (peers, other supervisors, self-ratings) are used.

(8) Raters are held accountable for their rating behavior.

---

systems) included in the figure. The following section is devoted to rater motivation to distort ratings.

Means

As noted above, means are those aspects of the appraisal system that may contribute to deliberate rating distortion. Though scant research exists on the features of appraisal systems that serve to inhibit or reduce the effects of IM behaviors by raters, some prominent features of appraisal systems seem particularly important in this regard. Table 5.1 presents a list of prescriptions for appraisal characteristics that are most likely to reduce or eliminate attempts to use IM behaviors in the appraisal process and to reduce the effects of any such attempts.

Criteria for appraisal must be relevant. If the criteria upon which ratings are based are irrelevant or, at best, loosely related to organizational goals, raters are likely to approach the appraisal process less seriously. When individual-level ratings are perceived to bear a direct relationship to other indices of organizational success (e.g., productivity, profitability) and administrative action and the accuracy of the ratings are deemed essential to monitoring organizational goal accomplishment, then the rater must balance the personal gains of rating distortion against the consequent costs to the organization of inaccurate diagnostic information. If appraisal data are not perceived as relevant to organizational goals, the rater may discount the importance of accurate ratings and rate in a manner designed to optimize personal goals.

Criteria for appraisal should be clearly defined and verifiable. The greater the specificity of the measurement system—or, conversely, the less the ambiguity in the performance levels—the smaller the impact of IM behaviors by raters. Greater specificity increases verifiability and thus inhibits rating distortion of all kinds. More specific criteria can also affect rater perception of how important accurate appraisal data are to the organization. If the organization has gone so far as to develop specific criteria, raters may feel more obligated to focus on behavior or outcomes relevant to these criteria. Conversely, if the criteria do not refer to specific behaviors or outcomes, but rather to personal traits of the ratee (e.g., dependability, attitude), the ratings are more likely to be contaminated by the personal biases of raters (Cummings & Schwab, 1973). Also, since in the case of trait ratings raters are asked to evaluate *persons* rather than job performance, raters may be more reluctant to give low ratings for fear that ratees may interpret those ratings personally. Unfortunately, many organizations continue to evaluate performance using formats that require personality ratings of ratees or with dimensions or factors that are not clearly defined (e.g., quality, quantity) (Bernardin & Pynes, 1990).

Nonverifiable criteria invite rating distortion by simply conceding to the rater that "performance is in the eye of the beholder." The absence of clearly defined, unambiguous criteria (e.g., output data, attendance records, errors) not only makes for a deficient representation of performance, but also serves as a de facto sanction of arbitrary and capricious rating behavior. One indirect method of verifying ratings, for example, is to obtain information on a group of individual ratees from personnel records in the form of absence or output data and to correlate these data with subjective ratings of these criteria. To the extent that subjective ratings correlate with data found in personnel records, increased confidence in the validity of the ratings would have some empirical justification (Bernardin & Beatty, 1984).

Train raters on the appraisal process and IM behaviors. If an organization has gone to the trouble of developing specific, verifiable criteria relevant to its goals, it may also have gone so far as to install a rater training program to stress the importance placed upon accurate ratings. A comprehensive program is one that involves raters from the start in the development of the rating scale and auxiliary criteria; provides raters with formal training in observation, attributions, and rating; and concludes with training on how to conduct the performance appraisal interview. Since the beneficial effects of rater training tend to dissipate rather quickly (Ivancevich, 1979), it is advisable to conduct "refresher" training periodically. Bernardin and Buckley (1981) have reviewed various types of rater training and offer caveats for those who see training as a panacea for appraisal problems. Training that focuses on the attributions of performance and possible constraints on performance has been shown to increase rater confidence in performance levels and could thus reduce the effects of ratee IM behaviors as well (Bernardin, 1989).

Conduct more frequent performance appraisals or maintain a performance diary. It may be advisable to conduct more frequent appraisals given the limited human ability to recall and process information (see Cooper, 1981). Research has shown that individuals tend to rate a person in a manner more consistent with their general impression of the person as the interval between observation and rating is extended (Wyer & Srull, 1989). Also, as has been the case with the features reviewed so far, more frequent appraisals underscore the importance placed on appraisal data by the organization. Diary keeping has been shown to increase rating effectiveness and to reduce the effects of a fallible memory (Bernardin & Beatty, 1984).

Determine the appropriate level of ratee aggregation for performance appraisals. Individual ratings of performance are inappropriate in circumstances where the interdependence among work group members precludes a clear determination of an individual's contribution. Moreover, the ambiguity in individual-level performance stemming from this interdependency might increase the effectiveness of ratee impression management behavior on the part of individual group members (Villanova & Bernardin, 1989). In such cases it is advisable to aggregate performance to the group level and rate at this level.

Avoid overall or global performance judgments. Decomposed   ratings are those that require raters to evaluate ratees' performance on multiple tasks or dimensions. Holistic judgments are global evaluations of performance. Most appraisal situations require a rater to make decomposed judgments of performance and then to make a single overall rating of performance. Research has shown that this rating procedure results in low agreement among raters with respect to overall ratee performance (Lyness & Cornelius, 1982). Longenecker, Sims, and Gioia (1987) found that raters faced with the combined decomposed-holistic judgment task "tended to inflate the overall rating rather than the individual appraisal items." And, not surprisingly, "although the overall rating was generally the last item on the appraisal form, this overall rating was determined first; then the executive went back and completed individual items" (p. 187). A better procedure would have raters provide the decomposed judgments and then have these judgments combined statistically into an overall evaluation (Bernardin & Kane, in press; Jako & Murphy, 1990).

Use multiple-rater systems. Single-rater systems (typically using the immediate supervisor as the sole rater) are the most common approach to performance appraisal in industry today (Bernardin & Pynes, 1990). However, peers, subordinates, higher-level supervisors, the ratee, and clients or customers could serve as possible sources of data for pooling performance information. Multiple-rater systems have several advantages. First, because different sources occupy different perspectives from which to observe ratee performance, the use of multiple raters provides a more complete representation of ratee performance; some sources occupy better positions than others to observe critical aspects of ratee performance. Second, multiple rater sources tend to be more accurate. Combining the judgments of different rating sources reduces the influence of bias present in any single rating. Finally, multiple-rater systems can highlight rating inconsistencies and thus serve as a deterrent to rating distortion.

Hold raters accountable for their rating behavior. Holding raters accountable for their ratings by establishing a performance feedback and formal appeals process is another way to reduce the impact of IM behaviors. A feedback and appeals process places the rater on notice that ratings will be discussed with ratees and that the rater may be required to defend his or her ratings. However, while having an operational feedback and appeals process might well reduce the incidence of deliberately deflated ratings, it may also have unintended side effects, such as a general hesitancy of raters to give low ratings (Larson, 1986, 1989). We discuss this issue at greater length below.

Rater Impression Management Motives

We have so far reviewed how characteristics of appraisal systems can foster or dissuade deliberate rating distortion. In this section we focus on factors in the appraisal context that provide motives for raters to manipulate their ratings purposely (see Figure 5.1).

Motives

Leary and Kowalski (1990) recently proposed a two-component model of impression management consisting of impression motivation and impression construction. *Impression motivation* is defined as the desire of individuals to generate specific impressions in others' minds in order to maximize social and material outcomes, maintain self-esteem, and/or cultivate a particular public identity. *Impression construction* is the process of choosing the kind of impression to create and deciding exactly what behaviors would be effective in transmitting such an image. Our concern in this section is largely with impression motivation among raters. Impression construction, or the choice of rating strategies by raters for impression management purposes, has received attention elsewhere (see Villanova & Bernardin, 1989).

Intended use of appraisal data. When appraisal data are used for important personnel decisions such as promotions, merit increases, or layoffs, rater motivation to distort ratings may be more pronounced due to the potential implications of ratings for ratee social, economic, and/or political status in the work group or organization (Ferris et al., 1989). Of course, since the implications of such ratings for the ratee are so significant, the rater is likely to approach the ratings in a more studied manner, perhaps mindful of the potential implications the ratings may have for future rater-ratee interactions (Bernardin & Villanova, 1986; Longenecker et al., 1987). To the extent that ratings are perceived as critical by management, there could also be greater accountability for raters and thus less motivation to distort ratings.

Rater role in the selection of work group members. Schoorman's (1988) data on escalation bias in performance appraisal suggest that raters tend to inflate the performance ratings of ratees for whom raters have agreed with and participated in the original hiring decision. What's more, Schoorman also found that raters gave lower ratings to those ratees for whom the raters disagreed with and participated in the decision to hire. While Schoorman's data were interpreted in terms of escalation of commitment to a previous decision, the findings are also consistent with an impression management explanation. That is, in the organization studied by Schoorman, raters' decisions to hire or reject applicants were known to the personnel director and the raters' supervisors. It is very likely that the impression management concerns of raters to appear accurate in their ability to forecast future employee success may have contributed to the rating bias. We would expect that more public disclosure of an employment decision by a supervisor would result in a correspondingly greater concern with the accuracy of the initial decision and serve as a catalyst for rater impression motivation.

Rater trust in the appraisal process. If raters have low trust in the appraisal process, they are more likely to use the ratings for impression management purposes. Bernardin and Orban (in press) administered a questionnaire called TAPS (Trust in the Appraisal Process Survey) to raters that asked them to indicate the extent to which the "typical supervisor" in the department or organization would purposely distort ratings (e.g., inflate ratings). The reasoning behind the questionnaire was that the "typical supervisor" conducts performance appraisals in the context of the way in which other raters approach the task. Bernardin and Orban found that to the extent that raters felt the typical supervisor would inflate ratings, they themselves tended to rate more leniently. If raters perceive that the appraisal process is used by other raters to "bask in the reflected glory" (Cialdini, 1989) of their subordinates' success, they are likely to follow suit themselves. Experimental data from Greenberg (1983, 1984) similarly illustrate that raters tend to inflate ratings of their subordinates' performance in order to convey an image of successful management. On the other hand, in a low-trust environment some raters may purposely deflate ratings as an attempt to minimize deviation from prescribed behavior. Cummings (1983) notes that interpersonal trust and trust between individuals and the organization can reduce rater use of performance appraisal as a control mechanism to correct deviant behavior.

Rater need for social approval. Some individuals may have a greater need for social approval and so respond more favorably to social influence attempts in order to maintain others' positive regard. They may also go to great lengths in order to avoid confrontation with others. Some research supports the view that particular leadership styles or traits may be related to rating inflation. Klores (1966) found that supervisors who scored higher on the "consideration" dimension of a leadership scale tended to make more lenient ratings of their subordinates. To the extent that this dimension is related to a need to maintain friendly relationships with subordinates or to avoid confrontations regarding judgments of performance, consideration may also be related to susceptibility to social influence attempts. A high need to avoid confrontation may also affect the way the rater attends to and stores performance-related information. Such a motivation, for example, may foster greater attention to the affective components of a supervisory-subordinate relationship and less attention to the observation and encoding of information related to performance. Such an orientation at the encoding, storing, and integration components of the performance appraisal process may facilitate greater reliance on other sources (ratees themselves) for information about performance and constraints on performance and ultimately less confidence in a rater's performance ratings. Such conditions would further increase the probability of inflated ratings.

Rater self-efficacy in providing negative performance feedback. In 1986 we published a study reporting the results of a survey we administered to actual participants of appraisal systems (administrators, supervisors, subordinates) (Bernardin & Villanova, 1986). We asked them to rate 20 factors (nominated by an independent group of similar respondents) thought to be potential causes of rating inaccuracy. We found that the factor deemed most responsible for rating inaccuracy in organizations from the perspective of subordinates (i.e., ratees) was that raters rate some employees higher than deserved as an attempt to please certain employees. Also, supervisors (i.e., raters) reported that a significant source of rating error stemmed from their desire to avoid confrontations with ratees. Laboratory research corresponds with our questionnaire findings; Fisher (1979) found that the ratings by raters who anticipated future contact with ratees exhibited greater leniency than the ratings by raters who did not expect any future contact.

In another study with actual appraisal participants, Napier and Latham (1986) found that raters perceived the use of incidents to support an unfavorable rating would reduce their own chances of promotion. They conclude, "Apparently, appraisers feared the organizational consequences of 'making waves' with their subordinates" (p. 833).

In addition to the leadership instrument discussed above, another instrument shown to be related to rating leniency is the Performance Appraisal Self-Efficacy Scale (PASES), which purports to measure a rater's expectation of personal efficacy regarding the appraisal process (see Table 5.2). High scores represent low self-efficacy and predict higher rating leniency (Bernardin & Kane, in press). The PASES may also predict susceptibility to IM behaviors, since many IM behaviors are directed at making the rater aware of ratee perspectives on levels of performance and attributions of effective and ineffective performance. Such IM behaviors could thus increase the rater's fear of confrontation over an impending appraisal and, for those raters with difficulties in this area, increase the probability that the rating will be adjusted. Raters who are generally uncomfortable in the role of judge or in making decisions about people may also be more willing simply to accept the perspective of the ratee on causes and levels of performance outcomes. The PASES could be used as a diagnostic instrument to identify raters who may be prone to leniency bias in order to avoid confrontations with subordinates. Raters so identified could be provided with some form of assertiveness training so that they might feel more confident in executing their appraisal responsibilities.

Table 5.2   Performance Appraisal Self-Efficacy Scale

Indicate the degree of discomfort you would feel in the following situations. Answer as honestly as possible what is true of you. Do not merely mark what seems "the right thing to say."

Rate each item on the following scale:
5 = high discomfort
4 = some discomfort
3 = undecided
2 = very little discomfort
1 = no discomfort

(1) Telling an employee who is also a friend that he or she must stop coming into work late.

(2) Telling an employee that his or her work is only satisfactory, when you know that he or she expects an above satisfactory rating.

(3) Talking to an employee about his or her poor performance.

(4) Conducting a formal performance appraisal interview with an ineffective employee.

(5) Asking an employee if he or she has any comments about your rating of his or her performance.

(6) Telling an employee who has problems in dealing with other employees that he or she should do something about it (take a course, read a book, etc.).

(7) Telling a male subordinate that his performance must improve.

(8) Responding to an employee who is upset over your rating of his or her performance.

(9) Conducting a formal appraisal interview with an effective employee.

(10) Letting an employee give his or her point of view regarding a   problem with performance.

(11) Giving a satisfactory rating to an employee who has done a satisfactory (but not exceptional) job.

(12) Having a subordinate disagree during an appraisal interview.

(13) Being challenged to justify an evaluation in the middle of an appraisal interview.

(14) Being accused of playing favorites in the rating of your staff.

(15) Recommending that an employee be discharged.

(16) Telling an employee that his or her performance can be improved.

(17) Telling an employee that you will not tolerate his or her taking extended coffee breaks.

(18) Warning an ineffective employee that unless performance improves, he or she will be discharged.

(19) Telling a female employee that her performance must improve.

(20) Encouraging an employee to evaluate his or her own performance.

Individuals are generally reluctant to transmit bad news to others (Tesser & Rosen, 1975), but being visible to the recipient of the bad news is particularly distressing. This was demonstrated in an experiment by Bond and Anderson (1987) in which subjects were asked to communicate either favorable or unfavorable feedback to a peer about his or her performance on an intelligence test. Also, subjects were led to believe that they would be either visible or not visible to the test taker. Bond and Anderson found that

subjects who were led to believe they were visible to the peer in the tes
failure condition took twice as long to deliver feedback as did subjects i
any other group. Also, subjects who were both visible and delivered negativ
feedback also reported greater discomfort than subjects in any other condi
tion. Of course, in most appraisal systems, performance feedback to subor
dinates is typically communicated by the immediate supervisor who als
completed the ratings. Insofar as the rater is required to justify the ratings
feels discomfort in conveying negative feedback, or perceives that negativ
feedback may harm future rater-ratee interactions, the rater will have ampl
incentive to distort ratings (Bernardin & Kane, in press; DeCotiis & Peti
1978).

Rater perceptions of leader-member relations. Raters' impression moti
vation is probably more acute in circumstances of poor leader-membe
relations. This was indirectly illustrated by Kipnis and Vanderveer (1971)
Further evidence for the effect of group composition on rating behavio
comes from the work of Mitchell and Liden (1982), who found that ʒ
poor-performing subordinate was rated more positively and the remainin
well-performing group members more negatively when the poor performe
possessed good social and/or leadership skills than when the poor performe
was low on these factors. Mitchell and Liden also report field data tha
suggest supervisors direct less severe responses toward group members whɔ
perform poorly but are well liked by other group members. Other evidenc
supports the contention that within-group variability in leader-member rela
tions can serve as a catalyst for rater impression motivation (e.g., Grey &
Kipnis, 1976).

Individual differences in justice motives or the costs associated witƗ
specific rating responses might mitigate the occurrence of opportunisti
rating behavior. For example, if ratings are tied to reward distributions, mor
"equity-sensitive" raters (Huseman, Hatfield, & Miles, 1987) may be mor
reluctant to distort ratings if such behavior results in a nonequitable distribu
tion of rewards. Likewise, if the group maintains a strong equity norm sucƗ
that deviations from this norm result in the withdrawal of group approva
(i.e., punishment), the rater may be less inclined to distort ratings for fear o
undermining group cohesiveness or the leader-member relationship (see Rei
& Gruzen, 1976; Walster, Berscheid, & Walster, 1973).

Rater commitment to the organization's mission. Another motivationa
variable that may be related to rater susceptibility to IM influence is rate
organizational commitment. Raters who embrace the organizational missioɲ
and strategic goals tend to be more performance oriented in their manageria

capacities and thus may be less susceptible to rater behaviors related to the affective components of manager-subordinate interaction. While managers high in organizational commitment may certainly seek to establish and maintain close working relationships with subordinates, such a goal is predicated on the assumption that such relationships are essentially good for business. Managers less committed to the organization and its mission may be primarily motivated to gain popularity, friendships, and generally amiable working relationships so as to avoid discord and confrontation.

Criteria used to evaluate raters' ratings. In some instances the ratings assigned to subordinates may be used by superiors to make inferences about the raters' supervisory behavior. High ratings may lead to different inferences as to what was responsible for the high ratings. The superior may infer that the ratings reflect an instance of effective supervision, or that the work group may consist of exceptionally talented members, or, simply, that rater leniency may be wholly responsible for the high ratings. Each of these inferences leads to a different image of the rater. The rater's impression management task then becomes one of anticipating superior reactions to different rating levels. If, for example, the rater believes his or her superior prefers lower ratings, the ratings may be manipulated to reflect a severity bias so that the superior may conclude the rater is a taskmaster. Of course, attempts to appease one constituency (e.g., superiors who prefer ratings that are normally distributed) may lead to antagonism with another (e.g., subordinates who desire high ratings; Villanova & Bernardin, 1989). When rating criteria in addition to rating level are adopted, such as agreement with other raters or peer ratings, the rater's attempt at impression management through ratings becomes more difficult because he or she does not have direct knowledge of the ratings provided by other raters or work group members. Moreover, if the organization has a corrective policy regarding incidents of rating disagreement (i.e., the ratings are analyzed and a rater found to be rating too high or too low is identified and counseled about his or her rating behavior), then the propensity to distort ratings deliberately might be mitigated by the perceived costs of such allegations.

Summary

When raters who are motivated to distort ratings are provided with the means to do so, they may use the ratings toward some political end. However, as we have tried to illustrate, many situational and dispositional factors influence the likelihood and magnitude of such rating distortion. The problems that rater IM strategies pose for human resources management professionals are daunting, but, nonetheless, increased awareness of the phenomenon serves at least to highlight the need for further understanding of the effects of IM on appraisals.

Given the myriad IM strategies available to raters and the resource constraints on personnel and human resources management departments, it may be wishful thinking to believe that an appraisal system could be designed that would be completely free of deliberate rating distortion. However, some progress toward that end could be made by incorporating some of the more positive characteristics discussed above. As noted by one of the participants in the Longenecker et al. (1987) study, "I guess the biggest thing is that people are led to believe that it is a management tool that works; it's got to start at the top" (p. 186).

References

Austin, J. T., Villanova, P., Kane, J. S., & Bernardin, H. J. (in press). Construct validation of performance measures: Definitional issues, development, and evaluation of indicators. In G. R. Ferris & K. M. Rowland (Eds.), *Research in personnel and human resources management* (Vol. 9). Greenwich, CT: JAI.

Bernardin, H. J. (1989). Increasing the accuracy of performance management: A proposed solution to erroneous attributions. *Human Resource Planning, 12*, 239-250.

Bernardin, H. J., & Beatty, R. W. (1984). *Performance appraisal: Assessing human behavior at work.* Boston: Kent.

Bernardin, H. J., & Buckley, M. R. (1981). Strategies in rater training. *Academy of Management Review, 6*, 205-212.

Bernardin, H. J., & Kane, J. S. (in press). *Performance appraisal: Assessing human behavior at work* (2nd ed.). Boston: Kent.

Bernardin, H. J., & Orban, J. A. (in press). Performance ratings as a function of trust in the appraisal, purpose for the appraisal, and rater individual differences. *Journal of Business and Psychology.*

Bernardin, H. J., & Pynes, J. P. (1990). *A survey of performance appraisal among the Fortune 1000.* Unpublished manuscript.

Bernardin, H. J., & Villanova, P. (1986). Performance appraisal. In E. Locke (Ed.), *Generalizing from laboratory to field settings* (pp. 43-62). Lexington, MA: Heath/Lexington.

Bond, C. F., & Anderson, E. L. (1987). The reluctance to transmit bad news: Private discomfort or public display? *Journal of Experimental Social Psychology, 23*, 176-187.

Cialdini, R. B. (1989). Indirect tactics of image management: Beyond basking. In R. A. Giacalone & P. Rosenfeld (Eds.), *Impression management in the organization* (pp. 45-56). Hillsdale, NJ: Lawrence Erlbaum.

Cooper, W. H. (1981). Ubiquitous halo. *Psychological Bulletin, 90*, 218-244.

Cummings, L. L. (1983). Performance-evaluation systems in the context of individual trust and commitment. In F. Landy, S. Zedeck, & J. Cleveland (Eds.), *Performance measurement and theory* (pp. 89-93). Hillsdale, NJ: Lawrence Erlbaum.

Cummings, L. L., & Schwab, D. P. (1973). *Performance in organizations: Determinants and appraisal.* Glenview, IL: Scott, Foresman.

DeCotiis, T. A., & Petit, A. (1978). The performance appraisal process: A model and some testable propositions. *Academy of Management Review, 3,* 635-645.

Fandt, P. M., & Ferris, G. R. (1987). *Impression management in organizations* (working paper). College Station: Texas A&M University.

Ferris, G. R., & Mitchell, T. R. (1987). The components of social influence and their importance for human resources research. In K. M. Rowland & G. R. Ferris (Eds.), *Research in personnel and human resources management* (Vol. 5, pp. 103-128). Greenwich, CT: JAI.

Ferris, G. R., Russ, G. S., & Fandt, P. M. (1989). Politics in organizations. In R. A. Giacalone & P. R. Rosenfeld (Eds.), *Impression management in the organization* (pp. 143-170). Hillsdale, NJ: Lawrence Erlbaum.

Fisher, C. D. (1979). Transmission of positive and negative feedback to subordinates: A laboratory investigation. *Journal of Applied Psychology, 64,* 533-540.

Gardner, W. L., & Martinko, M. J. (1988). Impression management in organizations. *Journal of Management, 14,* 321-338.

Giacalone, R. A. (1985). On slipping when you thought you had your best foot forward: Self-promotion, self-destruction, and entitlements. *Group & Organization Studies, 10,* 61-80.

Greenberg, J. (1983). Self-image versus impression management in adherence to distributive justice standards: The influence of self-awareness and self-consciousness. *Journal of Personality and Social Psychology, 44,* 5-19.

Greenberg, J. (1984). *Inflated performance evaluations as a self-serving bias* (working paper). Columbus: Ohio State University.

Greenberg, J. (1990). Looking fair versus being fair: Managing impressions of organizational justice. In B. M. Staw & L. L. Cummings (Eds.), *Research in organizational behavior* (Vol. 12, pp. 111-157). Greenwich, CT: JAI.

Grey, R. J., & Kipnis, D. (1976). Untangling the performance appraisal dilemma: The influence of perceived organizational context on evaluative processes. *Journal of Applied Psychology, 61,* 329-335.

Huseman, R. C., Hatfield, J. D., & Miles, E. W. (1987). A new perspective on equity theory: The equity sensitivity construct. *Academy of Management Review, 12,* 222-234.

Ivancevich, J. M. (1979). Longitudinal study of the effects of rater training on psychometric error in ratings. *Journal of Applied Psychology, 64,* 502-508.

Jako, R. A., & Murphy, K. R. (1990). Distributional ratings, judgment decomposition, and their impact on interrater agreement and rating accuracy. *Journal of Applied Psychology, 75,* 500-505.

Katz, D., & Kahn, R. L. (1978). *The social psychology of organizations* (2nd ed.). New York: John Wiley.

Kipnis, D., Schmidt, S. M., & Wilkinson, I. (1980). Intraorganizational influence tactics: Explorations in getting one's way. *Journal of Applied Psychology, 65,* 440-452.

Kipnis, D., & Vanderveer, R. (1971). Ingratiation and the use of power. *Journal of Personality and Social Psychology, 17,* 280-286.

Klores, M. S. (1966). Rater bias in forced-distribution ratings. *Personnel Psychology, 19,* 411-421.

Larson, J. R. (1986). Supervisors' performance feedback to subordinates: The impact of subordinate performance valence and outcome dependence. *Organizational Behavior and Human Decision Processes, 37*, 391-408.

Larson, J. R. (1989). The dynamic interplay between employees' feedback-seeking strategies and supervisors' delivery of performance feedback. *Academy of Management Review, 14*, 408-422.

Leary, M. R., & Kowalski, R. M. (1990). Impression management: A literature review and two-component model. *Psychological Bulletin, 107*, 34-47.

Liden, R. C., & Mitchell, T. R. (1988). Ingratiatory behaviors in organizational settings. *Academy of Management Review, 13*, 572-587.

Longenecker, C. O., Sims, H. P., & Gioia, D. A. (1987). Behind the mask: The politics of employee appraisal. *Academy of Management Executive, 1*, 183-193.

Lyness, K. S., & Cornelius, E. T., III. (1982). A comparison of holistic and decomposed judgment strategies in a performance rating simulation. *Organizational Behavior and Human Performance, 29*, 21-38.

Mitchell, T. R., & Liden, R. C. (1982). The effects of social context on performance evaluations. *Organizational Behavior and Human Performance, 29*, 241-256.

Napier, N. K., & Latham, G. P. (1986). Outcome expectancies of people who conduct performance appraisals. *Personnel Psychology, 39*, 827-837.

Ralston, D. A. (1985). Employee ingratiation: The role of management. *Academy of Management Review, 10*, 477-487.

Reis, H. T., & Gruzen, J. (1976). On mediating equity, equality, and self-interest: The role of self-presentation in social exchange. *Journal of Experimental Social Psychology, 12*, 487-503.

Schoorman, F. D. (1988). Escalation bias in performance appraisals: Consequences of supervisor participation in hiring decisions. *Journal of Applied Psychology, 73*, 58-62.

Stires, L. K., & Jones, E. E. (1969). Modesty versus self-enhancement as alternative forms of ingratiation. *Journal of Experimental Social Psychology, 5*, 172-188.

Tesser, A., & Rosen, S. (1975). The reluctance to transmit bad news. In L. Berkowitz (Ed.), *Advances in experimental social psychology* (Vol. 8, pp. 193-232). New York: Academic Press.

Villanova, P., & Bernardin, H. J. (1989). Impression management in the context of performance appraisal. In R. A. Giacalone & P. Rosenfeld (Eds.), *Impression management in the organization* (pp. 299-314). Hillsdale, NJ: Lawrence Erlbaum.

Walster, E., Berscheid, E., & Walster, G. W. (1973). New directions in equity research. *Journal of Personality and Social Psychology, 25*, 151-176.

Wayne, S. J. (1987). *An investigation of the determinants of exchange quality in supervisor-subordinate relationships.* Unpublished doctoral dissertation, Texas A&M University.

Wayne, S. J., & Ferris, G. R. (1990). Influence tactics, affect, and exchange quality in supervisor-subordinate interactions: A laboratory experiment and field study. *Journal of Applied Psychology, 75*, 487-499.

Wayne, S. J., & Rubenstein, D. (1987, August). *The influence of subordinate impression management behaviors on supervisor performance appraisal and exchange quality.* Paper presented at the annual meeting of the Academy of Management, New Orleans.

Wyer, R. S., & Srull, T. K. (1989). *Memory and cognition in its social context.* Hillsdale, NJ: Lawrence Erlbaum.

Zalesny, M. D. (1990). Rater confidence and social influence in performance appraisals. *Journal of Applied Psychology, 75*, 274-289.

6

Impression Management and Exit Interview Distortion

ROBERT A. GIACALONE
STEPHEN B. KNOUSE
D. NEIL ASHWORTH

Competition for goods and services is occurring on a global rather than national basis. Moreover, remaining competitive will primarily be a function of the effective use of human resources in the organization. Organizations are beginning to realize that it is an expensive proposition not only to attract competent workers but also to retain them by providing an environment conducive to the creativity and innovation that is critical for the firm's survival. Managing turnover is one of the keys to managing these crucial human resources. Judicious handling of turnover can ensure a consistent infusion of fresh ideas and new energy within the employee ranks. Replacement costs, such as recruiting, hiring, and paying market value for new employees, can be high, however (Casio, 1982; Mercer, 1988). Thus unlimited turnover is not cost-effective; replacement costs dictate an upper limit to acceptable turnover. Moreover, the psychological costs of turnover can include apprehension and distrust among employees who remain with the organization.

An Effective Separation Process: The Exit Interview

Turnover can be viewed as an organizational process that, like many organizational processes, can be improved by appropriate feedback loops (Steers & Rhodes, 1978). Feedback in the form of information obtained from employees who are being separated can have a positive effect on how their successors are treated, on hiring and retaining new employees, on identifying more efficient ways of conducting operations, and on identifying means of improving communication. One of the primary means of obtaining useful information is through the use of an exit interview.

An exit interview is "a discussion between a representative of an organization and a person whose employment with that organization has been terminated" (Goodale, 1982, p. 169). As a recruiting interview creates an opportunity to gather as much information as possible about a potential entrant into the organization, the exit interview may identify undetected problems that may be creating a negative effect on employee turnover. Such problems could involve such issues as the stridency of company regulations and policies as well as the overall impact of management philosophy.

The success of an exit interview, however, is a function of the organization's ability to conduct the interview effectively. While interview guidelines may vary among companies, the following items have received consistent support in the literature (see, e.g., Bruce, 1988; Embry, Mondy, & Noe, 1979; "Exit Interviews," 1986; Giacalone, 1989; Giacalone & Knouse, 1989):

(1) Do not wait until the employee's last day to conduct an exit interview when other issues may be perceived as more important (e.g., resolution of severance pay).

(2) Allow enough time during the interview to give an employee ample opportunity to discuss his or her feelings and answer questions from the organization's representative.

(3) Make sure the individual conducting the exit interview is personable, easy to talk to, and trusted by the employee. The interviewer should also be knowledgeable about company policies, procedures, and benefits in order to answer any questions competently.

(4) Focus in the exit interview on the job itself; avoid comments on the employee's personality.

(5) Provide open-ended questions that give the employee an opportunity to express him- or herself freely. A standardized format is recommended as a means of providing more consistency across interviews.

(6) Keep the goals of the exit interview realistic; do not expect to gain full disclosure of everything.

(7) Deal with positive aspects of the job ("What did you like about the job?") as well as any negative issues contributing to the separation.

(8) Compare the benefits, salary, and opportunities of the employee's new job with those of the old job. Explore how the old job could be changed to improve it.

It should be noted that following these guidelines will not only heighten awareness of potential problems within the company but may also help the company avoid wrongful discharge litigation. With the common law doctrine of freedom to discharge employees for any reason being seriously challenged in the courts, expensive, time-consuming litigation is becoming increasingly common. Employers have to be prudent about what they ask or reveal during the exit interview (Gilbert, 1987).

Distorted Information From the Exit Interview

The use of well-defined, consistent guidelines in conducting an exit interview can produce information that will be useful in the management of an organization's human resources. Realistically, however, there is a distinct possibility that information obtained from those separating from the organization will, in fact, be distorted to some extent. One reason for such distortion may be that there is a more pressing concern for information concerning future compensation and/or life and health insurance. The distortion may also arise from the fact that too much information is expected to be shared in a relatively short period. In any case, organizations need to be aware that distortion can occur and to be alert to the many ways in which it can be created. Following is a review of factors leading to response distortion as suggested by previous studies (see, e.g., Giacalone & Knouse, 1989).

In many exit interviews, personal considerations are paramount. For example, an individual may perceive some issues as involving his or her personal life, and may therefore be reluctant to provide any information. It may be that the separated employee is willing to address job conditions but will not discuss other individuals, or that he or she will want to avoid conflict at all costs (i.e., does not want to "burn any bridges").

A second cause of distortion can be attributed to an individual's anger with "forced separation." It would be logical, of course, to assume that employees who are leaving voluntarily will be more favorably disposed to provide useful information to an organization's representative. When an employee is forcibly terminated, there is always the risk that any information provided will be intentionally distorted for revenge purposes. This distortion could occur, for example, when an employee is forced to retire early or is unjustly accused of improper behavior.

Another factor that could distort information is an overwhelming concern by those being separated for the protection of employees who remain with the organization. It is possible that criticism of the company's operations or those in charge of the operations could produce changes in policies and procedures that would be regarded as detrimental to an individual's former coworkers. In other words, an interviewee may withhold important information or offer a biased view in order to minimize the likelihood that those remaining behind will suffer as a result of information he or she is being asked to provide.

Distortion in the exit interview may also occur when individuals fear that negative information may result in future reprisals from the organization in the form of negative recommendations. An individual leaving an organization and having to embark on a job search realizes that a prospective employer will want as much job-related information as possible from former employers. Thus he or she will want to avoid the even the remote possibility that a former employer will offer a negative recommendation, and possibly prevent him or her from gaining new employment (Knouse, 1983).

Finally, an individual who is about to be separated may simply lack incentive to cooperate with the organization in its search for useful information. There are those who may think that the exit interview is an exercise in futility, with no real benefits to be gained from the time invested (Garretson & Teel, 1982). In addition, and equally important, the separated individual does not expect to obtain any personal benefits (e.g., money, intrinsic rewards) from taking the time to respond to a series of questions from the organization.

Thus, although exit interviews can provide a useful vehicle for obtaining information that can be beneficial to the operations of a company and the human resources behind the operations, human resources professionals must realize that such information may not be forthcoming from those being separated by the company.

Distortion, Impression Management, and the Exit Interview

Although research and discussions of exit interview distortion have not been based on any one theoretical approach, impression management theory can provide a theoretical basis for explaining exit interview distortion. Essentially, the interviewee is motivated to create some impression (or hide an impression) that will provide him or her with short- or long-term benefits. In creating this impression, the interviewee may draw from a variety of tactics, such as ingratiation, enhancement, and self-presentation (Gardner & Martinko, 1988; Schlenker, 1980). Of primary interest is an understanding of why interviewees are motivated to distort information. In short, what interviewee role might the interviewee choose to play in the exit interview process?

Interviewees and Roles

In assessing the role of the interviewee during the exit interview, one could compare it with the role of a volunteer research subject. The comparative analysis of the roles both play yields striking similarities. First, both the research subject and the exit interviewee are expected to provide information to a person perceived to be powerful, leaving both in a rather powerless position (Weber & Cook, 1972). Second, both the volunteer subject and the interviewee have very little to gain from the experience. In many cases, the volunteer in behavioral research is taking part to fulfill course obligations or to avoid additional assignments. The exit interviewee is often simply fulfilling another obligation in making the transition out of the organization. Finally, both the exit interviewee and the research subject provide information that is unique to them, information that is often difficult to verify regarding veracity. This allows for distortion and/or outright falsification of information and attitudes.

We suggest that exit interviewees play roles in much the same way that research subjects do, reporting information that creates the impression that they believe is appropriate, given the roles they have chosen to play (see Stone, 1989). Distortion, therefore, can be conceptualized as the management of impressions based on the subject's role orientation.

Subject Roles in the Exit Interview

Research on subject roles has provided four distinct roles that subjects may play: apprehensive, good, faithful, and negativistic (Weber & Cook, 1972; Kruglanski, 1975). We now turn the discussion to the potential effects these roles have in the management of impressions during the exit interview.

Weber and Cook (1972) define the apprehensive role as one in which subjects are "apprehensive about how their performance will be used to evaluate their abilities or their socioemotional adjustment" (p. 275). The subject's role, then, leads him or her to mitigate, moderate, intensify, or falsify responses so as to protect the others' relatively positive (or neutral) perceptions of his or her abilities or adjustment. Such apprehension undoubtedly affects the role that an exit interviewee will take on. While in the experiment this apprehension is probably focused on abilities and adjustment (because the subject is aware of the psychological nature of the experiment), apprehension in the exit interview may extend beyond the parameters of psychological well-being. In fact, the apprehensive role in the exit interview may occur because of apprehension about what the *interviewer will do* with particular information. Such fears may focus on retaliation by the interviewee's current employer against the interviewee in a new job or on retaliation against the interviewee's friends remaining in the organization.

The good subject is said to attempt "to give responses that, in his opinion, will validate an experimental hypothesis" (Weber & Cook, 1972, p. 275). While such formal experimental hypotheses are virtually nonexistent in the personnel world, easy substitutes can be found in the form of leading questions by interviewers, unintentional nonverbal messages, or carefully planned programs into which the organization has invested much time and money.

The faithful subject is one who "believes that a high degree of docility is required in research settings and . . . further believes that his major concern should be to scrupulously follow experimental instructions" (Weber & Cook, 1972, p. 275). These faithful subjects, however, can be further distinguished into those who are *active* and those who are *passive*. The active faithful subject is motivated to help, and will therefore do all in his or her power not to act on any suspicions. On the other hand, the passive faithful subject stays generally uninvolved, and dispassionately follows instructions (Orne, 1962). From the standpoint of the exit interviewee, the essential facet of the faithful role is that no impression management is expected, because he or she is either indifferent or concerned with accuracy (Weber & Cook, 1972).

Finally, the negativistic subject is said to "want to confirm [a hypothesis] by corroborating some hypothesis other than the experimenter's or by giving responses that are of no use to the experimenter" (Weber & Cook, 1972, p. 275). Although the reasons for this role in experimentation remain unclear (see Fillenbaum & Frey, 1970; Masling, 1966), in the exit interview, the interviewee's motivations may be more goal directed. First, the interviewee may wish to create an erroneous impression so as to retaliate against upper management for perceived offenses. Such offenses may range from trans-gressions committed by management, of which it is unaware, to the firing of the interviewee or his or her friends. Second, the interviewee may wish to retaliate against lower management or other political enemies he or she may want to bring down or at least malign in some way. Finally, the interviewee may wish to help friends left in the organization to attain some of their goals (e.g., promotions or raises), and may therefore manipulate information for altruistic purposes.

From an impression management standpoint, none of the impression management strategies used can help the interviewer discern which role the subject is playing. They can, however, help us to understand better the motivation that causes interviewees to engage in manipulative techniques in order to affect the perceptions of management.

Beyond Subject Role Impression Management Effects

The subject role approach to understanding why interviewees seek to make particular impressions, however, does not take into account two important factors that may serve to intensify the use of impression manage-ment during the exit interview.

First, the notion of subject roles focuses on the role that the individual interviewee chooses to play during the exit interview. While this is obvious in the context of behavioral research, within the context of the exit interview it is unrealistically restrictive. Interviewee roles should not automatically be assumed to be for self-benefit alone; this would place the behaviors caused by these roles within the more restricted view of impression management as *self-presentation*. Certainly, the role that the interviewee takes on may explain why impression management is used in the context of the individual interviewee's goals. However, one must believe that interviewees may be additionally taking on roles in order to create impressions on behalf of others in the organization. These others most certainly include bosses, colleagues, and friends at the organization, but may also include the impression the interviewer has of members of the interviewee's new organization. A more nefarious goal may be to bring down political enemies in the organization by providing real or fictitious information to damage their images.

Second, because the stakes are potentially so much greater in an exit interview, the resulting distortion may be more motivated and thus stronger. The bias of the subject's information during behavioral research represents an attempt on the subject's part to deal with a short-term relationship with the researcher. Because there is essentially no long-term relationship, the impression that is made is of importance only for the duration of the research. In the exit interview, the impression made could have long-term repercussions for both the interviewee and others who might be affected by the information. It could be expected, therefore, that there is additional motivation to create appropriate impressions for the interviewer, since many more people may be affected (protection of friends and family directly or indirectly affected by the information provided), the reputation and status of the interviewee in a new job may be influenced, and there is a clearer link between the impression created during the interview and the fulfillment of the interviewee's goals (Leary & Kowalski, 1990).

Intentional and Unintentional Distortion

Although much research has fostered the concept of impression management as an intentional and manipulative attempt to control others (e.g., Tedeschi, Schlenker, & Bonoma, 1971) comparable to Machiavellianism, coolly exploitive and controlling, this perspective is but one viewpoint on impression management attempts. In fact, several researchers have noted that many impression management attempts are a result of habitual, overlearned, and unconscious behavior patterns (Hogan, 1982; Leary & Kowalski, 1990; Schlenker, 1980). As Leary and Kowalski (1990) note, "As employees enter the boss's office, they may unconsciously tuck in their shirttails, rake their hand through their hair, and smile" (p. 37).

Although understanding such impression management is rather simple, it nonetheless produces some interesting problems for the exit interviewer. First, just because interviewees are providing distorted information, they cannot be said to be lying. What the interviewee states *is truly believed* by him or her, either because he or she was misinformed or because the statements are congruent with his or her identity. The exit interviewer, therefore, cannot simply look for an organizational malcontent to report distorted information, as one might expect of the negativistic subject. Distorted information may indeed be conveyed by a well-intended exiting employee. Second, because distorted impressions created are not necessarily perceived as lies by the interviewee, usual means of informal screening may not be useful. Thus the potential nonverbal signals ordinarily evidenced by liars (see DePaulo, Stone, & Lassiter, 1985) may not exist, because the interviewee does not experience the information as a lie.

Recommendations for Improving the Exit Interview

Given the potential for information distortion through either intentional or unintentional impression management on the part of the employee being separated, what recourse is left to the employer? The answer is that the exit interview has too much potential value to be abandoned; there are steps that can be taken to reduce impression management distortion.

(1) Pay the employee being separated for participating in the exit interview.

One means of conceptualizing impression management is as a reward exchange process (Tedeschi & Norman, 1985). Each party is providing reinforcements to the other for his or her own ultimate gain. Paying the employee directly may provide a perceived benefit that is reciprocated with truthful information (at least as the employee sees it). When money is presented up front, the employee may reciprocate with the disclosure of a greater amount of information. Further, the employee may be less apt to feel that the interview is superficial or unimportant.

(2) Implement a program of several exit interviews occurring over time. A program of multiple exit interviews over time removes the employee who is being separated from the situation-specific influences of those last days on the job that may affect interview responses (Giacalone & Knouse, 1989). For example, if the employee is brought back for an interview (with pay) several weeks or even months after separation, the influence of such motives as immediate revenge or fear of retaliation against oneself or fellow employees would be lessened. Further, potential roles that the separating employee could take on, such as the apprehensive role or the role of the faithful subject, would be fairly far removed from the work situation factors that maintained them. In addition, multiple interviews provide more time and hence more opportunities for a greater amount as well as a greater variety of information to be brought up. Finally, the cues maintaining unintentional impression management may be weaker over time and thus less influential in controlling the responses of the interviewee.

(3) Consider using an "outsider" to conduct the exit interview.

Using an outsider, such as an independent consultant, as the exit interviewer can reduce fear of retaliation (Zarandona & Camuso, 1985). From the
role-taking perspective, an outsider would be less apt to elicit the apprehensive or faithful subject roles. Further, in terms of impression management,
the various motives to distort information based on employer-related and
work-situation factors would be diminished.

References

Bruce, S. D. (1988). Exit interview: Potent managerial tool. *Chemical Engineering, 95*, 105-108.

Casio, W. F. (1982). *Costing human resources.* Boston: Kent.

DePaulo, B. M., Stone, J. I., & Lassiter, G. D. (1985). Deceiving and detecting deceit. In B. R.
    Schlenker (Ed.), *The self and social life* (pp. 323-370). New York: McGraw-Hill.

Embry, W. R., Mondy, R. W., & Noe, R. M. (1979). Exit interview. *Personnel Administrator,
    24*(5), 43-48.

Exit interviews: An overlooked information source. (1986). *Small Business Report, 11*, 52-55.

Fillenbaum, S., & Frey, R. (1970). More on the "faithful" behavior of suspicious subjects.
    Journal of Personality, 38, 43-51.

Gardner, W. L., & Martinko, M. J. (1988). Impression management in organizations. *Journal
    of Management, 14*, 321-338.

Garretson, P., & Teel, K. S. (1982). The exit interview: Effective tool or meaningless gesture?
    Personnel, 59(4), 70-77.

Giacalone, R. A. (1989). The exit interview: Changing your expectations. *Supervision, 50*, 12-13,
    26.

Giacalone, R. A., & Knouse, S. B. (1989). Farewell to fruitless exit interviews. *Personnel, 66*,
    60-62.

Gilbert, K. R. (1987). Employee terminations: Risky business. *Personnel Administrator, 32*,
    40-46.

Goodale, J. G. (1982). *The fine art of interviewing.* Englewood Cliffs, NJ: Prentice-Hall.

Hogan, R. (1982). A socioanalytic theory of personality. In M. Page (Ed.), *Nebraska Symposium
    on Motivation* (pp. 55-59). Lincoln: University of Nebraska Press.

Knouse, S. B. (1983). The letter of recommendation: Specificity and favorability of information.
    Personnel Psychology, 36, 331-341.

Kruglanski, A. W. (1975). The human subject in the psychology experiment: Fact and artifact.
    In L. Berkowitz (Ed.), *Advances in experimental social psychology, 8*, 101-147.

Leary, M. R., & Kowalski, R. M. (1990). Impression management: A literature review and
    two-component model. *Psychological Bulletin, 107*, 34-47.

Masling, J. (1966). Role-related behavior of the subject and psychologist and its effects upon
    psychological data. *Nebraska Symposium on Motivation, 14*, 67-103.

Mercer, M. W. (1988). Turnover: Reducing the costs. *Personnel, 65*, 36-42.

Orne, M. T. (1962). On the social psychology of the psychological experiment: With particular
    reference to demand characteristics and their implications. *American Psychologist, 17*,
    776-783.

Schlenker, B. R. (1980). *Impression management: The self-concept, social identity, and inter-personal relations.* Monterey, CA: Brooks/Cole.

Steers, R. M., & Rhodes, S. R. (1978). Major influences on employee attendance: A process model. *Journal of Applied Psychology, 63*, 391-407.

Stone, E. F. (1989). Self-presentational biases in organizational research. In R. A. Giacalone & P. Rosenfeld (Eds.), *Impression management in the organization* (pp. 189-202). Hillsdale, NJ: Lawrence Erlbaum.

Tedeschi, J. T., & Norman, N. (1985). Social power, self-presentation, and the self. In B. Schlenker (Ed.), *The self and social life* (pp. 293-322). New York: McGraw-Hill.

Tedeschi, J. T., Schlenker, B. R., & Bonoma, T. V. (1971). Cognitive dissonance: Private ratiocination or public spectacle? *American Psychologist, 26*, 685-695.

Weber, S. J., & Cook, T. D. (1972). Subject effects in laboratory research: An examination of subject roles, demand characteristics, and valid inference. *Psychological Bulletin, 77*, 273-295.

Zarandona, J. L., & Camuso, M. A. (1985). A study of exit interviews. *Personnel, 62*(3), 47-49.

PART III

Negotiation, Conflict, and Justice

7

Establishing Fairness
in the Eye of the Beholder

Managing Impressions
of Organizational Justice

JERALD GREENBERG
ROBERT J. BIES
DON E. ESKEW

How important is a reputation for fairness? It is absolutely critical and essential to my effectiveness as a manager. In fact, a reputation for being fair is one of my primary assets as a manager. To protect this asset, I not only try to be as fair as possible, but in some situations, like with the recent budget cuts, I go out of my way to convince people that I have been fair.

(vice president of a bank)

Background: An Impression Management Approach to Fairness in Organizations

Scholars have long noted how the ideals of justice and fairness serve as guidelines for the harmonious distribution of society's resources in various types of social interaction (Cohen, 1986). For example, consider the admonitions to athletes to "play fairly" on the sports field, and to judges to "give fair sentences" in the courtroom. So too are practicing managers responsible for maintaining fairness in the context of interest to them—the workplace. As an example, consider how the fair determination of wages constitutes an important part of a manager's job (Greenberg & McCarty, 1990). In addition, managers are responsible for making fair employee selection decisions, for conducting employee appraisal interviews fairly, and for seeing that worker-management grievances are settled fairly, to name just a few domains of managerial activity in which considerations of fairness are emphasized (Folger & Greenberg, 1985). As sociologist Charles Perrow (1972) puts it, "The common purpose of an organization must always be a moral purpose, and to inculcate this moral purpose into the very fiber of the organization and into the members of it is the only meaningful task of the executive" (p. 77).

When viewed in this way, it is easy to understand how cultivating an image of fairness may be an important part of any manager's job. Simply put, effective managers need to behave fairly and—just as important—they need to *make sure that others are convinced of their fairness* (Greenberg, 1990b). In this chapter, we follow Leary and Kowalski's (1990) definition of impression management: "the process by which individuals attempt to control the impressions others form of them" (p. 34). More specifically, we focus on how managers in organizations attempt to cultivate and control the impressions of fairness that others form about them. Our analysis focuses on how managers cultivate impressions of fairness in the eyes of others (Baumeister, 1982; Goffman, 1959; Jones & Pittman, 1982; Schlenker, 1980; Tedeschi, 1986). Consistent with Leary and Kowalski's (1990) approach, we view managers as motivated to cultivate impressions of fairness because doing so helps them achieve their organizational objectives (as suggested in our introductory quote). However, creating an impression of fairness is often easier said than done. The major problem lies in the fact that fairness judgments rest in the eye of the beholder. Thus what one person may be convinced constitutes a just decision—be it a fair wage rate or an equitable grievance resolution—may be perceived as patently unjust by another. This is particularly so in organizations, where supervisors and subordinates are very likely to have different sources of information available to them, and to bring different values to bear on the situation. Add to this the fact that the norms of justice are themselves complex and multiply determined (Reis, 1986), and it is easy to anticipate how disagreements are likely to arise between various organizational members regarding what constitutes fair treatment.

It is the astute manager who realizes this and who tries to be fair, not necessarily by following any prescribed patterns of morality, but, instead, by focusing on what others believe to be fair. After all, others will be likely to believe that you are being fair if you have behaved in a manner that appears to be fair from their own perspective. In fact, the more an individual appears to have behaved fairly in the eyes of others, the more likely those others will be to attribute the characteristic of fairness to that person (e.g., "Based on his actions, he appears to be a fair person"). And we know from recent evidence that practicing managers are highly concerned about getting others to think that they are fair—even more than they are concerned about actually *being* fair in any objective sense (Greenberg, 1988). Thus "looking fair" is at least as important as "being fair." In other words, managers seem to be aware implicitly of the value of cultivating an image of fairness—that is, of convincing others that they are fair individuals. This aspect of our impression management perspective on fairness was captured by a senior vice president of a *Fortune* 500 firm in a comment to one of the authors: "What's fair is whatever the workers think is fair. My job is to convince them that what's good for the company is also good for them as individuals" (Greenberg, 1988, p. 155).

The position that fairness is in the eye of the beholder—that is, an impression management perspective of organizational justice—raises two basic questions. First, how can managers create a fair impression? And second, what are the effects of being perceived as fair? This chapter is organized around each of these themes.

How Can Managers Cultivate Impressions of Fairness? Questions Managers Should Ask Themselves

It is a major part of managers' jobs to make decisions that affect their subordinates' outcomes, be they pay-raise decisions, budget allocations, or job assignments (Mintzberg, 1973). When assessing the fairness of such decisions, employees are concerned not only with what outcomes result (e.g., how much they are paid), but also with *how* those decisions were made (e.g., what information was taken into account) (Folger & Greenberg, 1985). Indeed, a fair decision-making process may be considered the hallmark of a fair manager. However, since most managerial decisions are made in private and then announced publicly, it is often difficult for subordinates to observe directly whether or not their superiors acted fairly. Consequently, subordi-

nates may act as "intuitive detectives," searching for clues as to whether o
not their superiors act fairly (Bies, 1987). Most of these clues may be founc
in what managers say and do in their interactions with subordinates.

When attempting to judge their superiors' fairness, subordinates look fo
clues regarding how their superiors have behaved in dealings with subordi
nates. Based on previous conceptualizations and research evidence (e.g.
Folger & Bies, 1989; Leventhal, 1980; Tyler & Bies, 1990), we assert tha
this may take the form of looking for answers to six key questions regardin§
managerial behavior. Specifically, does the manager (a) adequately conside
his or her subordinates' viewpoints, (b) appear to be neutral, (c) appl'
decision-making criteria consistently, (d) give subordinates timely feedback
(e) provide adequate explanations for his or her decisions, and (f) trea
subordinates with respect and dignity? The importance of each of thes«
questions in creating an impression of fairness is considered below.

Does the Manager Adequately Consider Subordinates' Viewpoints?

When managers make decisions that affect their subordinates' outcomes
it is usually considered fair for them to allow the subordinates to have som«
say in those matters. Such participatory practices may take forms rangin§
from formal corporate profit-sharing plans to simple acts of asking individua
subordinates for their viewpoints (Greenberg & Folger, 1983). Allowin§
subordinates to have some input into the decisions influencing them may b·
considered fair because doing so enhances the chances that subordinates
opinions will be taken into consideration. Because subordinates' viewpoint
will be considered, there is an increased likelihood that they will get wha
they want. Indeed, just as litigants in court decisions prefer to select their ow
attorneys and the evidence used in presenting their cases, employees i
performance appraisal situations prefer to have some say over the informa
tion used as the basis for their evaluations (Greenberg, 1986b). Having th
opportunity to be heard concerning the making of crucial organizationa
decisions is a key determinant of their perceived fairness.

It is important to add that perceptions of managerial fairness are enhance
by giving subordinates a voice in the decision-making context not onl
because such a procedure provides them with fair opportunities to influenc
the system, but also because granting them those opportunities suggest
caring and personal sensitivity on the part of the manager (Lind & Tyle
1988). In other words, the mere act of allowing subordinates to express thei
opinions may be at least as important as any possible beneficial outcome
resulting from their expressing those opinions. The key is for managers t

demonstrate that they are concerned about their subordinates' viewpoints. By implementing procedures that take into account their employees' ideas (e.g., "suggestion systems"), managers may do a great deal to enhance their subordinates' impressions of their fairness. Managers must demonstrate that they care enough for their subordinates by allowing them to express their own feelings about matters of interest to them.

As a cautionary note, it is critical to point out that once employees' viewpoints are solicited, it must be made clear to them that those views are given serious consideration by their superiors. Workers may be quite sensitive to clues that their subordinates are listening to them (e.g., nodding in agreement and restating their ideas) and giving serious consideration to their input (e.g., explaining exactly what steps were taken in response to their suggestions). Managers who solicit and then ignore their subordinates' viewpoints run a serious risk of being perceived as more unfair than they would have been if they never provided any opportunities for input in the first place (Greenberg & Folger, 1983). With this in mind, it is not surprising that managers of employee suggestion systems have been advised to explain carefully the reasons behind all decisions to accept or reject each employee's submitted suggestion (Reutter, 1977). Indeed, demonstrating that others' opinions are seriously considered is a critical part of cultivating an image of fairness.

Thus to appear to be fair, managers should solicit and carefully consider in an ostensible manner their employees' viewpoints on matters of concern to them. As an industrial manager confided to one of the authors, "If you ask them [subordinates] for their points of view, you'd better be serious about considering that information. Otherwise, people will feel 'used' and you will be seen as unfair and unfit as a manager."

Does the Manager Appear Neutral?

As another sign of fairness, subordinates expect managers to be impartial and neutral in making decisions. Fairness demands suppressing personal biases that may influence decisions. Just as justice is expected to be "blind" in the courtroom, so too is it expected to be neutral in the workplace. Subordinates expect decisions to be made for reasons that exclude any personal benefits to the decision maker.

Being completely impartial and unbiased is, of course, very difficult to accomplish. After all, even the best-intentioned managers may be expected to show some partiality to their own personal viewpoints. Often, the result may be that subordinates believe they were treated unfairly, especially when the decisions made have negative consequences for them. Ironically, this may be the case even if the decision maker does not mean to be biased, but is simply perceived as such. As a bank manager told one of the authors, "If they [employees] don't think you were neutral, or if they think you were biased against them—even if you were neutral and you know you weren't biased—you will be painted as unfair."

So, then, what can managers do to promote impressions of impartiality? One effective technique is to make a show of neutrality by relying on procedures that ensure impartiality, such as random number drawing. Such a technique may be an effective means of assigning priorities to certain desired limited resources (e.g., access to specific vacation days). Because lotteries allow outcomes to be determined independently of the persons receiving them, they are well accepted as fair procedures. Of course, it would be considered essential for managers using lotteries to hold them in public where both the process and the outcomes can be monitored for the introduction of any additional biases. A manager who claims to have made an important decision by drawing lots, but who did so in private, surely cast doubt on the impartiality of the procedure. (In fact, it may be argued that one who intentionally violates neutrality standards by circumventing the randomness of procedures designed to preclude bias may be guilty of a more serious justice violation than those who simply seized the opportunity to exercise bias in a procedure that allowed for its occurrence.)

As an example of such a practice in operation, one of the authors uses a blind grading scheme for scoring essay exams in his MBA classes. Instead of writing their names on their papers (which the professor could use as a source of bias), students submit their exams with identifying code numbers that are decoded into students' names only later, after the grading has been done. In this manner, the professor cannot be charged with biasing the grades assigned by giving higher or lower scores than warranted to students who might be either favored or disfavored. Although one might argue that such a procedure gives undue attention to the threat of a counternormative, unprofessional action, it is countered by the fact that it ensures against any possible later claims of favoritism by students displeased with their scores. The blind coding procedure promotes the fairness of the instructor by demonstrating that he is enough concerned about the possibility of bias that he voluntarily instituted a procedure to combat it. This example clearly supports our point. Managers must both be neutral and *promote the neutrality of their actions* in their dealings with subordinates.

Does the Manager Apply Decision-Making Rules Consistently?

Few would argue with the idea that fairness demands treating like individuals in a like manner. For example, if one employee's wages are determined by his or her productivity, it would be unfair to base another employee's wages on the number of years he or she has been employed by the company. Research has shown that employees consider such equality of treatment to be a hallmark of fairness in their organizations (Greenberg, 1986a; Sheppard & Lewicki, 1987).

As an example of such a dynamic in operation, consider the recent case of the ongoing contract dispute between NFL football player Steve McMichael and his employer, the Chicago Bears. Although the Bears management claimed to have a policy of "never renegotiating" a player's contract, McMichael became enraged when his own request for renegotiation was denied after another player's contract had, in fact, been renegotiated. To quote McMichael: "Who's getting the most money is not what I'm worried about. I'm talking about equality and justice."

It is important to note that being completely consistent in decision making may make it difficult, if not impossible, for managers to incorporate the level of flexibility and concern for extenuating circumstances that most employees believe are needed to maintain fairness (Sheppard & Lewicki, 1987). In other words, consistency at the cost of flexibility might represent a serious threat to perceived fairness. Thus, whereas a manager may subscribe to a policy of consistently rewarding employees on the basis of their meritorious performance, rigidly adhering to this policy may be considered unfair if it automatically precludes consideration of special situations or extenuating circum–stances. Such unsympathetic reactions may themselves be considered unfair (Tyler & Bies, 1990). Obviously, then, the key is to exercise "consistency with flexibility."

Such a policy also can help managers promote fairness in the hiring and promotion of women and minorities. Unfortunately, women and minority group members are frequently excluded from consideration for some jobs although decision-making rules are applied consistently. The problem is that the decision rules themselves are often biased, or are interpreted in a biased manner to favor one group (e.g., white males) over another (e.g., women, minorities). To overcome such bias, managers sometimes rely on affirmative action policies—additional procedures and criteria that favor qualified women and minorities in hiring and promotion decisions when all other considerations are equal. To many employees, applying the "consistency with flexibility" policy to the hiring and promotion of women and minorities may appear to be very unfair even though such a policy may promote broader societal goals of workplace justice. In such situations, managing impressions of fairness may be difficult for managers, but it need not be impossible. For example, managers must always hire and promote females and minority candidates who are demonstrably well qualified so that hiring practices do not appear to be biased. In addition, managers must point out that whereas a consistency with flexibility policy may appear to be unfair on one dimension, it is also an attempt to eliminate bias in decision making—another key fairness concern.

Does the Manager Give Timely Feedback?

One of the things managers spend a considerable part of their time doing on the job is giving feedback to their subordinates (Mintzberg, 1973). Indeed, letting subordinates know the effects of their actions on organizational functioning is considered a key managerial function. In this regard, just as yesterday's newspaper may have little value, organizational feedback that is given in an untimely fashion may be useless. Late feedback may fail to help workers respond as they should, and giving untimely feedback may be the cause of serious performance problems down the line.

Beyond this, the untimely giving of feedback represents a key source of perceived injustice because of the disrespect it conveys to the recipient— "You were not important enough to respond to right away." Finding out that one's telephone messages and letters are consistently pushed to the back of a superior's response queue, for example, is certainly likely to be taken as a sign of disregard. By contrast, a subordinate who is given an immediate response by a superior is much more likely to believe that the superior was willing to treat his or her ideas as valuable enough to warrant immediate consideration. People believe that fairness demands a prompt response. For example, research by Bies (1986) found that MBA candidates being recruited for jobs frequently cited unduly long delays as sources of unfair treatment experienced in the recruitment process.

Because of the stress associated with many organizational interactions (e.g., performance appraisals, employment interviews), superiors who show consideration by providing prompt feedback tend to be perceived as behaving more fairly than those who respond in a more leisurely fashion. To the extent that fairness demands taking into account the interpersonal concerns of employees, showing sensitivity to those concerns by providing relevant information in a prompt manner is sure to enhance perceptions of fairness (Greenberg, 1990b).

It is with an interest in promoting an image of himself as "rigorous, but fair" in his dealings with students that one of the authors attempts to give very prompt and detailed feedback on his students' dissertation drafts. Given that the student may face a great deal of rethinking and rewriting in response to the professor's suggestions, it may be harder for the student to externalize any delays in completion of the project when the professor's comments are very prompt. Indeed, adding the "insult" of the delay to the "injury" of the major reworking would be fertile ground for claims of unfair treatment. However, to the extent that the feedback is timely, the student is more likely to accept as fair the delays caused by the need to improve the work itself.

There is one particular context that managers are likely to face in which timely feedback may be an especially potent determinant of fairness—that is, when the manager's delay affects the amount of time the subordinate has available to meet a deadline. For example, suppose a lower manager submits a draft of a report to a middle manager for approval three weeks before it is due on the desk of the upper manager. Instead of promptly commenting on the draft, the middle manager waits until the night before it is due to give the lower manager detailed comments. As the lower manager stays up all night hastily making corrections in order to incorporate them into the draft before the deadline, he or she cannot help but think of how unfairly he or she was treated by the middle manager's insensitivity to the demands on the lower manager's time. Of course, it would have represented a fairer distribution of the available slack time had the middle manager given feedback earlier, thereby allowing the lower manager more time to make corrections. If in business "time is money," as they say, then it is no wonder that claims of unduly long delays in feedback may represent the misuse of a valued resource. As a corporate etiquette expert has said, "Wasting the time of any businessman is equivalent to robbing his wallet. Keeping him waiting is bad practice and bad manners" (Alihan, 1970, p. 14).

Does the Manager Provide an Adequate Explanation for the Decision?

When announcing their rulings, judges typically provide explanations for their decisions. By doing so, they provide good evidence that they have considered and taken into account the information relevant to the case at hand. Analogously, it is considered quite useful for managers to provide clear explanations for the decisions they make. Not only do employees tend to expect such accounts, but because so many business decisions are made in private, the decision makers' explanatory accounts may constitute the major way for employees to evaluate the fairness of superiors' actions (Bies, 1987). In other words, employees judge the fairness of the decisions in light of the explanations offered. Indeed, several research studies (e.g., Bies & Shapiro, 1987, 1988) have shown that people receiving undesirable outcomes (e.g., being turned down for a job) are much more likely to accept those outcomes as fair when the decision makers provide sound explanations for the outcomes than when no explanations are offered (see also Giacalone, 1988; Giacalone & Pollard, 1987).

Interestingly, when managers fail to give explanations for their decisions it is almost certain that perceptions of unfairness will result. This is in part because subordinates tend to expect explanations; they believe they have explanations coming to them, almost as "a right" (Bies & Moag, 1986). When no explanation is forthcoming after a decision is made, subordinates are likely to wonder why it was made, and to draw many possible worst-case readings of the decision maker's motives (e.g., "He is favoring his friends and harming his enemies"). Thus the mere act of not explaining an outcome for which an explanation is normatively expected may tend to sensitize subordinates to the possibility of some unfairness—not because any injustice actually occurred, but because nothing was said when an explanation was perceived to be forthcoming.

It is important to point out that it is not enough simply to provide an explanation; the explanation provided must be perceived as adequate (Bies & Sitkin, in press; Higgins & Snyder, 1989). That is, the information must "fit the facts" and have sufficient detail to be convincing. Moreover, the information must be communicated sincerely. That is, subordinates must believe that managers really mean what they are saying. Research has shown that when corporate officials present bad news in just the right manner, they can do a very effective job of warding off what otherwise would be very negative reactions (Bies, Shapiro, & Cummings, 1988). For example, a recent study by Greenberg (1990a) compared employee theft rates in three manufacturing plants during conditions in which a 15% pay cut was in effect for all employees. In one plant, the pay cut was announced without any explanations whatsoever. In a second plant, some minimal information was given to explain why the pay cut was necessary. This information was provided in a dispassionate, businesslike fashion. Finally, in the third plant, a highly elaborate explanation of the facts was provided to explain the need for the pay cut. This information was presented in a highly sensitive manner, showing a great deal of remorse for the adverse effects the action would have on employees. It was found that although employee theft rates were higher during the time of the pay cut than either before or after the pay cut, the amount of theft was influenced greatly by the explanations given for the pay cut. Even the plant at which workers were given a minimal, businesslike explanation for the pay cut had a lower theft rate than the plant where workers were given no explanation. However, the lowest theft rates occurred when the most thorough, interpersonally sensitive explanations were provided. Apparently, a thorough explanation can have a profound effect not only on judgments of organizational fairness, but on profitability as well.

Do Managers Treat Subordinates With Respect and Dignity?

As suggested by the above findings, subordinates are likely to pay a great deal of attention to how they are treated interpersonally. Certainly, fairness demands consideration of how managers go about making decisions, but it also requires attention to interpersonal treatment (Tyler & Bies, 1990). For example, does the manager show concern for the employees' rights of privacy when tests are administered (whether for purposes of testing for illegal drugs or vocational placement)? Does the company management express any regret for having to lay off a segment of the work force? In general, are managers courteous and respectful in their dealings with employees? It is not that subordinates expect to be treated with kid gloves, but rather that they expect to be treated as individuals who have certain rights, and who deserve respect. Such interpersonal treatment is of considerable importance in subordinates' assessments of managers' fairness (Folger & Bies, 1989).

The failure to treat employees with respect and dignity most assuredly undermines impressions of a manager's fairness. For example, publicly ridiculing an employee about substandard performance may be seen as an unfair invasion of the employee's privacy inasmuch as discussions of job performance are widely regarded to be a private matter between superior and subordinate. Employees who feel that they may be humiliated by a superior are likely to decry those actions as unfair. To the extent that employees believe they have the right to be treated with dignity on the job, acts in clear violation of such standards may label the offender as being patently unfair.

This fact is demonstrated in a recent study by Greenberg (in press), in which different amounts of interpersonal sensitivity were demonstrated by an experimenter in the process of attempting to explain a state of underpayment. Whereas one group was shown callous disregard for the outcomes (e.g., "That's the way it is"), the other was shown considerable amounts of interpersonal sensitivity (e.g., "I'm terribly sorry about what's happening"). Interestingly, those treated with courtesy and dignity were more likely to accept the same poor outcomes as fair than those who were treated less courteously. The bottom line: Impressing others with one's fairness demands treating them with dignity and respect.

Summary

We have identified six key questions subordinates are likely to ask in forming their impressions of their managers' fairness. Three of the questions focus on how managers make decisions (i.e., adequately considering subordinates' viewpoints, appearing neutral, being consistent), and three focus on communication (i.e., providing timely feedback, giving adequate explanations, and treating subordinates with respect). The answers to these questions are likely to provide insight into whether one is conveying an impression of fairness to others. In the case of subordinates' impressions of their managers' fairness, the answers may be determined by many important factors. Simply stated, whether one will be perceived as fair will depend on the judgments made about how one acts. As we will see, such judgments may prove critical to organizational functioning.

What Are the Consequences of Cultivating Fair Impressions? Reaping the Benefits, and Suffering the Liabilities, of Looking Fair

Thus far we have argued that there are various things managers can do to promote their images of fairness. The underlying assumption has been that such images are somehow good, and are worth striving for. Certainly, people are interested in feeling that they have behaved fairly because fairness is a desired characteristic, and people like to think of themselves as being fair (Greenberg, 1990b). However, this private self-image of fairness may not be simply an egoistic illusion (see Greenwald & Breckler, 1985), but a perception actually based on one's own fair actions with others (see Bem, 1967). To the extent that a manager is believed to be fair, he or she can be expected to enjoy several benefits at the individual, managerial level as well as at the overall organizational level. However, as we will also argue, being perceived as fair is not an unequivocally positive state; there are also several important negative consequences likely to be associated with being perceived as fair.

Fairness as a Key to Managerial Power

Suppose that you are a manager who has a record of treating subordinates consistently, as we have described in the first part of this chapter. That is, suppose you have adequately considered your subordinates' viewpoints, appeared neutral, acted with consistency, given timely feedback, provided adequate explanations, and treated subordinates with dignity and respect. Such consistently fair treatment is sure to be acknowledged by subordinates, who would simply refer to you, their superior, as "a fair person." As we will see, having earned this label of fairness entitles a manager to certain power advantages in interpersonal relations with subordinates. Indeed, in the minds of many, fairness is inextricably tied to effective leadership. For example, in commenting on General Eisenhower's performance as supreme commander in Europe during World War II, former British Prime Minister Harold Macmillan was quoted as saying, "He had an indispensable quality of leadership, that is, *fairness*" (Hollander, 1985, p. 504).

One way fairness may facilitate individual leadership effectiveness is through the halo effect it creates. That is, fairness as a characteristic is likely to generalize to other positive characteristics. Thus someone who is believed to be fair is also likely to be perceived as honest, honorable, ethical, and, in general, highly trustworthy (Messick, Bloom, Boldizer, & Samuelson, 1985). Being seen as possessing these traits may well facilitate the acceptance of one's actions. Consider the analogy of a military leader guiding troops through a dark tunnel to an unknown destination at the other end. Which leader will be more effective in gaining the support of the troops, one who has won them over with fairness or one who has not so impressed them? Obviously, the more effective leader will be the one who is able to command support due to a record of fairness, the one whose reputation for trustworthiness will be unchallenged in the face of uncertainty.

In an organizational setting, imagine a situation in which a manager is attempting to institute a new performance appraisal program (for a discussion of the role of impression management in performance appraisals, see Villanova & Bernardin, 1989). Certainly, such an event may constitute a situation in which employees will be distrusting and uncertain of the consequences for themselves (e.g., "Will the new system possibly yield lower evaluations of my job performance, resulting in lower raises?"). Because such fears may lead to distrust of the system, it is important for managers to provide the kind of assurance that will facilitate the acceptance of change. There can be little doubt that the managers who will be particularly effective will be those whose reputations for past fairness lead subordinates to give them the benefit of the doubt in the unknown present situation. "He was fair before," subordinates might think, "so there's reason to believe he'll continue to be fair." In other words, as Greenberg (1990b) has noted, cultivating an impression of fairness may result in a manager's accumulation of "idiosyncrasy credits" (Hollander, 1958)—tolerance for ostensibly deviant acts—that subsequently may be spent to gain acceptance of questionable new policies or to "buy" forgiveness for unfair acts. Such willingness to accept a manager's actions in an unknown situation—or to forgive past actions—may be considered an especially potent source of organizational power.

One of the authors has, over the years, worked diligently to cultivate an impression of fairness as an instructor in the eyes of his students. He listens to their arguments regarding exams and class procedures, refrains from showing favoritism, and so on. On one occasion, several years ago, he, along with other instructors teaching in the same program, was ordered by the program director to implement a new exam procedure requiring several changes to safeguard against cheating—stationing multiple proctors throughout the exam room, requiring students to deposit all their personal belongings in a distant part of the room, and so on. For the most part, the students disliked the system because it created a very distrusting atmosphere. When it came to evaluating their instructors that term, the students tended to express their dissatisfaction with instructors who were believed to have instigated and supported the new testing procedures. However, the author's students assumed from his past reputation that he would not have instituted such a plan without being ordered to do so—or, at least, so they stated on their evaluation forms. As a result, the author's reputation for fairness provided him some degree of immunity from the widespread rejection that swept the program that term. Clearly, such reputational power was well spent in this episode.

Fairness as a Key to Improved Organizational Functioning

Despite our emphasis thus far on the individual managerial benefits likely to result from cultivating impressions of managerial fairness, this is not to say that impressions of fairness might not also operate at an organizationwide level. That is, just as individuals might become more effective as managers because of their personal reputations for fairness, so too can organizations benefit because of their corporate reputations for fairness. Indeed, just as individuals may have (and work to promote) certain identities, so too may corporations (or, at least, some of their subunits) enjoy identities as being fair. In such cases, the benefits of having a reputation for fairness may be widespread. Imagine, for example, a company that has a reputation for treating its various stakeholders (e.g., customers, shareholders, employees) fairly. As we will demonstrate, the benefits of being perceived as fair at this level are considerable.

One source of benefits derived from a corporate image of fairness comes from support by customers. For example, it has been claimed that the general public will recognize and support firms that fulfill society's ethical expectations—that is, "socially responsible" firms (Murray & Montanari, 1986). At the negative extreme, widespread boycotts of products of corporations that mistreat either their employees or the environment have been known to have adverse effects on profitability (Lydenberg, Marlin, Strub, & the Council on Economic Priorities, 1986). At the other extreme, data suggest that socially responsible corporate behavior pays off. For example, it has been established that an investment of $30,000 in Dow-Jones stocks in 1952 would have grown to $134,000 by 1986, whereas had the same amount of money been invested in 15 highly socially responsible companies, it would have grown to more than $1 million in the same time (Burns, 1987). Although it is difficult to claim unequivocally that such differential stock performance is caused by greater customer acceptance of socially responsible behavior, the possibility is nevertheless intriguing.

Can it also be said that corporations with images of fairness benefit because of the increased support they receive from current employees? Although this is widely assumed to be the case, most of the relevant research has been conducted by companies preferring to treat such internal data as proprietary. As a result, we have mostly secondary accounts of such associations. In this regard, consider the following observations by an expert on corporate image:

> The effect of an enhanced reputation among employees, improving their morale and productivity, has also been studied and found substantial. But the information is held as confidential. In that case, it has been learned that employees react quite positively to working for a company they are proud of, that an employee's stature in the community goes up when the company's reputation is improved. This effects not only the employees, but their families and friends as well. (Garbett, 1988, pp. 254-255)

In contrast with the scarcity of research on the effects of corporate reputations on current employees, there is a considerable literature noting the role of company images on prospective employees, particularly as it involves the recruitment interview. Of the many mechanisms through which job seekers may learn about the image of prospective employers, the college recruitment interview represents one of the richest and most potent sources of information. Part of the reason for this is that the recruiters usually represent the applicants' primary source of information about the company, often leading them to perceive the recruiters as symbols of their organizations (Rynes, Heneman, & Schwab, 1980). Not surprisingly, research has shown that interviewees tend to project both the positive and negative individual characteristics they perceive in the interviewers onto the companies they represent (e.g., Harris & Fink, 1987; Rynes & Miller, 1983). Thus it is essential that an organization promote its image of fairness through the actions of its corporate recruiters. Indeed, the very same actions being advocated for practicing managers to enhance their perceived fairness may well be recommended for corporate recruiters.

It is especially important to note that the current generation of first-time job seekers, referred to as the "baby bust" generation by David Cannon, a career counselor at a Canadian university, is different from its predecessors in the earlier, "baby boom" generation in that they place a higher value on justice and integrity as work values (Hladun, 1990). Knowing this, recruiters are encouraged to promote their companies' fairness actively in their solicitation efforts. Although it may never have been seen as harmful to promote a corporation's image as fair (at worst, it may have been seen as merely vacuous self-puffery), we are saying that it is now, given current work values, likely to be especially beneficial.

Evidence for this may be seen in a recent study by Schwoerer and Rosen (1989), who observed the reactions of would-be job applicants to different corporate recruiting brochures. One such brochure touted the company's interest in "fair treatment for all employees," whereas the other made no such claim. It was found that the applicants held much more positive impressions of employers who expressed an interest in fairness, and were slightly more willing to pursue jobs with such companies than with those companies that did not express an interest in treating workers fairly. These results support the idea that knowledge about the fairness of a prospective employer's treatment of employees is likely to be a major determinant of job applicants' employment decisions. A company's image of fairness does, in fact, facilitate the corporate recruiting process.

A negative case helps underscore this point. The career counselor mentioned above, David Cannon, cites a case in which a large Canadian company promised a graduating student from Queens University a job at the company's Toronto office (Hladun, 1990). However, when the woman visited the Toronto office, she was told that a recent corporate reorganization now required her to work in another city. Naturally, the new employee felt unfairly treated. How much negative publicity could one disgruntled employee generate for the company? Apparently, a considerable amount: The company witnessed a precipitous drop in the number of recruits from Queens University who signed up for on-campus interviews in each of the years following the event.

Given the heightened sensitivity job applicants are likely to have for unfair job treatment, it is not surprising that one incident had such profound effects on others. After all, when one has little knowledge about a company, one may give considerable weight even to possibly idiosyncratic information when making employment decisions. Not surprisingly, Cannon advises today's recruiters to demonstrate the honest, ethical, and interpersonally sensitive treatment of recruits we have been advocating throughout this chapter.

Possible Liabilities and Limitations
of Fair Impressions: A Caveat

Although the benefits of being perceived as fair may be considerable, it is important to note that there are also several negatives associated with being perceived as a fair person (Greenberg, 1990b). What are these liabilities?

At the personal level, it has been noted that there is a burden associated with always having to justify one's actions as fair. Each action a "fair person" takes must be seen as an act of fairness, thereby requiring him or her repeatedly to justify the actions taken as fair. In other words, having an image requires renewing it by behaving in a manner consistent with it and by making certain that others are so aware (Greenberg, 1990b). Having to do this is somewhat restrictive. As one expert put it, "Infamous people aren't leaders over the long term. Leaders can't get drunk at an office party; they have to act in the way people expect them to act" (Labich, 1988, p. 66). Our point is not that it may be so terribly difficult to be fair repeatedly, but that it could be limiting to have to position one's actions consistently as such.

There is yet another way an impression of fairness may be seen as constituting a liability—namely, because of the raised expectations it is likely to cause. Imagine, for example, an individual whose primary identity is centered on an image as a fair and moral person. Then, imagine that this person is found guilty of some moral offense. Consider the very painful results of having to confront charges that challenge one's central identity. If our story line appears somewhat unoriginal, if not positively worn out, it is no doubt the result of familiar memories from recent history concerning certain political leaders (e.g., Nixon) and TV evangelists (e.g., Bakker and Swaggart). Naturally, any fallen and disgraced individual is likely to feel shamed, but not as much as those who have fallen from loftier perches positioned at the pinnacle of their identities. Thus the more a person promotes an image of fairness, the more fairness is expected of him or her by others, and the more that person will be held accountable for any perceived fairness violations.

Although this argument has been couched in individual terms, the same point can be made regarding reputations of fairness at the organizational level (Greenberg, 1990b). For instance, the American press is an institution historically regarded as safeguarding freedom and democracy; it is expected to report stories to the public fairly and dispassionately. For this reason, there is likely to be considerable disenchantment with the press when it is perceived to be biased or proactive, actively creating stories, rather than unbiased and reactive, passively reporting stories. This was apparently the case before the 1988 U.S. presidential election, when Republican vice presidential candidate Dan Quayle was repeatedly questioned by reporters about his motives for joining the National Guard (allegedly, to avoid being drafted and having to serve in the Vietnam War). A poll taken at the time reported that 55% of those surveyed believed that the press was treating Quayle unfairly ("Poll," 1988). Given that the press is expected to promote justice (i.e., it is "expected to know better"), it is not surprising to find such a public outcry alleging injustice leveled against the press in response to its perceived unfair hounding of a public figure. This is clearly a case of a "holier than thou" image returning to haunt those who embrace it most dearly. Indeed, the same liability of raised expectations that may penalize otherwise fair individuals for apparent acts of unfairness appears to hold the potential for challenging the fairness of institutions as well.

Finally, we should note that being perceived as fair is not always believed to be the most effective way to achieve organizational goals. For example, in *The Soul of a New Machine*, Kidder (1981) recounts the success of Tom West's Data General engineering team in introducing a new minicomputer in record time. Many of the engineers viewed West's management style as often unfair—arbitrary and without any apparent concern for the psychological welfare of team members. West reasoned that showing more interpersonal concern would actually interfere with the team objective in this crisis situation (the introduction of a new minicomputer was necessary for Data

General to stay in business). In other words, fairness was not believed to be the optimal impression to cultivate when trying to motivate team members under such conditions. Of course, to the extent that fairness demands giving full consideration to others' feelings and the opportunity to have a voice in decisions, time pressure and the need for swift, decisive actions may dictate against the practicality of such so-called fair actions in crisis situations. This is not to say, however, that other considerations of fairness might not prevail under crisis situations (e.g., the use of timely feedback may be especially critical under such circumstances). Thus, just as leadership theorists have recognized that the appropriateness of leadership style is dependent upon the situation that the leader faces (e.g., Fiedler, 1978), it may be noted that concerns about fairness—and the specific aspects of fairness emphasized— may likewise be contingent upon situational factors. After all, managers may well attempt to manage impressions of themselves as being "tough, but fair." Although research relevant to this point has not yet been conducted, it remains an intriguing possibility that impressions of fairness–at least in some forms–might be not only sought less aggressively, but avoided altogether.

Conclusion

There are many positive characteristics that people may desire to have attributed to them. On the job, for example, people may wish to be seen as competent, hardworking, and—as we have been arguing—fair. It has been contended that impressions of fairness constitute an important aspect of a manager's identity. Managers will be successful in cultivating impressions of themselves as fair to the extent that they make and communicate their decisions in certain ways that their subordinates are likely to be sensitive to (namely, by adequately considering subordinates' viewpoints, appearing neutral, acting with consistency, giving timely feedback, providing adequate explanations, and treating subordinates with dignity and respect). Demon-strating fairness in this manner is expected to enhance both an individual's managerial power and the general effectiveness of his or her organization.

It is important to conclude by cautioning that any apparent irony concern-ing the manipulation of impressions of fairness is merely illusory. Although some may take the view that it is inherently contradictory to speak of fairness and manipulation in the same breath, we believe that it is no more unfair to attempt to promote an image of fairness than it is to promote any other desirable aspect of oneself. Indeed, it may be considered no more unscrupulous for persons to attempt to present themselves as fair than it would be for them to present themselves as punctual, well dressed, neat, or polite. In the case of managerial fairness, it is often so unclear what actions a manager has taken, and exactly what would constitute fairness under such circumstances, that it is possible that the fairness of the actions would go unnoticed in the absence of the manager's self-promotional efforts to make clear how his or her actions took into account considerations of fairness. Thus, as we stated at the opening of this chapter, "looking fair" may be at least as important as "being fair."

References

Alihan, M. (1970). *Corporate etiquette*. New York: Weybright & Talley.

Baumeister, R. F. (1982). A self-presentational view of social phenomena. *Psychological Bulletin, 91*, 3-26.

Bem, D. J. (1967). Self-perception: An alternative explanation of cognitive dissonance phenomena. *Psychological Review, 74*, 183-200.

Bies, R. J. (1986, August). Identifying principles of interactional justice: The case of corporate recruiting. In R. J. Bies (Chair), *Moving beyond equity theory: New directions in research on organizational justice.* Symposium conducted at the meeting of the Academy of Management, Chicago.

Bies, R. J. (1987). The predicament of injustice: The management of moral outrage. In L. L. Cummings & B. M. Staw (Eds.), *Research in organizational behavior* (Vol. 9, pp. 289-319). Greenwich, CT: JAI.

Bies, R. J., & Moag, J. S. (1986). Interactional justice: Communication criteria of fairness. In R. J. Lewicki, B. H. Sheppard, & B. H. Bazerman (Eds.), *Research on negotiation in organizations* (Vol. 1, pp. 43-55). Greenwich, CT: JAI.

Bies, R. J., & Shapiro, D. L. (1987). Interactional fairness judgments: The influence of causal accounts. *Social Justice Research, 1*, 199-218.

Bies, R. J., & Shapiro, D. L. (1988). Voice and justification: Their influence on procedural fairness judgments. *Academy of Management Journal, 31*, 676-685.

Bies, R. J., Shapiro, D. L., & Cummings, L. L. (1988). Causal accounts and managing organizational conflict: Is it enough to say it's not my fault? *Communication Research, 15*, 381-399.

Bies, R. J., & Sitkin, S. B. (in press). Excuse-making in organizations: Explanation as legitimation. In M. L. McLaughlin, M. J. Cody, & S. J. Read (Eds.), *Explaining one's self to others: Reason-giving in a social context*. Hillsdale, NJ: Lawrence Erlbaum.

Burns, S. (1987, April 15). Good corporate citizenship can pay dividends. *Dallas Morning News*, p. C1.

Cohen, R. L. (1986). *Justice: Views from the social sciences*. New York: Plenum.

Fiedler, F. E. (1978). The contingency model and the dynamics of the leadership process. In L. Berkowitz (Ed.), *Advances in experimental social psychology* (Vol. 11, pp. 60-112). New York: Academic Press.

Folger, R., & Bies, R. J. (1989). Managerial responsibilities and procedural justice. *Employee Responsibilities and Rights Journal, 2*, 79-90.

Folger, R., & Greenberg, J. (1985). Procedural justice: An interpretive analysis of personnel systems. In K. Rowland & G. Ferris (Eds.), *Research in personnel and human resources management* (Vol. 3, pp. 141-183). Greenwich, CT: JAI.

Garbett, T. F. (1988). *How to build a corporation's identity and project its image.* Lexington, MA: Lexington.

Giacalone, R. A. (1988). The effect of administrative accounts and gender on the perception of leadership. *Group & Organization Studies, 13*, 195-207.

Giacalone, R. A., & Pollard, H. G. (1987). The efficacy of accounts for a breach of confidentiality by management. *Journal of Business Ethics, 6*, 393-397.

Goffman, E. (1959). *The presentation of self in everyday life.* Garden City, NY: Doubleday.

Greenberg, J. (1986a). Determinants of perceived fairness of performance evaluations. *Journal of Applied Psychology, 71*, 340-342.

Greenberg, J. (1986b). Organizational performance evaluations: What makes them fair? In R. J. Lewicki, B. Sheppard, & M. Bazerman (Eds.), *Research on negotiation in organizations* (Vol. 1, pp. 25-41). Greenwich, CT: JAI.

Greenberg, J. (1988). Cultivating an image of justice: Looking fair on the job. *Academy of Management Executive, 2*, 155-158.

Greenberg, J. (1990a). Employee theft as a reaction to underpayment inequity: The hidden cost of pay cuts. *Journal of Applied Psychology, 75*, 561-568.

Greenberg, J. (1990b). Looking fair vs. being fair: Managing impressions of organizational justice. In B. M. Staw & L. L. Cummings (Eds.), *Research in organizational behavior* (Vol. 12, pp. 111-157). Greenwich, CT: JAI.

Greenberg, J. (in press). Stealing in the name of justice: Informational and interpersonal moderators of theft reactions to underpayment inequity. *Organizational Behavior and Human Decision Processes.*

Greenberg, J., & Folger, R. (1983). Procedural justice, participation, and the fair process effect in groups and organizations. In P. B. Paulus (Ed.), *Basic group processes* (pp. 235-256). New York: Springer-Verlag.

Greenberg, J., & McCarty, C. L. (1990). Comparable worth: A matter of justice. In G. Ferris & K. Rowland (Eds.), *Research in personnel and human resources management* (Vol. 8, pp. 265-301). Greenwich, CT: JAI.

Greenwald, A. G., & Breckler, S. J. (1985). To whom is the self presented? In B. R. Schlenker (Ed.), *The self and social life* (pp. 126-145). New York: McGraw-Hill.

Harris, M. M., & Fink, L. S. (1987). A field study of applicant reactions to employment opportunities: Does the recruiter make a difference? *Personnel Psychology, 40*, 765-784.

Higgins, R. L., & Snyder, C. R. (1989). The business of excuses. In R. A. Giacalone & P. Rosenfeld (Eds.), *Impression management in the organization* (pp. 73-85). Hillsdale, NJ: Lawrence Erlbaum.

Hladun, H. (1990, March). The class of '90: Today's grads need special handling. *Canadian Business*, pp. 99-100.

Hollander, E. P. (1958). Conformity, status, and idiosyncrasy credit. *Psychological Review, 65*, 117-127.

Hollander, E. P. (1985). Leadership and power. In G. Lindzey & E. Aronson (Eds.), *Handbook of social psychology* (3rd ed.) (Vol. 2, pp. 485-537). New York: Random House.

Jones, E. E., & Pittman, T. S. (1982). Toward a general theory of strategic self-presentation. In J. Suls (Ed.), *Psychological perspectives on the self* (Vol. 1, pp. 231-262). Hillsdale, NJ: Lawrence Erlbaum.

Kidder, T. (1981). *The soul of a new machine.* Boston: Little, Brown.

Labich, K. (1988, October 24). Making leaders at Wharton. *Fortune*, pp. 66-69.

Leary, M. R., & Kowalski, R. M. (1990). Impression management: A literature review and two-component model. *Psychological Bulletin, 107*, 34-47.

Leventhal, G. S. (1980). What should be done with equity theory? In K. J. Gergen, M. S. Greenberg, & R. H. Willis (Eds.), *Social exchange: Advances in theory and research* (pp. 27-55). New York: Plenum.

Lind, E. A., & Tyler, T. (1988). *The social psychology of procedural justice.* New York: Plenum.

Lydenberg, S. D., Marlin, A. T., Strub, S. O., & the Council on Economic Priorities. (1986). *Rating America's corporate conscience.* Reading, MA: Addison-Wesley.

Messick, D. M., Bloom, S., Boldizer, J. P., & Samuelson, C. D. (1985). Why are we fairer than others? *Journal of Experimental Social Psychology, 21*, 480-500.

Mintzberg, H. J. (1973). *The nature of managerial work.* New York: Harper & Row.

Murray, K. B., & Montanari, J. R. (1986). Strategic management of the socially responsible firm: Integrating management and marketing theory. *Academy of Management Review, 11*, 815-827.

Perrow, C. (1972). *Complex organizations.* Glenview, IL: Scott, Foresman.

Poll: News on Quayle is unfair. (1988, August 29). *Columbus Dispatch*, p. 2A.

Reis, H. T. (1986). Levels of interest in the study of interpersonal justice. In H. W. Bierhoff, R.L. Cohen, & J. Greenberg (Eds.), *Justice in social relations* (pp. 187-209). New York: Plenum.

Reutter, V. G. (1977). Suggestion systems: Utilization, evaluation, and implementation. *California Management Review, 19*, 78-89.

Rynes, S. L., Heneman, H. G., III, & Schwab, D. P. (1980). Individual reactions to organizational recruiting: A review. *Personnel Psychology, 33*, 529-542.

Rynes, S. L., & Miller, H. E. (1983). Recruiter and job influences on candidates for employment. *Journal of Applied Psychology, 68*, 147-154.

Schlenker, B. R. (1980). *Impression management: The self-concept, social identity, and interpersonal relations.* Monterey, CA: Brooks/Cole.

Schwoerer, C., & Rosen, B. (1989). Effects of employment-at-will policies and compensation policies on corporate image and job pursuit intentions. *Journal of Applied Psychology, 74*, 653-656.

Sheppard, B. H., & Lewicki, R. J. (1987). Toward general principles of managerial fairness. *Social Justice Research, 1*, 161-176.

Tedeschi, J. T. (1986). Private and public experiences and the self. In R. Baumeister (Ed.), *Public self and private self* (pp. 1-20). New York: Springer-Verlag.

Tyler, T. R., & Bies, R. J. (1990). Beyond formal procedures: The interpersonal context of procedural justice. In J. Carroll (Ed.), *Applied social psychology and organizational settings* (pp. 77-98). Hillsdale, NJ: Lawrence Erlbaum.

Villanova, P., & Bernardin, H. J. (1989). Impression management in the context of performance appraisal. In R. A. Giacalone & P. Rosenfeld (Eds.), *Impression management in the organization* (pp. 299-313). Hillsdale, NJ: Lawrence Erlbaum.

8

Impression Management in Negotiations

JAMES A. WALL, JR.

About 15 years ago, I read James Michener's *Centennial*—all 1,086 pages of it. And of all the plots, and stories, only one episode stays with me: The old chief, Lame Beaver, went out onto the barren plain and took up a position where the enemy—Pawnee—charge would be heaviest. There, he hammered a stake into the ground, tied his leg to it, and waited, rifle in hand—looking tough but very vulnerable. He wasn't going to back down; he couldn't make concessions; he was standing his ground.

The first wave of Pawnee charged and swerved to avoid him, in an attempt to draw his fire. He simply watched. A second wave caught him from the rear and left a lance in his armpit. He wrenched it out and laid it beside him. Then came a second lance into his leg. This was not a good beginning.

Rude Water, the Pawnee chief, led the third charge. Assuming Lame Beaver was badly wounded, he rode straight at his bloody, tethered opponent. Lame Beaver took careful aim and shot Rude Water dead. Denied their chief, the Pawnee were routed.

Two facets of this story appeal to me. First is the impression set by Lame Beaver; he is tough, and by tethering himself to that stake he communicates, "I'm bad, mighty tough. I'll die; only the rocks last forever; but I'll go down fighting." A second facet enthralls me—the student of negotiation. As he stood firm, but alone, Lame Beaver communicated a vulnerability that allowed him to decoy in and immobilize his opponent. This is a classic strategy of war and negotiation.

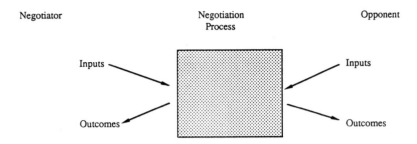

Figure 8.1. The Negotiation Process

Lame Beaver's heroics illustrate an overlap between impression management (i.e., controlling the impressions formed of oneself by others) and negotiation, namely, creating an impression that assists one's interaction with an opponent. Yet the impression management-negotiation overlap is more complicated than this. Specifically, there are two aspects to consider. First, negotiators interact not only with opponents but also with constituents and other third parties. Therefore, negotiators must consider their impression management before these individuals.

Second, in many negotiations, the image or impression that negotiators take *from* the negotiation is as important as the image they take into or develop within it. For example, parents in parent-child negotiations are very careful to leave the impression that they are caring/loving even though they are cheap and will not capitulate to buying the third pair of Reeboks.

As a starting point, this chapter will first look in some detail at the negotiation process and the parties involved in the negotiation. Subsequently, attention will be given to the use of impression management *in* the negotiation and the importance of the impressions taken from it.

Negotiation Process

Most people have a general feel for what a negotiation is, so here I will simply add some structure that will be useful later: Negotiation is a *process* in which two or more parties exchange goods or services and attempt to agree upon the rate of exchange for them (Wall, 1985).

As Figure 8.1 shows, each party—here called *negotiator* and *opponent*—participating in the negotiation takes certain inputs (i.e., goods and services) into the negotiation and derives outputs from it. In the negotiation process—which can involve maneuvers, tactics, strategies, demands, threats, concessions, give-and-take, stonewalling, and so on—the parties attempt to hammer out an acceptable exchange between their inputs and outcomes.

In this definition, a distinction is drawn between the negotiation process and the inputs (and outcomes) for an important reason. It must be kept in mind that each party's payoffs spring from two principal sources: the ongoing negotiation process as well as the outcomes of the negotiation. For example, while negotiating with another supervisor, a production supervisor might lose face in the process. He responds with friendly banter to the other supervisor's curses. He spends considerable time in the opponent's office. And he revamps the production schedule to fit with the opponent's needs. In short, the production supervisor comes across as a wimp *in* the negotiation. Yet as a *result* of the negotiation, he might be able to smooth many of the peaks and valleys in his production runs, reduce costs, and obtain raises for his workers.

Likewise, each party's costs are the sum of the inputs into the negotiation and the costs of the negotiation process. We must also keep in mind that most negotiations have more than two participants.

Negotiation Paradigm

As can be seen in Figure 8.2, the typical negotiation has five players and ten relationships. The players or parties include the negotiator, the opponent (opposing negotiator), the negotiator's constituent(s), the opponent's constituent(s), and a third party (mediator, arbitrator, or the like).

Among the parties there are ten potential relationships. In these each party receives payoffs and incurs costs as she or he interacts with the other parties. The difference between the payoffs and costs yields a net payoff to each party. Since each party—negotiator, opponent, negotiator's constituent, opponent's constituent, and perhaps a third party—can interact with more than one other, his or her total net payoff from the negotiation is a rough summation of the net rewards occurring from all relationships. For instance, textile salespersons often find their negotiations with buyers to be very stress-

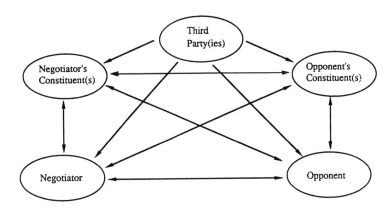

Figure 8.2. The Negotiation Paradigm

ful, even hostile, and quite unrewarding. Yet they like their jobs because their constituents—vice presidents of marketing and plant managers—are quite supportive and openly express their appreciation for valiant sales efforts. They also pay the salespeople a great deal for their sales.

While there are five parties in most negotiations, the following pages will concentrate on the negotiator (bear in mind that this generic term can refer to production managers, salespersons, labor negotiators, CEOs, purchasing agents, lawyers, financial agents, and so on).

Negotiator-Opponent Interaction

The negotiator's relationship with the opponent is the most thoroughly studied of the relationships in negotiation. In this process the negotiator—like Lame Beaver—attempts to develop an image that enhances his or her payoffs. One option the negotiator often employs is to bargain toughly so as to create and exploit a tough image.

Looking Tough via Tough Bargaining

In using this approach, the negotiator assumes that tough bargaining (making small and infrequent concessions) reduces the opponent's aspirations and discourages him or her from negotiating toughly. The negotiator who uses this approach feels that it pays to be tough, opening with a high demand, conceding little, and thereby driving down the opponent's goals.

With these lower goals, the opponent is expected to strive for less, settle for less, and be content with what he or she receives.

Does this strategy work? Sometimes it does, yet all too often the tough bargaining strategy evokes tough opponent responses. This being the case, when should this form of toughness be avoided? Usually, it should be avoided whenever the opponent has the power to retaliate. If the opponent has power, he or she will probably use it, at considerable cost to the negotiator.

The negotiator should also avoid this tack when he or she is in a very powerful position or whenever the opponent is not very dependent on the relationship with the negotiator. In the former case, it is a waste of time—or perhaps overkill—to bargain toughly when one clearly occupies a dominant position. Resentment—or its cousin, rebellion—can result.

In the latter case, being tough when the opponent is not dependent risks driving the opponent from the interaction. For instance, an overbearing purchasing agent might find that her supplier reacts to tough bargaining by selling scarce items to the agent's competitors. In this case the supplier can abandon his negotiation relationship with the agent or raise the demands (e.g., an exclusive buyer-seller contract) for remaining.

A final rule for eschewing *toughness through bargaining* is to avoid it whenever the opponent is engaging in appropriate behavior. When appropriate behavior occurs it should be rewarded, not punished. No doubt this comes across as obvious to some, yet this principle is violated all too frequently by negotiators who are attempting to squeeze the last concession out of an opponent. And sometimes it comes from negotiators who interpret the opponent's cooperativeness as a sign of weakness.

I recall vividly a recent negotiation between a home buyer and seller. It was a sellers' market, and I could tell the seller was in the driver's seat. He listed the house at a high but reasonable price, finding a buyer who offered $10,000 less. In the subsequent negotiation, both the buyer and seller conceded to, and tacitly agreed at, a point about $4,000 below the listed price. *Then* the seller asked to advance the closing date. The buyer conceded. The seller called for an additional $500 for the riding lawn mower that he was leaving. The buyer paid it. Finally, the seller demanded $100 for the propane left in the fuel tank. The buyer backed out unequivocally, muttering, "I don't want to live in such a greedy bastard's house!"

If the negotiator does choose to create a tough image by bargaining toughly, there are many other tough ploys (other than small, infrequent concessions) available. One is the *preemptive concession*. Here the negotiator concedes before an outside event or the opponent's action requires it. Such an early concession allows the negotiator to appear strong even though he or she has conceded to an opponent. A management negotiator, for instance, can retain a powerful image before the union by giving a wage increase prior to an arbitrator's order to do so.

Another option for appearing tough is through nondeferential behavior. An executive, for example, upon entering a conference room, might remove his jacket prior to negotiating with mufti-clad colleagues. A stronger tack would be to arrive late; still stronger would be a failure to appear.

Deadlines also provide a nice vehicle for impression management. The negotiator can accept deadlines but then become entrenched or ask for extensions as they draw near. The deadlines can be ignored if the negotiator wishes. Or a stronger tactic is to set them. For maximum impact, a negotiator can set the deadlines and then ignore them.

An offensive but sometimes effective tactic for looking tough within bargaining is for the negotiator to ask a vague, complex, insulting, or even stupid question to catch the opponent off guard. By doing so, the negotiator communicates that he or she is powerful enough to ask questions that impose on the opponent. Also, this places the opponent in the position of responding aggressively or conceding the negotiator's power with an attempt to deal with the question.

Developing a Tough Image Outside the Negotiation

Since bargaining toughly has its risks (Lame Beaver would concede this point), it is often preferable for negotiators to cast a tough image outside of their bargaining. To develop this posture, negotiators can acquire status or develop abilities and skills that are valued by their constituents and opponents. Likewise, negotiators can voice early disclaimers to prevent any future loss of status, or they can strengthen their position by building alliances with other parties.

Perhaps one of the simplest, but most effective, impression management ploys is stockpiling. Here negotiators accumulate resources prior to and during the negotiation that will prove useful as they bargain. The stockpile can consist of the goods and services that the negotiator intends to trade to the opponent (e.g., a production manager builds inventories with products that the marketing VP wants to sell) or of outcomes provided by the opponent (e.g., a diamond company stockpiles diamonds prior to a negotiation with its miners). At times, shrewd negotiators will acquire chips from their constituencies (or allies), stockpile them, and then trade them to opponents for chips the negotiators can use as leverage with their constituencies.

In addition to stockpiling, strengthening their stand with their constituencies is one of the most potent image-building maneuvers negotiators can undertake. They can meet openly and visibly with the constituents, meet as a team, or even hold a rally to strengthen their positions with the constituents, and, more important, to demonstrate that strong position to the opponents.

Another technique negotiators often employ is the establishment of cooperative arrangements, bonds, alliances, and coalitions with third parties. Negotiators can gain third-party assistance via negotiations, threats, rewards, or use of their other power bases—referent, expertise, co-oriented, and legitimate (French & Raven, 1959).

As negotiators enhance their salient ties with their constituencies and other third parties, they can also enhance their images by developing salient outside options for themselves. If negotiators can display their independence (or detachment) from the negotiation, they can usually enhance their power within it.

Soft Impressions

The focus of the chapter thus far on tough impression management is for the most part understandable, because we in Western cultures believe this is the image negotiators should develop toward opponents. (Eastern cultures place more emphasis on appearing warm, complex, and interesting; Adler, 1991.) Yet in many instances it is advantageous to communicate softer impressions.

The gentle image has high utility whenever the negotiator is attempting to open or begin negotiations with the opponent. Likewise, such an impression can be useful if future relationships/negotiations are important. In this latter situation, tough posturing might prove successful in initial negotiations, but it risks alienating the opponent. Even if the opponent is not alienated, he or she will probably adjust to the tough posturing, thereby reducing its subsequent effectiveness. In addition, demonstration of a tough image early in a negotiation may motivate the opponent to abandon the negotiation or to seek alternative relationships.

In the negotiation, soft imaging proves quite useful to the negotiator whenever high joint outcomes are possible. In such a case, the implied cooperativeness raises the opponent's aspirations and motivates him or her to seek agreements—perhaps via logrolling (an exchange of concessions in which the cost of the opponent's concession is low but the benefit to the

negotiator is high; likewise, the cost of the negotiator's concession is persc
ally minimal but the benefit to the opponent high; Pruitt, 1981)—that v
raise individual and joint outcomes.

If the opponent responds favorably to the cooperative imaging—by seeking integrative agreements, by conceding, or by posturing agreeably—then
the negotiator should retain the soft impression. Why? Because these are
behaviors that should be reinforced, and soft (or positive) imaging is a strong
reinforcer.

Soft imaging is also advisable when the negotiation is highly visible to the
opponent's constituency or is being observed by important third parties.
When they are being watched, opponents are very sensitive to threats to their
own images or reputations and will retaliate against the negotiator's tough
image to save face before constituent and third-party audiences.

Finally, soft posturing can at times be used to set the opponent up for future
exploitation. More about this later.

If a soft image is sometimes desirable, then how does the negotiator
develop it? For the most part the negotiator can use tactics opposite to those
of tough imaging. For instance, the negotiator can express deference with
gestures, eye movements, dress, and facial expressions. Likewise, he or she
can set no deadlines, observe those set by the opponent, be friendly, and make
no surprising moves. Complementary moves include lowering demands,
hinting at weak commitments, appearing inconsistent, and falling back
quickly from positions of proclaimed importance.

Within the bargaining and in implementing agreements, the negotiator can
also take several steps. Some of the most effective are those that win the
opponent's trust. For instance, negotiators can openly discuss their goals and
objectives, or even more openly admit where they are vulnerable to the
opponent.

To improve affective ties, negotiators can banter with opponents to put
them at ease and emphasize common backgrounds, tastes, occupations,
clothing, weight, height, and baldness. Or, over time, negotiators can simply
attempt to build friendships with opponents.

On occasion, negotiators can flatter their opponents—both privately and
publicly—and attempt to make them look efficacious to their constituents.
As an example of this last ploy, the negotiator can proffer a straw image of
toughness before the opponent and his or her constituent. Then the negotiator
can allow the opponent to call his or her bluff, and thereby appear tough to
the constituency and his or her peers.

Other soft tacks include making offers the opponent can refuse, not raising or pressing embarrassing issues, and demonstrating one's reliability. In addition, the negotiator can use the demand-debasement ploy. Here the negotiator makes a demand and observes how it plays out with the opponent and his or her constituency. If the demand does not fare well—perhaps it strains the opponent-constituent relationship—the negotiator can then debase it. That is, the negotiator can follow the original demand with several new ones that, by virtue of their numbers, debase the perceived importance of the original demand.

Negotiator-Constituents Interaction

Most observers believe that negotiators concentrate on their interactions with opponents. Here, the battle is won or lost; here, negotiators take better than they give; and here, they strike fruitful accords.

Seasoned negotiators, on the other hand, see the picture quite differently. From experience, they know that the relationship with the constituent (the person or persons represented by the negotiator or opponent) is equally important. Most negotiators are responsible to their constituents and receive their marching orders from them. Constituencies, for the most part, are very powerful; in most instances, the constituents provide the negotiator's monetary and social remunerations, and they have the power to fire the negotiator. In almost every case, constituents can make the negotiator's life miserable.

Given that constituents are influential, what types of impressions do negotiators wish to present to them? Before opponents, negotiators seek to appear tough, perhaps reasonable, and, in appropriate situations, soft. What impressions do they seek to create for their constituents? The answer—in one word—is *competence.*

In the short run, an image of toughness would suffice. Constituents appreciate tough negotiators because they believe assertive negotiators are advancing or protecting constituency interests. Even if the tough negotiator fails, he or she—as the wounded warrior—is perceived as defending "our position."

Because they equate toughness with competence in the short run (perhaps in a negotiation or two), constituents are likely to leave tough negotiators in place, support them, reward them when they do well, tolerate their failures, and, most important, allow them sufficient latitude in their bargaining.

But negotiators realize that successful negotiations (not toughness) are the key to an enduring image of competence. To be successful, a negotiator must converse openly with the opponent to establish what the opponent wants from the negotiator and his or her constituency. Likewise, the negotiator must communicate to the opponent rather openly his or her own needs and expectations, to seek out acceptable overlap in their positions.

The negotiator as well as the opponent realize that the keys to successful long-term negotiations and to images of competence lie in (a) communication of needs, (b) searches for overlap in the needs, (c) trades that are acceptable to both sides, and, usually, (d) costly concessions from both sides.

For the constituents, these four activities generate substantial apprehension. Physically and conceptually, the constituents are far removed from the negotiation. They have limited information about the opponents and their constituents; consequently, they do not understand the opponents' perspectives, demands, needs, and values. Whenever their negotiator communicates these to the constituents—speaks for the opponent—and seeks areas of mutual agreement, the constituents distrust him or her. Many have been heard to ask, "Are you our representative or theirs? Whose side are you on?"

Understandably, constituents also second-guess the negotiators' bargaining tactics, strategies, and agreements. That is, they frequently feel and complain that the negotiator is being too soft and is demanding too little. The opponent appears to be getting too much, and the compromises as well as the agreements seem to favor the opponent's side.

Victimized by these apprehensions, negotiators face a tricky impression management dilemma. Appearing tough pleases the constituency but risks generating countermeasures from the opponent. Aiming for long-run benefits irks the constituents in the short run but builds a base for an image of competence.

How do negotiators cope? In different ways. Some say, "To hell with the long run; it's then you're dead. Look tough; be tough!" A good example is the representative from a rustbelt state who, along with some congressional colleagues, launched a hard campaign/negotiation in the House of Representatives to enact a steel import quota against Japan. His stand was so uncompromising and unrealistic that it failed; yet, his constituents loved him.

Other—wiser—negotiators capitalize better on their impression management. They, along with opponents who face the identical dilemma, waltz through a feigned-toughness ritual. Specifically, both act tough publicly to impress their constituents. Then, having gleaned both constituencies' confidence, they privately conduct their bargaining. Once they strike an accord, the negotiator and opponent carry it to the constituents for ratification. Impressed significantly by their representatives' toughness and somewhat by their agreement, the constituents nod their acceptance.

Most negotiators, however, eschew these ploys and methodically build an image of "competence" before their constituents. If possible, they develop a track record of success *within* the constituency before representing it in a negotiation. Prior to and during the negotiation they cultivate a network of colleagues within the constituency upon whom they can rely.

Once in the negotiator position, they devote considerable time to reporting back to the constituents and educating them on the opponents' position. As they do so, they strive to come across as authorities. They appear to be in charge of the situation. They understand the opponents; they do not represent them. The negotiators stress that they bargain the way they do because *they* know it is the correct way to proceed. It is the route a competent person would take.

Negotiator-Opposing Constituents Interaction

So far, I have held that negotiators generally should present a tough image to opponents but should modify this to fit the occasion. Before the constituents they should appear competent, perhaps toughly so. Now consider another party in the negotiation paradigm—the opponent's constituents. What impression should the negotiator impart to them?

The answer is rather speculative because no one, to date, has dealt with the question. We are on somewhat solid ground, however, when we say that few negotiators concern themselves with their relationship to the opposing constituents. They realize it is wise not to alienate these parties, but they do not invest time, energy, or resources in posturing before them.

It seems advisable, however, for negotiators to reflect on their image here and to give an impression of being a *reliable nemesis*. That is, the negotiator should come across as one who is difficult to understand, but also one who is somewhat predictable—one who can be understood, and perhaps be controlled.

The journey to this prescription is through a process of elimination. First, the negotiator does not want to come across as tough to the opposing constituents. This image motivates the opposing constituents to pressure the opponent toward tough negotiations. A soft stance, on the other hand, prompts the opposing constituents to exploit the negotiator. They simply perceive the negotiator as a cherry to be picked; therefore, they pressure their negotiator (the opponent) to do what is obvious, to exploit the situation. Finally, for the negotiator to appear totally unreliable and unpredictable tempts the opposing constituency to break off the negotiation. For the most part, they, like any constituency, want a relationship that produces a productive, manageable exchange, and if they do not find it in this relationship, they will simply seek a more suitable one.

Given the above deductions, it seems advisable for the negotiator to come across as a reliable puzzle to the opposing constituents. That is, he or she should appear as a moving target, oscillating within an acceptable behavioral bracket. This said, how can negotiators create this image? It's tricky. Negotiators must bear in mind that their images before the opponents and their own constituencies are the most important ones. These should not be jeopardized by any attempt to project the correct image before the opposing constituency.

With this in mind, negotiators can tactfully *alter* various facets of their behavior. They can abruptly raise their demands, hold to them for a while, and then recede to the original point. Another option is to shift from small—salami—concessions to large ones and then perhaps come back to slicing the concessions thinly.

Alternatively, negotiators can send up trial balloons, somewhat at random, seemingly ignoring the opponents' responses. Or negotiators can shift between asking many questions and giving all the answers. They can discuss issues on a abstract level and then turn to a concrete perspective. The issues can be simplified and then made more complex. Structured agendas can be used, then freewheeling discussions insisted on; deadlines proposed, later ignored. Sometimes negotiators can arrive late; at other times, early. Sometimes they can banter, then turn to a serious face, then don a somber one. Even alterations of dress are fair game—on most occasions the negotiator can be sartorially resplendent; on others, quite casual.

As negotiators alter their demands, agendas, timing, banter, and dress, they must keep their opponents abreast of their tactics. Confusion must be avoided. More important, negotiators must supply their opponents with information that can be used to educate the opposing constituency. Such education enables the opponent to appear efficacious and to seem "understandable."

In the following example, note the value of keeping the opponent abreast of negotiator intentions. A salesman for a plumbing wholesaler begins with reasonable concessions (e.g., giving a 10% discount for a large order, promising early delivery times, and allowing the retailer to return unsold items). Abruptly he shifts to very small "salami" concessions (e.g., 1% discounts on copper tubing), then for no apparent reason returns to reasonable concessions. When the opposing constituents (i.e., the buyer's bosses) learn of this shifting—by observation or via the opponent's reports—they are puzzled.

In such a case a confidential explanation—fabricated or valid—to the buyer would prove beneficial: "Hey, look, my boss thought I was letting him down, not bringing home enough margin. So I came on a little tough, cut the salami thin a few times. That made them feel better. And you [the buyer] did what I knew you would do, raised holy hell and threatened to take your business elsewhere. So now I go back and tell my boss that if we want to make this sale I have to stick with being reasonable."

The buyer, thus assured, can now educate his constituents: "Look, the salesman was just cutting it thin a few times to impress his boss. That's nothing to worry about. We're back on the path again. He'll give us some good bargains, and we'll buy most of our pipes from him."

As the negotiator constructs a reliable nemesis image before the opposing constituency and transmits explanations to the opponent, he or she must also take great care not to confuse his or her own constituency. The reason? A confusing, puzzling negotiator is seldom perceived as competent.

Interactions With Third Parties

Frequently, negotiator-opponent bargaining is observed and influenced by third parties. In labor negotiations the third party can be an NLRB mediator or arbitrator. When the dispute is between two neighbors, the third party could be a community mediator. The plant manager can serve as a conciliator or fact finder in a negotiation between an engineer and a production manager. A judge overseeing a civil case might first mediate between the plaintiff and defendant, then rule on the case in court. Parents often observe sibling disputes and then order that a problem be settled *now*, or *else*. Further examples could be given, but these few already foster the question of interest: What image should negotiators lay out to these third parties?

An intuitive prescription—and a very practical, precautionary one—is that negotiators should cast an image of politeness before powerful third parties. Most negotiators realize there is modest tangible payoff for such impression management and assume the appropriate posture. For instance, community mediators are addressed politely and are given a seat at the head of the table. Attorneys, in pretrial mediations, leave their coats on even when the judge does not. Subordinates seldom call their bosses by first names or put their feet on their bosses' desks.

In addition to presenting a polite image, negotiators should attempt to come across as reasonable. Third parties in our society place a strong emphasis on fairness. While they want a settlement, they also want the agreement to be fair and the process—the negotiation as well as their own interventions—to be correct, just. Unlike many societies, ours is one that places strong emphasis on distributive justice (people should get what they deserve) and procedural justice (what they get should be obtained fairly).

Strongly guided by these norms, third parties—be they fact finders, mediators, arbitrators, or observers—are not neutral. Rather, they tend to favor the negotiator who is making fair demands, who is behaving appropriately, or who will be fair in living up to any accord.

How do third parties consciously or inadvertently determine what is fair? Usually their benchmark is the opponent's behavior. Seldom do third parties conclude that the negotiator is being reasonable or unreasonable. Rather, they perceive the negotiator as more reasonable or less reasonable than the opponent.

Consequently, the goal for the negotiator is to appear *more* reasonable than the opponent, and not necessarily to appear perfect. This "relative fairness" can be illustrated by a story: Two fishermen had started cleaning their catch and now smelled like fish to a nearby bear. When the bear started to chase them, one of the fisherman stopped abruptly and began to strap on some track shoes. The other yelled, "You fool, you can't outrun a bear in track shoes!" To which the first fisherman retorted, "I don't have to outrun *him*. I only need to outrun *you*."

The fisherman's track shoes gave him an edge in outrunning his friend. How can negotiators appear more reasonable than their opponents? There are a number of tacks. If the opponent is being *quite* aggressive, the negotiator need only appear somewhat reasonable, perhaps by explaining his or her own aggressiveness. On the other hand, when the opponent is coming across as quite compliant, the negotiator needs to work harder at appearing reasonable. For example, the negotiator might find it necessary to listen calmly to the opponent's comments, ask polite questions for clarification, probe for areas of mutual benefit, refrain from threatening the opponent, and smile at bad jokes.

Other ploys include explaining the constituency's goals to the third party, being prompt, observing the third party's deadlines, apologizing to the opponent, making the first concession, volunteering an early concession, retracting a demand, announcing forthcoming moves, and signaling shifts in bargaining style. All of these create an aegis of reasonableness.

Negotiators might also apply impression management directly to the third party. Ingratiation (i.e., signaling one's likability; Jones & Pittman, 1982) is

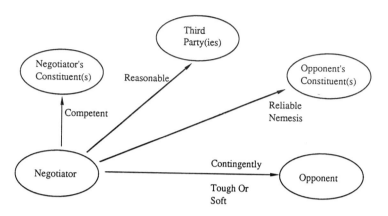

Figure 8.3. Negotiator's Image to Other Parties

commonly used by negotiators in attempting to win the approval of third parties. For instance, the negotiator might make statements to the third party that signal the negotiator's positive traits and intentions. A slightly different tack would be to compliment—but not flatter—the third party. Or the negotiator might express attitudes, values, and convictions that are consistent with those of the third party. Sometimes even subtle imitations of the third party's behavior have payoffs. For example, drinking coffee instead of tea, if coffee is the third party's preference; wearing an out-of-date sport coat if the third party is not particularly fashionable; or taking notes on a pad, holding a stiff physical posture in discussions, using a pencil instead of a pen—all of these subtle imitations can assist negotiator-third-party camaraderie (for descriptions of several impression management approaches, see Jones & Pittman, 1982; Leary & Kowalski, 1990).

These prescriptions and proscriptions must be tempered with two cautions. First, impression management of the third party, like any ingratiation, can be pushed so far that it backwashes. Consequently, negotiators, as they attempt to appear to be reasonable professionals, must be very careful not to come across as self-serving. Such an image dilutes, neutralizes, or overshadows the reasonableness image.

More important, negotiators must maintain a delicate balance among the images they create. Recall that negotiators seek to come across as competent to their constituents (see Figure 8.3). To opponents they should appear contingently tough or soft, to opposing constituencies they should seem reliable puzzles, and to third parties they should purport to be reasonable.

Can negotiators maintain all these images simultaneously? They should try. Realistically, there are many times when the images grate against each other. Appearing tough to the opponent may sacrifice looking reasonable to a third party (e.g., a mediator). Seeming reasonable to a third party can generate an image of weakness and incompetence to the constituency.

When impression management trade-offs are necessary or inevitable, negotiators must consider the priorities of their images. For most negotiations, impression before the opponent should have top priority; the image before the constituency, second; that to the third parties, next; and the one before the opposing constituency, last (but not unimportant). The logic for this ranking is, I hope, obvious. Negotiations with opponents should be of top priority for negotiators. If they are successful in that relationship, amicable relations and payoffs from the constituency probably will follow. The opposite is not true; good relations with the constituency do not yield productive negotiations.

The relationship with and image before the constituency are next in importance because constituencies have considerable power over negotiators. Negotiators serve at their constituencies' pleasure, take directives from constituents, and are rewarded by them.

Impression management of third parties must be considered next in importance because these outsiders have less impact on the negotiation—process as well as outcomes—than do the constituents and opponents, but probably more impact than the opposing constituents.

Finally, opposing constituencies, because they are farthest removed from the negotiation, usually have the least impact on it. Consequently, negotiators should give the lowest priority to impression management before them. Specifically, appearing a reliable puzzle to the opposing constituency should not sacrifice any of the other images.

Self-Impression

Thus far, this chapter has examined negotiators' impression management of opponents, constituents, opposing constituencies, and third parties. Another important target of impression management is the negotiator him- or herself. Leary and Kowalski (1990), after reviewing Greenwald and Breckler's (1985), Hogan, Jones, and Cheek's (1985), and Schlenker's (1985) works, refer to this as controlling impressions of one's self. Negotiators, like most of us, wish to maintain self-images of *efficacy* (more conventional terms include *winner, achiever,* or one who *dares to be great*). They develop this image from (a) effective performance; (b) symbols, rewards, and indicators that they are efficacious; (c) vicarious observations of others' effectiveness; and (d) perceiving themselves as acting efficaciously (Bandura, 1982).

Since the first two of these elements entail impression management, they will be examined here. First, consider performance. Negotiators develop a self-percept of efficacy by negotiating well with the opponent and hammering out acceptable agreements. Likewise, a feeling of success comes from pleasing the constituents, dominating the opponents, puzzling the opposing constituents, and winning third parties' assistance.

Admittedly, the self-percept of efficacy is not the primary objective of these behaviors (more important may be promotions, praise from colleagues, future employment, bonuses, and the like), but it is a nice perquisite. We all like to see ourselves as potent, useful, effective—as people who matter.

Negotiators also enhance their self-percepts by surrounding themselves with symbols, rewards, and indicators of their efficacy. For example: Many company negotiators drive expensive cars—cars that announce they are doing okay. In one case I recall, a negotiator's car announced this too loudly, and he was told by his boss (constituent) to trade in his $55,000 Corvette for a more appropriate car, such as a Buick.

Also, negotiators frequently use jargon that is elaborate and confusing to their opponents. For example, toolies—hand-tool salespersons to industrial users—frequently are accused of bombarding their customers with detailed specifications. Management negotiators in labor negotiations like to rely on elaborate statistics. Are these tacks intended to impress and confuse opponents, or do they serve as self-image boosters? I think the latter often dominates.

Another observation: Negotiators (Henry Kissinger is a good example) often surround themselves with large entourages. Perhaps these are useful in negotiations with their opponents. Perhaps they impress constituents and third parties. But they also, I feel, build the negotiator's self-image.

Is negotiator enhancement of self-perceived efficacy useful to the organization and to productive bargaining? That is, should negotiators frame themselves as efficacious? To some extent, the answer is yes. As Bandura (1982) and other scholars note, people with a strong sense of efficacy work harder to succeed and are more likely to overcome obstacles. Also, they are more likely to persist when faced with adverse experiences. As they work and persist, people with high opinions of themselves also tend to gain new skills for the management of stressful or threatening experiences.

Such attributes prove quite useful to negotiators. Their job is a tough one, stressful, and, as some would say, high in intrarole conflict. They are caught between the demands of their constituencies and those of their opponents. Quite often they must trade off the short run against the long. Concomitantly, they must maintain oft-conflicting images before constituents, opponents, opposing constituents, and third parties.

A strong self-image—even if self-induced—is a useful survival tool in such an arena. Moreover, feeling confident and effective improves negotiators' bargaining. And self-confident negotiators are more likely to stand up to their constituents, develop trusting relationships with opponents, assume moderate levels of risk, and be suitably assertive in negotiation.

This is the positive side of negotiators' self-impressions. On the downside, they can be quite deluding. Negotiators who successfully build strong "efficacious" impressions before themselves can become very rigid. As they do, they tend to ignore relevant corrective feedback. Specifically, they may ignore indications that negotiations are not going well, that their constituents are displeased with them, or that they are projecting the wrong image to several parties. Sometimes when receiving feedback, they distort it so that it is consistent with their self-images. I vividly recall a conversation I had with a senior administrator a few years back. He waxed eloquent as to how he had gotten the upper hand in a negotiation with his superior. She, he noted, "couldn't get in a word, not even edgewise." Later, I learned he had totally alienated his superior; yet he perceived himself as dominant.

A strong self-image also interferes with reality testing. To make the point here, I borrow from Janis's (1982) concept of "groupthink." Self-impressed negotiators have a tendency to ignore and distort corrective feedback; they also fail to probe reality and test their assumptions. Consequently, they conclude that they are in control (perhaps invincible), that others are of minor consequence, that obstacles do not exist, and that progress is being made in negotiations. In short, they are blind because they do not look and will not see.

As with groupthink, negotiators who blind themselves with their own positive self-image can begin to make poor decisions, base incorrect behavior on these decisions, ignore corrective information, and blissfully negotiate themselves toward disaster. As they do so, they might shout, "How am I doing?" but they never hear the answer.

Recapitulation

Since this discussion will now shift conceptual gears, it seems appropriate to reiterate the previous points. So far, the role of impression management in the negotiation *process* has been addressed. As they bargain, negotiators should build contingently tough or soft images before opponents, appear competent to their constituencies, appear as understandable nemeses to opposing constituencies, and appear reasonable to third parties. Add to this the idea that negotiators do build an image of efficacy before themselves—an image that has advantages as well as disadvantages. All of these impressions, I have held, affect the negotiation process.

Impressions as Inputs and Outcomes

Just as images or impressions can be developed *within* the negotiation process, they can also be brought into—serve as inputs to—it. Specifically, the negotiator can bring a tough image to the interaction with the opponent just as he or she can develop that impression within it. Prior to representing their constituents, negotiators can develop an image of competence and then rely on this as they negotiate. The strategically astute negotiator takes steps to develop a reasonable image before a mediator prior to negotiation.

Moving a step further, I should point out too that images are *outcomes* of the negotiation. That is, negotiators take various images from a negotiation. For example, look at the outcomes in this negotiation: As he bargains with his boss, a loyal, competent subordinate demands two additional computer workstations for his unit. He argues logically but assertively that delays in his unit are the result of insufficient computer units; deadlines can be met only if he receives the units. As he states his argument, the subordinate loses his temper and accuses the boss of being unsympathetic recently to his unit's computer needs. The boss reacts hostilely, countering with a demand for an apology. She explains that money is tight, and as a result everyone feels neglected. Coming across as sympathetic, she promises to review her subordinate's request. After some additional discussion, the subordinate apologizes and agrees to work diligently to meet future deadlines, but once again stresses the need for more units.

Consider now the inputs, process, and outcomes in this brief negotiation (Figure 8.4). For the subordinate, his inputs are an image of loyalty and competence and a demand for two computer units. The boss enters with power and resources. In the negotiation process, both parties rely on logic.

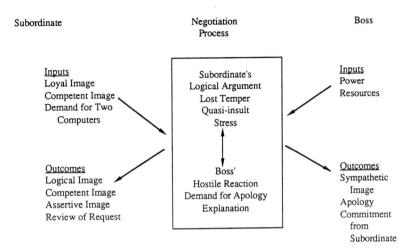

Figure 8.4. Example of Negotiation Inputs, Process, and Outcomes

Tempers flare, but the boss as well as the subordinate emerge unscathed. As for outcomes, the subordinate probably retains an impression of loyalty and competence but probably picks up an image of assertiveness. His other outcome is a promised review of his request. From the boss's perspective, she takes a sympathetic image—and probably one of dominance—from the negotiation, an apology, and a commitment from her subordinate to meet future deadlines. Here, then, we see that images serve as outcomes as well as inputs to the negotiation process.

Exchange of Images

If images serve as inputs to the negotiation and as outcomes from it, then the obvious question is, Can images be exchanged for images? The answer is yes! *Images can be exchanged for images and images are exchanged for other utilities.* Let us first deal with trading images. Impression management theory has long recognized that images or impressions are formed through interactions. In these interactions parties tend to negotiate their identities with one another (Leary & Kowalski, 1990; Tedeschi & Melburg, 1984). For example, to obtain an identity as a leader and to convince others to assume the identity of subordination, a person must appear to be somewhat selfless.

Negotiator's   Opponent's

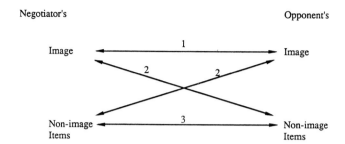

Figure 8.5. Exchanging Images and Other Utilities in Negotiations

In other words, people will not give the image of authority to someone or assume a self-percept of subordination themselves unless the person in question (the potential leader) takes on or creates an image of generosity.

Another example: Management negotiators in a labor negotiation will not allow the union representative to look tough at the expense of management's apparent weakness. They will trade the "tough" image for one of "generosity" or "toughness" (as we saw earlier, both parties can appear tough in a negotiation), but management will not give "tough" and take "weak."

Images are also exchanged for other inputs and outcomes, that is, for other items that have utility. The impression management literature as well as daily observations are replete with examples of these trades. In ingratiation (Tedeschi & Melburg, 1984) a negotiator seeks to obtain a favorable—perhaps cooperative—image by giving items rather freely to the opponent. Had the subordinate in the preceding example given a strong commitment up front to meet deadlines in exchange for an image of high loyalty, then this exchange would be classified as ingratiation.

On a more negative note, reflect on the price some people will pay to appear tough. In his book *Goodbye Darkness*, William Manchester (1979) tells how a young Marine lieutenant paid the ultimate price to look tough by foolishly charging a Japanese machine-gun emplacement instead of waiting for it to be flanked by another platoon. I also recall reading how Gordon Liddy once held his hand over a lit candle—letting his flesh burn and the stench fill the room—to prove his toughness. These are examples of items—a life, burnt flesh—exchanged for image.

Is the reverse possible? Are images traded for other utilities? Yes! In supplication, negotiators take on a weak image to glean tangible outcomes. No doubt this went on repeatedly in France as mayors of small towns negotiated with SS (German occupation troops) commanders in the early 1940s. And in self-promotion, an individual—student, subordinate, intern, or whatever—risks coming across as conceited (Giacalone & Rosenfeld, 1986) in order to improve his or her image.

To complete the paradigm, recall that nonimage items are exchanged for others in many negotiations. Management raises workers' salaries to keep them on the job. A daughter agrees to clean her room for $2.00. The United States removes cruise missiles from Britain as the Soviet Union moves its SRBM back, behind the Urals. Or Britain turns Hong Kong over to China so as to retain peaceful relationships.

Figure 8.5 summarizes the above discussion. As arrow 1 depicts, the negotiator—as any party—trades images with the opponent. Images are traded for nonimage utilities (arrows 2). Finally, as most people perceive negotiations, utilities are traded for utilities (arrow 3).

Strategic Use of Impression Management

The most intriguing aspect of impression management emerges when we look at negotiations from a long-run perspective. Over the long term, negotiators develop impressions in one round of a negotiation, take these images away from that round, and use them as inputs into the second round. Here the images are maintained, used, traded, or modified; again they are output-ted. In turn the residual images are used strategically in the next negotiation round. The sequence is repeated, and as this happens, impression management becomes a central element of the negotiation strategy.

Let me illustrate this sequencing with a few concrete examples. A simple strategy for a union negotiator would be to give some major concessions when the economy is depressed so as to develop an image of cooperativeness with the management negotiator. Having developed the cooperative image and taken it from the initial negotiation, the union representative could use it to glean high outcomes—perhaps through logrolling—in a negotiation during an economic expansion.

Consider a more complex example. A DEA agent wants to identify the major drug distributor in his city, and he knows a minor pusher has that information. How does he get it? After he arrests the pusher, does the agent rely on a tough image and try to sweat the information out of the pusher? Only if he is stupid. An alternative—a smart one—is to establish a very soft image in the negotiation. The agent, for instance, might announce through the press that he has only circumstantial evidence in the case (i.e., that he is in a weak position). The agent could then negotiate a generous plea bargain in which he accepts probation (down from 10 years in prison for the pusher) in exchange for discrete information on a *minor* drug distributor. At the conclusion of the negotiation, the pusher "walks" and the DEA agent comes across as a Milquetoast. With this image in hand, the DEA agent arrests the minor distributor and nails him with a stiff sentence. The distributor's peers (the pusher's constituents) perceive that the pusher capitulated—rolled over to—a soft DEA agent. They seek to kill the pusher—stoolie—forcing him to leave town or negotiate for protection from the DEA agent. The agent then trades entrance into an informant-protection program for information about the major distributors. With this information the DEA agent cracks a major drug ring.

Finally, think of Lame Beaver alone on that barren plain. In his first encounter with the Pawnee braves he paid a high price—lances in the armpit and leg—to look vulnerable. This image, however, allowed him to be victorious in the second, conclusive contest.

Conclusion

Most people, both lay and scholarly, probably perceive impression management and negotiations to be distinct, quite separate. In the former process, an actor attempts to establish a favorable identity before an audience. In the latter, two or more parties attempt to agree on the rate of exchange for items they are trading.

The processes, however, have significant overlap. As shown in this chapter, negotiators can and should use impression management to develop different images before their opponents, their own constituencies, their opponents' constituencies, and other parties. This impression management entails more than the development of images in the negotiation per se. It also involves taking a favorable image into the negotiation, trading images with the opponent, and capitalizing on images taken from each negotiation.

It is my hope that this coverage of impression management in negotiations improves our grasp of both processes. Currently the relevance of both to interpersonal, organizational, and interorganizational relations is being increasingly recognized. Perhaps this discussion of the interplay between them will enhance the interest in and study of their influences.

References

Adler, N. J. (1991). *International dimensions of organizational behavior* (2nd ed.). Boston: PWS-Kent.

Bandura, A. B. (1982). Self-efficacy mechanism in human agency. *American Psychologist, 37,* 122-147.

French, J. R. P., Jr., & Raven, B. (1959). The bases of social power. In D. Cartwright (Ed.), *Studies in social power.* Ann Arbor: Institute for Social Research, University of Michigan.

Giacalone, R. A., & Rosenfeld, P. (1986). Self-presentation and self-promotion in an organizational setting. *Journal of Social Psychology, 126,* 321-326.

Greenwald, A. G., & Breckler, S. J. (1985). To whom is the self presented? In B. R. Schlenker (Ed.), *The self and social life* (pp. 126-145). New York: McGraw-Hill.

Hogan, R., Jones, W. H., & Cheek, J. M. (1985). Socioanalytic theory: An alternative to armadillo psychology. In B. R. Schlenker (Ed.), *The self and social life* (pp. 175-198). New York: McGraw-Hill.

Janis, I. J. (1982). *Victims of groupthink: A psychological study of foreign policy decisions and fiascoes.* Boston: Houghton Mifflin.

Jones, E. E., & Pittman, T. S. (1982). Toward a general theory of strategic self-presentation. In J. Suls (Ed.), *Psychological perspectives on the self* (pp. 231-262). Hillsdale, NJ: Lawrence Erlbaum.

Leary, M. R., & Kowalski, R. M. (1990). Impression management: A literature review and two-component model. *Psychological Bulletin, 1,* 34-47.

Manchester, W. (1979). *Goodbye darkness.* Boston: Little, Brown.

Pruitt, D. G. (1981). *Negotiation behavior.* New York: Academic Press.

Schlenker, B. R. (1985). Identity and self-identification. In B. R. Schlenker (Ed.), *The self and social life* (pp. 65-99). New York: McGraw-Hill.

Tedeschi, J. T., & Melburg, V. (1984). Impression management and influence in the organization. In S. B. Bacharach & E. J. Lawler (Eds.), *Research in the sociology of organizations* (pp. 31-59). Greenwich, CT: JAI.

Wall, J. A. (1985). *Negotiation: Theory and practice.* Glenview, IL: Scott, Foresman.

9

Impression Management and Organizational Conflict

M. AFZALUR RAHIM
GABRIEL F. BUNTZMAN

We won't pull any punches. We are not here on some exercise. And we're not
walking away until our mission is done, until the invader is out of Kuwait.
(President George Bush, speaking to American troops stationed in
Saudi Arabia, November 22, 1990; "Bush Raises Specter," 1990)

By word and deed, George Bush attempted to send a clear message to
Saddam Hussein that the occupation of Kuwait would be very costly. The
president also tried to rally support for military intervention in his American
constituency and among Western allies and coalition members in the Persian
Gulf. George Bush prepared himself and his allies to deal with the conflict
effectively, in part by using impression management to gain support for his
position in the Persian Gulf. As is often the case in conflict situations,
impression management was attempted by parties on both sides of this issue.

Impression management and conflict are both part of organizational life.
Just as with other interrelationships among variables in organizations, such
as decision making, recruiting, goal setting, and performance, it behooves
the members of organizations to understand the relationship between the
impression and conflict management processes. This is so because with such

knowledge comes an opportunity for increased success and satisfaction with organizational life.

While both impression management and conflict management are sufficiently interesting in and of themselves to warrant separate discussions, the relationship between them is especially interesting. It should be emphasized here that to date very little research has been done to integrate the two. As a result, much of the discussion we present here is speculative, because it is based on the separate theories of impression management and conflict management.

Defining Impression Management

Much more thorough analyses of self-presentation/impression management are available elsewhere (see, for example, Giacalone & Rosenfeld, 1989), but, briefly, impression management (self-presentation) has to do with how we manage verbal and nonverbal communication to convey a positive image of self to others. It is no doubt obvious that others' perceptions of ourselves can have an impact upon their interpretations of our intentions, abilities, and acts, including our intentions to act in ways detrimental to their interests, our abilities to prevail in conflict with them, and the meanings of our actions. Thus impression management can be expected to occur in all phases of the conflict process.

Impression management covers a wide variety of behaviors and tactics, including, for example, ingratiation, self-description, accounts, apologies, entitlements, and enhancements (Gardner & Martinko, 1988). Ingratiation is used to enhance others' perceptions of one's personal qualities; self-descriptions may be positive, negative, or neutral; accounts are often used to justify an event, deny it occurred, or deny responsibility; apologies admit responsibility while seeking to limit repercussions; and entitlements maximize an actor's responsibility for positive events. The intention of all of these in general is to enhance the perception of the actor in the eyes of his or her audience.

The foregoing are not the only impression management tactics available. Others include intimidation, self-promotion, exemplification, and supplication (Gardner & Martinko, 1988). Intimidation is used to cause the actor to be perceived as dangerous, self-promotion leads to the actor's being seen as competent, exemplification tactics make the actor appear morally worthy, and supplication is used to portray the actor as pitiful. All of these and more have their places in the creation and management of conflict. We now turn to an examination of organizational conflict, including a definition of conflict and a review of conflict management styles and mechanisms.

Defining Organizational Conflict

Conflict is defined as an interactive state manifested in incompatibility, disagreement, or difference within or between social entities—individuals, groups, organizations, societies. Conflict occurs when a social entity (hereinafter referred to as a person) is required to engage in an activity that is incongruent with his or her needs or interests. Conflict also occurs when a person holds a behavioral preference the satisfaction of which is incompatible with another person's implementation of his or her preference. Another possible source of conflict is some mutually desirable resource that is in short supply, such that the wants of everyone may not be satisfied fully. Differences in attitudes, values, skills, and goals can also cause conflict. Some examples of conflict behaviors are interference, rivalry, verbal abuse, tension, frustration, and annoyance (Rahim, 1986).

Organizational conflict can be classified as intrapersonal, interpersonal, intragroup, or intergroup. For the practitioner, we believe that a knowledge of the relationship between impression management and interpersonal conflict is useful in dealing effectively with day-to-day activities. The literature on interpersonal conflict is concerned mainly with the styles of handling conflict rather than the intensity or amount of conflict. Following is a discussion of these styles that organizational members can use to deal with their conflicts with superiors, subordinates, and peers.

Styles of Handling Interpersonal Conflict

There are various styles of behavior by which interpersonal conflict may be handled. The idea of the styles of handling interpersonal conflict in organizations was first conceptualized by Mary P. Follett (1926/1940), who found three main ways of dealing with conflict: domination, compromise, and integration. She also found other ways of handling conflict in organizations, such as avoidance and suppression. Blake and Mouton (1964) presented a conceptual scheme for classifying the modes of handling interpersonal conflicts into five types. They described the five modes of handling conflict on the basis of the attitudes of the manager: concern for production and for people. Their scheme was reinterpreted by Thomas (1976), who considered the intentions of a party (cooperativeness, i.e., attempting to satisfy the other party's concerns; and assertiveness, i.e., attempting to satisfy one's own concerns) in classifying the modes of handling conflict into five types.

Using a conceptualization similar to those of the above theorists, Rahim (1983) and Rahim and Bonoma (1979) differentiated the styles of handling conflict on two basic dimensions: concern for self and concern for others. The first dimension explains the degree (high or low) to which a person attempts to satisfy his or her own concern. The second dimension explains the degree (high or low) to which a person wants to satisfy the concern of others. It should be pointed out that these dimensions portray the motivational orientations of a given individual during conflict (Rubin & Brown, 1975). A study by Van de Vliert and Kabanoff (1990; see also Ruble & Thomas, 1976) provides support for these dimensions. Combination of the two dimensions results in five specific styles of handling interpersonal conflict, as shown in Figure 9.1.

The styles of handling interpersonal conflict are described as follows:

(1) *Integrating:* This is characterized by collaboration between the parties, that is, openness, exchange of information, and examination of differences to reach a solution acceptable to both parties. "The first rule . . . for obtaining integration is to put your cards on the table, face the real issue, uncover the conflict, bring the whole thing into the open" (Follett, 1926/1940, p. 38). This style has two distinctive elements: confrontation and problem solving (Prein, 1976). Confrontation involves open and direct communication that should make way for problem solving. As a result, it may lead to creative solutions to problems.

(2) *Obliging:* This style involves attempting to play down the differences and emphasizing commonalities to satisfy the concern of the other party. There is an element of self-sacrifice in this style. It may take the form of selfless generosity, charity, or obedience to another person's order. An obliging person neglects his or her own concern to satisfy the concern of the other party.

(3) *Dominating:* This style is associated with a win-lose orientation or with forcing behavior to win one's position. A dominating or competing person goes all out to win his or her objective and, as a result, often ignores the needs and expectations of the other party. Dominating may mean standing up for one's rights and/or defending a position that the party believes to be correct. A dominating supervisor is likely to use a position of power to impose his or her will on subordinates and command their obedience.

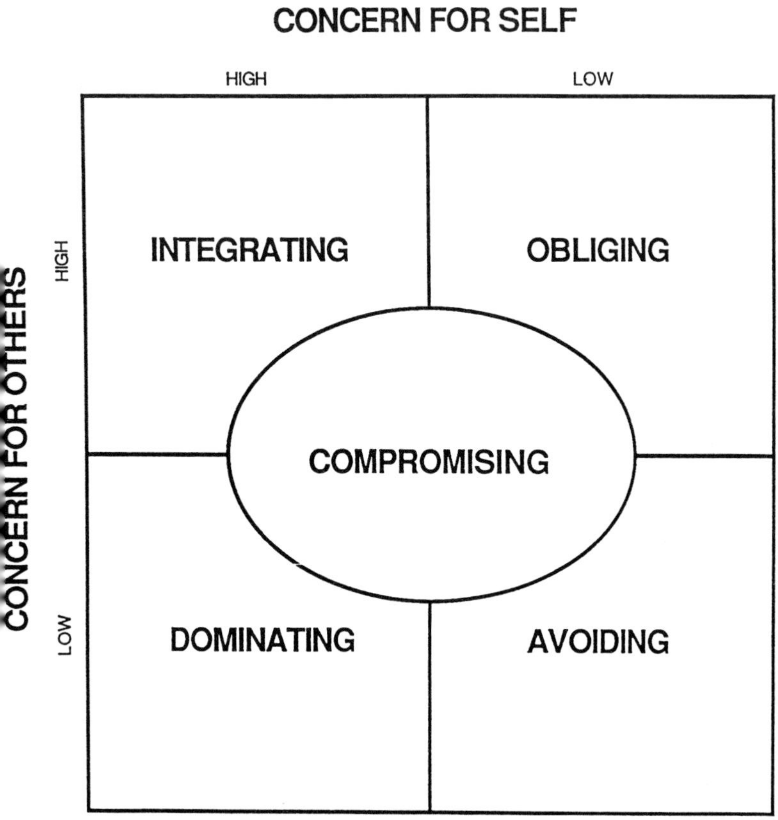

CONCERN FOR SELF

Figure 9.1. A Two-Dimensional Model of Styles of Handling Interpersonal
Conflict

SOURCE: From "Managing Organizational Conflict: A Model for Diagnosis and Intervention" by A. Rahim
and T. V. Bonoma, 1979, *Psychological Reports, 44*, pp. 1323-1344. Reprinted by permission.

(4) *Avoiding:* This may take the form of postponing an issue until a better time or
simply withdrawing from a threatening situation. An avoiding person fails to
satisfy his or her own concern as well as the concern of the other party. This
style is often characterized as an unconcerned attitude toward the issues or
parties involved in conflict. Such a person may be unwilling to acknowledge
in public that there is a conflict that should be addressed.

(5) *Compromising:* This involves give-and-take, or sharing, whereby both parties give up something to make a mutually acceptable decision. It may mean splitting the difference, exchanging concessions, or seeking a quick middle-ground position. A compromising party gives up more than a dominating party but less than an obliging party. Likewise, such a party addresses an issue more directly than would an avoiding party, but does not explore it in as much depth as would an integrating party.

Further insights into the five styles of handling interpersonal conflict may be obtained by organizing them according to the integrative and distributive dimensions of labor-management bargaining suggested by Walton and Mc-Kersie (1965). The integrative dimension (integrating-avoiding) represents the extent (high or low) of satisfaction of concerns received by the two parties, that is, their *joint gains or losses.* The distributive dimension (dominating-obliging) represents the extent of the satisfaction of concerns received by one party *at the expense of the other party.* In the integrative dimension, integrating style attempts to increase the satisfaction of the concerns of both parties by finding unique solutions to the problems acceptable to them. At the other end of the continuum, the avoiding style leads to the reduction of satisfaction of the concerns of both parties as a result of their failure to confront and solve their problems. In the distributive dimension, whereas dominating style attempts to obtain high satisfaction of concerns for self (and to provide low satisfaction of concerns for others), obliging style attempts to obtain low satisfaction of concerns for self (and to provide high satisfaction of concerns for others) (see Figure 9.2).

Compromising style represents the point of intersection of the two dimensions. In other words, it is a middle-ground position where both parties receive an intermediate level of satisfaction of their concerns from the resolution of their conflicts.

It is generally agreed that the above design for conceptualizing the styles of handling interpersonal conflict is a noteworthy improvement over the simple cooperative-competitive dichotomy suggested by earlier researchers (Deutsch, 1949). It is also an improvement over the other typologies: three styles, such as nonconfrontation, solution orientation, and control (Putnam & Wilson, 1982), and four styles, such as yielding, problem solving, inaction, and contending (Pruitt, 1983).

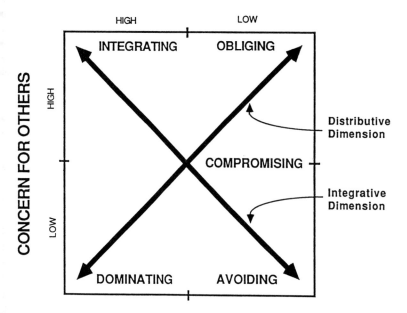

Figure 9.2. Integrative and Distributive Dimensions of Styles of Handling Interpersonal Conflict

The management of interpersonal conflict involves enabling organization members to learn the five styles of handling conflict so that different situations can be addressed effectively. Although some behavioral scientists suggest that integrating or problem-solving style is most appropriate for managing conflict (e.g., Blake & Mouton, 1964; Burke, 1969; Likert & Likert, 1976), it has been indicated by others that, for conflicts to be managed functionally, one style may be more appropriate than another, depending upon the situation (Hart, 1981; Rahim & Bonoma, 1979; Thomas, 1977). Rahim (1983) has described situations in which each of the styles is appropriate or inappropriate. In general, integrating and, to some extent, compromising styles are appropriate for dealing with strategic or complex issues. The remaining styles can be used to deal with tactical or day-to-day problems. The above discussion on the styles of handling conflict and the situations in which they are appropriate or inappropriate is a normative approach to managing conflict.

Relationships Between Impression Management and the Styles of Handling Interpersonal Conflict

However common it may be, the use of impression management in conflicts is not inevitable. In general, the motivation to use impression management may be especially strong if one or more of the following conditions holds: if managing impressions might be beneficial for goal attainment, if the outcomes are highly valued, or if one wishes to maintain or create a positive image (Leary & Kowalski, 1990). In conflicts, therefore, our motivation to use impression management will be higher if we think it will help us to "win" the dispute, when the stakes are high, or if our image can be enhanced by a victory or damaged by a defeat. George Bush would appear to have had all of these motives for impression management in the Persian Gulf crisis.

There are a number of ways we might go about analyzing the conflict management process, and the role of impression management therein. Here we adopt Thomas's (1976) process model of dyadic conflict as a loom upon which to weave together the separate threads of conflict management and impression management. According to Thomas, conflict is a five-stage process: a party's frustration, conceptualization of the situation, and behavior (response), the other party's reaction, and the outcome, that is, the final agreement or disagreement between parties and its effects.

Frustration

This is caused by an actual or anticipated interference of the other party in the attainment of the first party's goals. Frustration is a basic tension that is uncomfortable for the individual. As a result, the individual is motivated to do something about it. But what is to be done?

Conceptualization

The first aspect of this stage is the individual's definition of the issue involved; the second aspect is his or her awareness of action alternatives and their outcomes. The first aspect "appears to involve some assessment of the primary concerns of the two parties—the party's own frustrated concern and his perception of the concern which led the other party to perform the frustrating action" (Thomas, 1976, p. 896).

In this stage of conflict an individual seeks answers to a number of questions whose basic thrust is to determine why the conflict and consequent frustration have occurred. Why am I experiencing conflict? What issues underlie the conflict? What would I like to get out of this conflict? What would the other party like to obtain? How do I expect the other party to behave during this conflict? Impression management has the potential to influence responses to these kinds of questions, and therefore may influence the course of the conflict.

It may be difficult to own up to, or to get the other party to own up to, the real cause of some conflicts. Most organizational conflicts are issue based, but it is possible sometimes for personal differences (personality differences, personal grudges, and the like) to form the basis for conflicts. Since it is not terribly flattering to admit that a personal matter is the basis of a conflict causing inconvenience and expense to others and to the organization, the party with a "personal" grudge may well disavow such a motive with denials and affirmation of loftier goals. In such a case we might expect to hear exemplifications and accounts to justify the conflict. Because the underlying cause is not admitted, the conflict may not be satisfactorily resolved.

In general, impression management is rarely an unambiguous form of communication (Moberg, 1989), and a conflict in which the adversaries are prone to rely on impression management to disguise the true basis of the dispute may be especially intractable. It should be obvious that if one party fails to state honestly his or her reasons for frustrating the other, then the ability to conceptualize the conflict properly will be impaired. If the conflict is not properly conceptualized, if we do not understand the root cause, then we cannot effectively deal with the basic issues relating to the conflict.

Behavior

Conflict interactions are a dynamic process in which one party's behaviors serve as a stimulus for the other party's behaviors. In this section, we discuss this pattern of one party's behavior and reactions to the other's behavior. Impression management may influence a person's initial behavior and his or her reaction to the other party's behavior during conflict. Behaviors, the specific acts taken, are important in two ways—as a means of controlling the outcome itself, and also as a means of communicating to the other party, either truthfully or as a bluff, what else one might do. Whether through verbalizations in the conflict setting, artifactual displays, expressive behaviors, or purposive behaviors, a person may attempt to affect the other party's conceptualization, level of aspirations, or behaviors and conflict aftermath. Thus the U.S. president's sending another 100,000 troops to Saudi Arabia and Saddam Hussein responding in kind were behaviors with messages.

Both continued to use impression management to influence others at home and abroad to gain support for their respective positions.

Verbal self-presentations are vocalized statements designed to present an image to another party that is favorable to the sender. Thus a civil greeting, expression of concern for the other party's comfort, and so on may be intended to create an image of compassion or concern that might disarm the other party, or at least soften him or her so that some sort of compromise or true problem solving is possible. Or a verbal presentation may be calculated to demonstrate to the other side that one is not intimidated and therefore is not an easy target. As an example, we recall an experience one of the authors had in working with an entrepreneur. This entrepreneur on many occasions was required to negotiate with organizations whose resources were far greater than his own. Thus he would often attend meetings with adversaries either alone or with just one assistant while the other side would be represented by a team of three, four, or five people, including accountants, lawyers, engineers, and other professionals. As a meeting was about to begin, this businessman would proceed to point conspicuously to each of the other side's representatives and count them off. "Let's see," he would proclaim, "one, two, three, four, five. Okay, the sides are even. Let's get started." His message was clear, and it contained several points: First, he was not intimidated by their numbers; second, he had done his homework and therefore did not need a large team to back him up; and third, he felt in control of the situation. Artifactual displays are not behaviors, but they often are presented as meaningful stimuli during the period of direct interaction. These include physical appearance and situational context, such as plush offices and private conference rooms.

Expressive behaviors include "body language" and other nonverbal communication, such as smiles, frowns, and firm handshakes. Again, these may be used in a deliberate fashion to communicate friendliness, hostility, sympathy, and so on to make an impression upon others, and, as always, may be used in a truthful or misleading manner. A firm handshake and a pat on the back, for example, can be used to convey sympathy and trust in the message sender. This can be useful in pursuing an avoidance style, for example, by inducing the other party not to pursue conflict aggressively.

Purposive behaviors, like expressive behaviors, tell something about the personality and character of the individual. A manager who sends letters of congratulations to subordinates, for example, is using purposive behaviors whose effect, if successful, is to create an impression that the manager is aware of and cares about those individuals. Like other modes of impression management, purposive behaviors can be useful in establishing a climate in which to pursue a particular conflict management strategy.

In conflict, perhaps we find it necessary to fire the most liked coworker in a unit, or find ourselves in a conflict with others because we must take an unpopular stand or a stand that puts our own job in jeopardy. Impression management at the conceptualization stage is useful to structure the adversary's perception of the conflict "appropriately" to elicit the desired behaviors from the other side.

As discussed before, each of the five styles of handling conflict is appropriate, depending upon the situation. A party may conceptualize the issues involved in conflict as complex, and conclude that the synthesis of ideas of both parties is needed to come up with effective solutions. In this case, the party would probably try to use integrating style. This party is likely to use impression management so that the other party may also feel encouraged to use the integrating style. Because the parties use the integrative dimension, they can come up with a win-win solution to their common problem.

Avoiding style is appropriate when the issue is trivial or the potential dysfunctional effect of confronting the other party outweighs the benefits of resolution. Persons may use avoiding style if they think they are less powerful than the other party. Not all avoiders are weak, however. Even a strong party may profit from conflict avoidance, for the simple passage of time may itself take its toll on the strength of the weaker party. Delays may allow the stronger party to consolidate his or her position, and further discourage the weaker one. However, a party who is aware that delays are intentional and are designed to put him or her at a disadvantage may not willingly stand for them. Thus impression management by the avoider can sometimes play a role in the success of the avoidance strategy. We are aware, for example, of a certain manager who repeatedly informed subordinates of his intentions to get to the bottom of a certain superior-subordinate dispute, advising not only the subordinates but others sympathetic to them that he would resolve the matter satisfactorily for them. The subordinates' employment contracts nearly expired while they waited passively for the expected favorable resolution. (The superior's expressions of concern and sympathy may have been intended for other audiences—the intermediaries who had spoken on behalf of the employees.) In any event, the superior did not seem to have been sincere in retrospect. As it happened, the manager was forced to commit himself publicly to his antiemployee position while time still remained for an internal appeals process. Thus this delaying tactic was not completely successful.

There are other reasons avoidance may be the preferred style of handling interpersonal conflict, and one of them is our "gut feeling" that we cannot solve the problem because we cannot "get a handle on it." Managerial intuition plays an important role in decision making (Issack, 1978; Simon, 1987). If intuition leads one party to conclude that the adversary has not fully owned up to the cause of the conflict, or emotions are running too hot, then one or both parties may use this style. A manager choosing to make an unpopular move may disavow responsibility for the action due to "financial exigency," the press of competition, or other external causes. Impression management may be used to fix blame or credit internally or externally (Zaccaro, Petersen, & Walker, 1987). An external attribution serves to relieve the manager of responsibility and tends to eliminate the basis of conflict. The manager expresses regret at not being able to give raises, or at having to terminate employees, but "blames" external events. In this case, the "victim" of the manager's decision is asked to conceptualize the conflict as an impersonal one, between organizations in which this person is a helpless victim. The conflict is externalized, and the manager avoids having to cope with the disgruntled employee. This tactic is also available to adversaries who are peers and subordinates.

A dominating style is useful when a speedy decision is needed, when an issue is important to the party, or when a superior believes that the subordinates lack expertise to make technical decisions. It is well established that a show of force may deter aggression in some circumstances. Since there is less likelihood of aggression against one party by another if each is believed to be about equally powerful (Buntzman, 1990; Tedeschi & Bonoma, 1977), a party attempting to avoid conflict may, paradoxically, engage in posturing intended to convince a stronger party that he or she is dealing with an equally powerful adversary, hoping thereby to dissuade the stronger party from aggression. At the same time, a powerful party bent on using the dominating style of conflict management may try to project a strong, capable, and decisive persona to convince the opponent that resistance would be futile. In that event, the weaker party might resort to the obliging or avoiding style of handling conflict. At least this is what the United States and its allies hoped for in the Persian Gulf crisis.

An ingratiating impression management style may have several purposes. Ingratiation may serve as a signal to the other side that one is conceding an issue, as in an obliging style of conflict management. However, ingratiation must be interpreted in context, for, like other kinds of tacit bargaining, impression management behaviors may be open to a variety of interpretations, as noted earlier (Moberg, 1989). Another reason for ingratiation may be to build credibility, to convince another party of one's sincerity in wanting to find a compromise solution.

A number of other impression management techniques may also be appropriate at various times, depending on the issues confronted and the message to be conveyed. For example, one may wish to appear aloof, above the fray so to speak, to convince others of the loftier goals and rectitude of one's own position. An appeal to superordinate goals almost requires one to project an image of vision and concern for the organization as a whole.

Outcome

This is the final event in the conflict episode. Many conflicts are not easily forgotten, especially those in which one party has sought to dominate the other. If one party has won, then the other has lost. One has saved face, and the other has lost it. Here a loser may express satisfaction with the outcome. Since he is not accepting something unpalatable, there is less loss of face than if he grudgingly and powerlessly must accept an unpalatable outcome. Here he can be gracious and magnanimous in defeat. Thus impression management is all the more critical to the losing party, which will try to put the best face it can on the loss. The loss may be minimized to make it seem as though not much was lost, or the losing party may attempt to identify a superordinate goal that was preserved even though the party's immediate goal of winning the conflict was lost. Thus we have the candidate who, in losing an election, proclaims, "Today, the voters are the winners because they had the opportunity to express themselves and make a choice," or the department on the losing side of a budgetary dispute whose manager pro-claims, "At least we made them sit up and take notice, and specify what they were looking for." While the victory itself will have conferred some status automatically upon the prevailing party, the victor may wish to avoid long-term problems. Thus "statesmanlike" pronouncements may proclaim a new era of cooperation and a healthful clearing of the air. Conciliatory statements about the other party may be issued. These may help to defuse the conflict aftermath, and make it easier for the vanquished to cooperate in the future.

Recently, the president of a university had no choice but to grant tenure to a professor who had appealed a denial of tenure that originated with the college dean, was supported by the vice president of academic affairs, and ultimately was supported by the president. The denial was appealed through the university's grievance process and reversal was recommended by the grievance committee to the board of regents of the university. Asked by the regents for his opinion on the matter, the president wrote in part: "I have permitted Dr. X's appeal to be given exposure to every avenue available as outlined in the Faculty Handbook. . . . I encourage you to accept the committee's recommendation . . . and to award tenure to Dr. X."

On the surface, the president's letter appeared to imply that the appeal process was carried out through "every avenue available" out of consideration for the grievant, as condemned prisoners are allowed every possible appeal prior to an execution. Those familiar with the case, however, recognized the president's letter as an artfully contrived instrument of impression management, as explained below.

The facts of the case included a finding by a committee earlier in the grievance process that the decision to deny tenure was probably arbitrary and that tenure should be granted. Thus the president "allowed" the appeal to go forward not for the grievant's sake, but for the sake of the dean, vice president, and president himself, who evidently hoped that the earlier finding and recommendation supporting the professor would not be supported later on. Further, there was no provision in the faculty (employee) handbook for discretion on the part of the president in allowing or disallowing an appeal to go forward. Literally the president was correct—he did allow the appeal to go forward by failing to accept the first committee's recommendation. More correctly, perhaps, he forced the appeal to go forward. However, the impression from the president's letter was that he was in control of the process and allowed the grievance to proceed out of concern for the faculty member. It remains to be seen whether the professor who won his tenure will allow this small, face-saving deception to prevail or will act to correct the impression with his own letter. Impression management for the purpose of deception is not without risk, as a reputation as a manipulator may ruin one's career (Kotter & Schlesinger, 1979). In this case the already-damaged credibility of the president could suffer yet another blow, and he could suffer even more loss of face.

"Usually the resolution of conflict leaves a legacy which will affect the future relations of the parties and their attitudes toward each other" (Filley, 1975, p. 17). If the conflicting parties use integrating style, this will lead to a constructive management of conflict. A problem-solving or integrating approach to conflict management may lead to greater commitment to the agreement reached between parties. This is a win-win situation in which there should be no loss of face. Impression management will be directed at increasing the stature of the parties through entitlements.

A victor who has used an avoiding style and who is concerned with his or her postconflict image may express regret for delays. In fact, he or she may use as an excuse for the delays his or her concern that all necessary data be collected before proceeding with the conflict. Retrospective excuses in which some other person or thing is blamed for an outcome are not uncommon. Here the concern is to avoid seeming insensitive and overbearing. Thus a dominator may express concern for loss of life or property that might have occurred if quick and decisive (but unpopular) action were not taken. Grace and generosity in victory are the hallmarks of this style.

A compromise has sometimes been labeled a no-win/no-lose proposition, because both sides receive less than they originally sought. Thus there is still the potential to lose face, and the impression manager can be expected to cast the settlement in the best light with excuses, justifications, and symbolic behaviors that send the message that they have really gotten a good settlement, one that is entirely acceptable. Of course, if the resolution is especially popular, impression management may well include entitlements wherein the person attempts to take credit for the resolution of the conflict.

Discussion

Knowledge and awareness of impression management can be used in several ways by those managing organizational conflicts. For example, impression management can be used by a person proactively, to inform others of his or her resolve, abilities, or intentions. Impression management may be employed reactively, following impression management by adversaries to the same purpose. However, the adversaries in an organizational conflict may not be the only ones involved in the dispute. Others may be brought in as mediators or arbitrators of disputes. For example, higher-level managers may be expected to mediate or arbitrate disputes among subordinates. In some cases, of course, professional arbitrators from outside the organization may be brought in. Whether the third parties are internal or external, it is not unlikely that they too will be targets of impression management.

If we find ourselves as the third party brought in to adjudicate a dispute, we should be aware of the ways in which we might be unduly influenced by skillful impression management by a disputant. There should be no doubt that third parties may be influenced by impression management. Even something as subtle as the pattern of concessions made in collective bargaining prior to arbitration has been shown to influence an arbitrator's impression of the reasonableness or unreasonableness of the parties and, most important, his or her final determination of an appropriate award.

What prescriptions might there be for the effective use of impression management in conflict situations? The literature on bargaining and negotiation provides us with some guidelines. From that literature we know that a tough bargaining stance tends to lead to higher outcomes than a soft one, while at the same time toughness leads to deadlocks more frequently. Provided one is willing to risk a deadlock and its consequences—such as costly delays and escalations of the conflict—talking tough, shows of force, and the like are recommended impression management tactics. That same literature, however, informs us that the "norm of reciprocity" (tit for tat) can exert a powerful influence on others. If one has the hope or expectation that the other side might be reasonable, and room to maneuver from one's initial negotiating position, then a soft approach, meaning concessions, may be indicated. Body language and verbal language can be used to convey an impression that one is reasonable and "ready to do business." In Western society the norm of reciprocity can be quite a powerful force to induce the other side to make concessions.

However, a soft stance may result in a less favorable solution than a hard stance, although such a solution will likely be reached sooner and with less likelihood of a deadlock. There is the danger that the adversary will interpret a concession as a sign of weakness and then seek to exploit it. Thus a party who softens his or her position in the hope of moving a dispute forward should know that he or she risks creating the wrong impression in that way. If concessions are to be made, our advice would be to make only small concessions until a pattern of quid pro quo behavior has been established.

The manager will have to decide in any given situation which impression, firm or reasonable, should be conveyed, and then select carefully the words, symbols, and behaviors to convey that meaning. Clearly, this is a complex task, but one that, properly managed, can result in increased probability of a successful conflict management episode.

Impression management is obviously closely allied with the conflict management process in organizations. Unfortunately, there has been little or no scientific research explicitly linking these two concepts, although we have been helped in our discussion by reference to related ideas, such as bluffing and deception, from bargaining and negotiation literature.

Like so many other tools available to the practitioner, impression management can be used properly or improperly. The question is not whether to use impression management in the management of conflict but how to use it properly so that appropriate outcomes are achieved for the organization and its employees. We hope this chapter has provided some insights for managers and employees into how impression management may be used or misused in the management of conflict, as well as some ideas about tactics that can be used in defense of misused impression management. A comprehensive discussion of the ethics of conflict management is beyond the scope of this chapter. The reader who is interested in this issue is referred to the article by Rahim, Garrett, and Buntzman (in press).

A number of research questions present themselves in the areas of impression management and conflict. An important area of future research concerns carefully evaluating the impact of impression management training on the effective selection and use of the five styles of handling interpersonal conflict with superiors, subordinates, and peers. We need both laboratory and field studies in this area.

References

Blake, R. R., & Mouton, J. S. (1964). *The managerial grid*. Houston, TX: Gulf.

Buntzman, G. F. (1990). Power and politics in privatization negotiations. *International Journal of Conflict Management, 1*, 93-112.

Burke, R. J. (1969). Methods of resolving superior-subordinate conflict: The constructive use of subordinate differences and disagreements. *Organizational Behavior and Human Performance, 5*, 393-411.

Bush raises specter of Iraq making, using nuclear arms. (1990, November 23). *Louisville Courier Journal*, p. 1.

Deutsch, M. (1949). A theory of cooperation and competition. *Human Relations, 2*, 129-151.

Filley, A. C. (1975). *Interpersonal conflict resolution*. Glenview, IL: Scott, Foresman.

Follett, M. P. (1940). Constructive conflict. In H. C. Metcalf & L. Urwick (Eds.), *Dynamic administration: The collected papers of Mary Parker Follett* (pp. 30-49). New York: Harper & Row. (Original work published 1926)

Gardner, W. L., & Martinko, M. J. (1988). Impression management: An observational study linking audience characteristics with verbal self-presentations. *Academy of Management Journal, 31*, 42-65.

Giacalone, R. A., & Rosenfeld, P. (Eds.). (1989). *Impression management in the organization*. Hillsdale, NJ: Lawrence Erlbaum.

Hart, L. B. (1981). *Learning from conflict: A handbook for trainers and group leaders*. Reading, MA: Addison-Wesley.

Issack, T. F. (1978). Intuition: An ignored dimension of management. *Academy of Management Review, 3*, 917-922.

Kotter, J. P., & Schlesinger, L. A. (1979). Choosing strategies for change. *Harvard Business Review, 57*(2), 106-114.

Leary, M. R., & Kowalski, R. M. (1990). Impression management: A literature review and two-component model. *Psychological Bulletin, 107*, 34-47.

Likert, R., & Likert, J. G. (1976). *New ways of managing conflict.* New York: McGraw-Hill.

Moberg, D. (1989). The ethics of impression management. In R. A. Giacalone & P. Rosenfeld (Eds.), *Impression management in the organization* (pp. 171-187). Hillsdale, NJ: Lawrence Erlbaum.

Prein, H. C. M. (1976). Stiljen van conflicthantering [Styles of handling conflict]. *Nederlands Tijdschrift voor de Psychologie, 31*, 321-346.

Pruitt, D. G. (1983). Strategic choice in negotiation. *American Behavioral Scientist, 27*, 167-194.

Putnam, L. L., & Wilson, C. E. (1982). Communicative strategies in organizational conflicts: Reliability and validity of a measurement scale. In M. Burgoon (Ed.), *Communication yearbook, 6* (pp. 629-652). Beverly Hills, CA: Sage.

Rahim, M. A. (1983). A measure of styles of handling interpersonal conflict. *Academy of Management Journal, 26*, 368-376.

Rahim, M. A. (1986). *Managing conflict in organizations.* New York: Praeger.

Rahim, M. A., & Bonoma, T. V. (1979). Managing organizational conflict: A model for diagnosis and intervention. *Psychological Reports, 44*, 1323-1344.

Rahim, M. A., Garrett, J. E., & Buntzman, G. F. (in press). Ethics of managing interpersonal conflict in organizations. *Journal of Business Ethics.*

Rubin, J. Z., & Brown, B. R. (1975). *The social psychology of bargaining and negotiation.* New York: Academic Press.

Ruble, T. L., & Thomas, K. W. (1976). Support for a two-dimensional model for conflict behavior. *Organizational Behavior and Human Performance, 16*, 143-155.

Simon, H. A. (1987). Making management decisions: The role of intuition and emotion. *Academy of Management Executive, 1*, 57-64.

Tedeschi, J. T., & Bonoma, T. V. (1977). Measures of last resort: Coercion and aggression in bargaining. In D. Druckman (Ed.), *Negotiations: Social psychological perspectives* (pp. 213-241). Beverly Hills, CA: Sage.

Thomas, K. W. (1976). Conflict and conflict management. In M. D. Dunnette (Ed.), *Handbook of industrial and organizational psychology* (pp. 889-935). Chicago: Rand McNally.

Thomas, K. W. (1977). Toward multi-dimensional values in teaching: The example of conflict behaviors. *Academy of Management Review, 2*, 484-490.

Van de Vliert, E., & Kabanoff, B. (1990). Toward theory-based measures of conflict management. *Academy of Management Journal, 33*, 199-209.

Walton, R. E., & McKersie, R. B. (1965). *A behavioral theory of labor negotiations: An analysis of a social interaction system.* New York: McGraw-Hill.

Zaccaro, S. J., Petersen, C., & Walker, S. (1987). Self serving attributions for individual and group performance. *Social Psychology Quarterly, 50*, 257-263.

PART IV

Diversity: Gender and Cultural Applications

10

Start With a Rational Group of People . . .

Gender Effects of Impression Management in Organizations

LAURIE LARWOOD

> The game site is resplendent with symbolism.
> (Harrigan, 1977, p. 211)

Start with a rational group of people, not the few who are reputed to enjoy discrimination or who prefer to discriminate. Assume with me that this rational group of people is bent on acting to its own advantage as defined by expectancy theory researchers (see Matsui, Kagawa, Nagamatsu, & Ohtsuka, 1977; Vroom, 1964). Add, if you like, the limitations on expectancy offered by observers who believe that people's actions are governed in part by the intention to maintain justice—perhaps the system called equity (see Adams & Freedman, 1976; Greenberg, 1989) or your choice of another exchange (Larwood & Blackmore, 1977; Larwood, Kavanagh, & Levine, 1978).

AUTHOR'S NOTE: Correspondence and requests for reprints should be sent to Laurie Larwood, Dean, College of Business Administration, University of Nevada, Reno, NV 89557-0016.

Is it possible that, in this alert, purposeful, and fair world, impression management[1] could still influence judgment and behavior in organizations—particularly judgment and behavior with respect to something so obvious and basic as gender? Judgments and reactions based on gender are generally heavily proscribed by law and local regulations. Why would they still take place?

The intention of this chapter is to review briefly the persistence of gender discrimination in the face of legislative and regulatory attempts to end it. Thereafter, the chapter shows how some of the most important theoretical descriptions of discrimination, those involving role theory and rational bias theory, relate to forms of impression management. Final sections suggest practical ways in which impression management can be diminished and offer an interpretation of some everyday events in terms of impression management, role theory, and rational bias.

Setting the Scene

To understand the origin of gender effects in impression management at work, it is useful to consider briefly the recent gender history of Western business organizations. In the earlier part of this century, Asian, European, Latin American, and North American businesses were almost exclusively run by men (Davidson & Cooper, 1984). There has been significant change in the past two decades (the current extent of this change will not be known until analysis of the 1990 U.S. Census results, but an indication that equality has not been achieved can be gathered in the following paragraphs), but as recently as 1970, men were 96.5% of salaried managers in durable goods manufacturing, 93.8% in nondurable manufacturing, and 85.4% in finance, insurance, and real estate (Sommers, 1974). The women in those positions were generally subordinated to the men and earned less even when equally prepared and in equal positions (see Larwood & Wood, 1977, p. 13). For example, women salaried managers in nondurable goods manufacturing earned just 49% of what their male associates took home. Women were most strongly represented in low-paying and generally low-status professions—representing 73.5% of clerical workers and 96.6% of service workers in 1970 (Hedges & Bemis, 1974).

Recent changes in organizations have been largely toward closing the gender gap: in the direction of equality of preparation, representation at each level, and equal salary. The changes have been spurred by several factors, including declines in real disposable personal income, making two-earner families necessary; family planning practices, making long-range careers more feasible for women; the women's movement, which made inroads in helping both sexes to recognize the need for equality; and prominent government regulations outlawing sexual and racial discrimination (see Ledvinka, 1982, pp. 17-133).

The operative phrase here is *toward closing the gap*. The gap is not closed, and it shows no likelihood of quickly disappearing. Between 1970 and 1980, census data indicate that women in the United States increased from 38% to 42.6% of the work force. In that same decade, women's gains were disproportionately high in 60 of 503 occupations (Bianchi & Rytina, 1984; cited in Reskin & Roos, 1987). One calculation found that, overall, the ratio of women's wages to men's increased from .58 to .60 in the period. Although women managers as a whole increased from 51% to 55% of men's wages, professional women dropped from 64% to 63% in the same period (Tienda & Ortiz, 1987). More recent census data are not yet available, but estimates indicate that women are moving toward 45% of the U.S. work force, and that they now (as of 1988) earn 65% of the wages of men in comparable jobs—69% for equivalent hours worked (Horrigan & Markey, 1990). Despite progress, the gap continues.

Stereotyping and Impression Management

The gap discussed above fits neatly with our consensual concepts of sex role stereotyping. Stereotypes provide a sort of social icon or roughly drawn cartoon that people use as a general reference point to substitute for their lack of knowledge of specific details. For instance, not knowing a Mexican worker named José, I can imagine that his behavior parallels my stereotype of Mexicans when someone mentions him in a discussion. The less I know of the individual and the less experienced I am with Mexicans, the more comfortable I am in applying the broad strokes of the stereotype. Unfortunately, stereotypes can be far from the average they are meant to represent, and are seldom accurate when applied to individual cases. José turns out not to take siestas on the job, but is instead a sophisticated university graduate from Monterrey; his parents own a steel mill.

In the case of sex roles, the stereotype has not caught up to reality; it provides an explanation of the gap between men and women in the workplace, but is a poor description of modern career women. Sex role stereotypes, in the most general terms, still insist that women are warm and interpersonally skilled, while men are tough and objective. Women lack career motivation, according to the stereotype, but are quite willing to support others, particularly their husbands and other family members. By this stereotype, women enter and leave the work force casually, do not seek career preparation, do not care about moving up, prefer support staff positions, and are paid according to their lower productivity (Brenner, Tomkiewicz, & Schein, 1989; Colwill, 1987; Fagenson, 1990; Larwood & Wood, 1977). Men are paid more because they are bottom-line driven; they are competitive, but only about what matters. There is, of course, some basis in truth for the assumption that the average male worker differs from the average female worker (Olson & Frieze, 1987)—although not to the extent observed in position and salary differentials. Without belaboring the distance between sex role stereotypes and reality, it is important to recognize that we all apply them on occasion when other more valid information is lacking.

The gender effects of impression management come into organizational life at two levels. They enter most obviously when individuals can enhance their association with stereotypes to their own advantage—for instance, when a man, by seeming masculine, can leave the impression of being tough when a situation requires that attribute. Alternatively, gender effects are also apparent when impression management is called on to demolish this relationship, as when a woman intentionally promotes a tough image to set herself apart from the female stereotype. The two gender effects at this simple level might be labeled *first order*, as they primarily concern an individual's manipulation of his or her own image relative to the stereotype. Not surprisingly, these two effects are known technically as the "association principle"— in other words, "people claim desirable images" but "disestablish personal association with undesirable images" (Schlenker, 1980, pp. 105-106).

A *second-order* or *rational bias* effect occurs when the stereotype is applied by an intermediary who is distinct both from the person being stereotyped and from the person thought to believe in the stereotype. Here the intermediary is concerned with how he or she will be viewed by someone else as a result of the intermediary's behavior toward other persons being stereotyped. For instance, a human resources manager may be concerned with the stereotypes held by the vice president for whom a new recruit is sought. Should a male nurse be hired by a personnel manager who knows that the head of the nursing staff believes that men who go into the field are not sufficiently masculine? The result may make the human resources manager appear less competent than he or she would prefer. In a sense, the association principle described above works through the human resources manager's intention to be associated by the head of the nursing staff with his or her behavior toward the male nurse. First- and second-order impression management effects are examined in detail below.

Gender and Impression Management: First-Order Effects

First-order effects depend on the would-be impression managers' assumptions that someone important to them, such as their superior, relies on stereotypes in evaluating them. That important person, whom we might label a *power holder* relative to the impression manager, might be manipulated through the stereotypes. As noted above, first-order effects represent people's attempt to change the perception others have of them by altering the relationship between the image they project and the stereotype others seemingly hold. Since the stereotype is more likely to depict the situation accurately as it existed in previous decades than it now does, we might categorize first-order impression management as supporting tradition (supporting the stereotypic gap between men's and women's behavior, with consequent differences in positions and pay) or as supporting change (resisting the stereotype). See Table 10.1 for some examples.

Supporting Tradition

Although there has been no research specifically to the point, it might be expected that those who enjoy their current situation would resist changes in it. More specifically, those who feel that they are benefiting from the stereotype would seek to enhance it—or at least would defend it. The section of Table 10.1 labeled "Supporting Tradition" gives examples of individuals who are advantaged by the current stereotype and might prefer to maintain it. A woman who chooses to be a secretary because she enjoys the full traditional meaning of that role may be immediately displeased by assignment to a female boss (who signifies change), or by being joined by a male secretary (cutting into the femininity the woman associates with the role of secretary). She is unlikely to agitate for training to move into management or for opening the advancement ladder to secretaries. Similarly, male impression managers who enjoy the macho image of a male-only job would place that image at risk with the power holder if they invited a woman to join them as an equal.[2] Because our understanding of ourselves is derived in part from

Table 10.1 Examples of First-Order Effects

Supporting Tradition	
(Those below strive for the impression that the stereotype is correct.)	
Traditional Jobs	(A1) Women secretaries who *enjoy* the interactions with their bosses in the work process and who are afraid it will change.
	Male miners who *enjoy* the macho image of the work and are afraid it will become softer.
(Those below strive for the impression that the stereotype is usually correct, but that they are unusual and fit the job anyway.)	
Non-Traditional Jobs	(B1) Women bosses who *enjoy* the image of being as hard-driving as any man.
	Male preschool teachers who *enjoy* the relationships and the ability to be gentle in working with children.
Supporting Change	
(Those below strive for the impression that the stereotype is wrong and that they should not be placed in such a job.)	
Traditional Jobs	(A2) Women secretaries who *dislike* being stuck in a subordinate service role with no promotion ladder.
	Male miners who *dislike* the uncompromising conditions in which they work.
(Those below strive for the impression that the stereotype is wrong, and that they therefore are appropriate to their jobs.)	
Non-Traditional Jobs	(B2) Women bosses who *dislike* the assumption that their femininity is suspect as a result of the job.
	Male preschool teachers who dislike the assumption that they could not survive under the stresses of a "real job."

our behavior, the impression manager's own self-image as macho might also be at risk here.

What is the anticipated result of first-order effects for those supporting tradition? The interaction of gender and impression management can be anticipated as one in which the individual will make an effort to enhance the apparent correctness of the stereotype—at least the part of the stereotype that seems particularly advantageous. Thus those in traditional jobs can generally promote the entire stereotype.

Those in nontraditional jobs are in a more precarious position. They probably did not immediately fall into their jobs, but worked hard to get there. Consequently, they must be more selective, showcasing the importance of those parts of the stereotype that benefit them, while simultaneously ignoring or downplaying the parts that would emphasize that they are themselves in a precarious position. A woman boss might enjoy pointing out that her job is tough and that it takes an unusual woman to handle it—she would not point out that the tough quality of the job makes it seem stereotypically difficult for women to function appropriately in it.[3]

Supporting Change

Similar to those enjoying their relationship to the stereotype, those who dislike it will predictably manipulate the situation to their advantage. In this case, however, they will support change, rather than resist change. For example, a woman secretary who is ambitious to move up in the organization may look forward to any change that disassociates her and her position from the stereotypic role of women secretaries supporting men as bosses.

From the point of view of the secretary who is in a traditional "woman's job," activities that gnaw at any part of the stereotype will be beneficial. Every move in this direction will assist the impression manager in removing herself from the power holder's neat stereotypic compartmentalization of "woman—therefore, secretary."

In contrast, someone who is in a nontraditional role, such as a male secretary, can be expected to be more cautious. Since he acquired his role voluntarily and probably at some effort, he is not interested in demonstrating that the employer does not need a secretary. Instead, he seeks only to diminish the influence of those parts of the stereotype that negatively affect him—such as those suggesting perhaps that he is lacking in ambition for taking such a position.

Manifestations of Impression Management

How could impression management be carried out in these circumstances? It is directed toward the attention of the superior or person in charge of the situation. Consequently, impression management will normally have some combination of three elements:

(1) *Pointing* toward the importance (or inadequacy) of the stereotype. For instance, a male impression manager enjoying the traditional male role may use sports or martial imagery to describe the work situation, by which he identifies it as masculine (see Case, 1988; Harrigan, 1977, pp. 69-87). In contrast, a male in a nontraditional role disliking the stereotype of the role may point out how the stereotype does not really encompass the most important aspects of the job.

(2) *Calling attention to one's own stereotypic (or nonstereotypic) qualities.* In this process, a woman secretary who enjoys the stereotype might intentionally act it out by developing and vocalizing her nurturing relationship toward her male boss. Contrasting with this, a woman boss disliking the traditional stereotype might seek to legitimate herself by pointing out the unusual individual qualities that suit her for the position.

(3) *Identifying the stereotypic shortcomings of others.* Others who do not "look" stereotypically appropriate to their roles may be ridiculed by the impression manager for their apparent deficiency. This disassociates the impression manager from the one who is inadequate and may build awareness of the seeming accuracy of the stereotype. Similarly, others might be damned by associating them with a stereotype that does not seem to fit the task.

A Practical Note for Employers

On the surface, it may not seem possible to deal with individual subtle efforts to enhance or detract from the stereotype. A careful supervisor digests all of the information available and assesses it on the basis of his or her knowledge and experience. Additional or omitted remarks and activities cannot help but influence one's decisions as supervisor.

Fortunately, an easily remembered solution is available—although it is more readily described than practiced. Since gender-based impression management runs along stereotypic lines, the supervisor must understand that the stereotype does not represent direct or valid information, despite being broadly used as a surrogate for it. Consequently, when there is any doubt or room for alternative decisions, supervisors should make every effort to ignore stereotyping, instead gathering specific factual information. They should ask whether their gut-level preferences are based in part on subjective reactions to stereotypes, or whether they have objective data. Is the person using football imagery accurately reflecting what is needed in the office? Or is the competitive and physical male sport an irrelevant metaphor when the office should correctly be referred to as a cool but cooperative work site and people's efforts judged accordingly (Harrigan, 1977)?

This approach will not eliminate efforts at impression management, but it will lessen their impact. It will also allow people to be hired, developed, and promoted without respect to gender. On the other hand, the supervisor's effort at objectivity is unlikely to alter the internal relationships of personnel toward one another, and this is likely to be a contributing element in office performance.

Gender and Impression Management: Second-Order Effects (Rational Bias)

With second-order effects, a three-party interaction occurs. Here again, the power holder is believed to be aware of and concerned with stereotypes, and thus it is in the subordinate's interest to be concerned as well. Again, a subordinate impression manager is likely to attempt to alter the impression that the superior power holder has of him or her—but based on interaction with a third party.

The third party is the person evaluated according to the stereotype by the power holder—even though the third party may not report directly to the superior. *Instead, the subordinate is concerned with the power holder's impression of the subordinate, gained by observing the subordinate's interaction with the third party* (Larwood, Gutek, & Gattiker, 1984). Although the consequence may be sex bias and discrimination, the subordinate may be more interested in generating the impression of his or her competence or likability—and avoiding the impression that he or she opposes the values of the power holder.

If all of this seems complicated, imagine the following scenario: A woman contacts the personnel manager of a manufacturing firm and asks for a position as head of the shipping department in a major factory. The personnel director believes that the vice president for operations (to whom both would report) is biased against women in nontraditional jobs. Although the woman looks very competent, a nearly equally competent male is also available (see Figure 10.1). The vice president has asked to interview only the top candidate. If the personnel director sends the woman, this counterstereotypic decision will call attention to his judgment (Heider, 1944). Clearly, the personnel director can minimize his risk with the vice president by sending in the male. In making this decision, the personnel director considers the importance to himself of maintaining the impression of competence and good judgment held of him by the vice president. Not surprisingly, the personnel director will generally decide in favor of the male candidate.

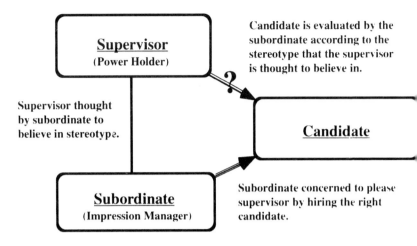

Figure 10.1. Second–Order Effects (Rational Bias)

This effect is referred to as *rational bias*, meaning that the bias does not depend on the personnel director's own stereotyped view of the third party, but rather on his or her reasoned expectation of the reaction of the power holder. As indicated in Figure 10.1, an interest in pleasing the supervisor (the vice president in the example above) may be sufficient for the subordinate (the personnel director in this example) to discriminate against the third person—particularly if the supervisor is known to prefer discrimination.

Nonetheless, rational bias depends on the perceptions and situation of the subordinate impression manager—not those of the power-holding supervisor. The supervisor can affect the subordinate's situation, however, making him or her feel more or less secure in the job and more or less able to operate independently. Similarly, the supervisor can alter the perception that he or she supports the stereotype by asserting directly a preference against discrimination. Without some unusual activity by the supervisor, however, the subordinate's actions will be based on the anticipation of normative consensual beliefs and actions by the supervisor. Given a nation with a history of stereotypic discrimination (as most developed nations have) and a workplace with a history of firing at will, the normative expectation is that impression managers will benefit by discrimination. That is, without knowledge that the superior or other important power holder prefers nondiscrimination, the subordinate must assume that he or she risks less by discriminating.

A series of studies has now supported these assertions (Larwood, 1984; Larwood & Gattiker, 1985; Larwood, Szwajkowski, & Rose, 1988a, 1988b; Szwajkowski & Larwood, in press), finding evidence for each of the following:

(1) More important situations result in greater stereotypic discrimination by impression managers anxious to please their superiors.[4]

(2) Power holders (such as the vice president in Figure 10.1) can affect the situation in several ways:

   (a) Power holders who are themselves women or minorities signal the need for less discrimination against that group (sometimes reverse discrimination).

   (b) Power holders who have used a woman or minority as intermediary to contact the impression manager signal the need for less discrimination.

   (c) Power holders who have gone to extraordinary lengths to assert a credible preference against discrimination do indeed diminish discrimination by the impression manager (reversing discrimination in the research findings).

(3) The situation of the power holder relative to the impression manager is also important:

   (a) More stereotypic discrimination is likely to result when the subordinate impression manager is in a weak position relative to the power holder— that is, when more attention must be paid to the wishes of the power holder.

   (b) More discrimination occurs when prior encounters with the power holder were unsatisfactory.

   (c) More discrimination is likely to occur in new, untested relationships.

Can Second-Order Effects Be Ended?

As with first-order impression management, it is not possible to assure elimination of second-order effects entirely—or even to be certain when they are taking place. Those engaging in rational bias are unlikely to identify themselves directly, since identification may undermine effectiveness and the activities are often illegal (Culbert & McDonough, 1980, p. 7). Additionally, impression managers run the risk that the unstated preferences of the power holder are actually opposed to discrimination. Under these conditions, the emphasis in second-order impression management seems most likely to be on limiting risk by quietly making discriminatory assumptions and thus decisions based on gender (as well as on race, ethical code, religion, or anything else in which there seems to be a prevailing norm). In this manner, punishment either for not discriminating (when the power holder prefers discrimination) or for discriminating (when the power holder opposes it) is eliminated.

Because second-order impression management effects depend on assump tions that the impression manager makes about the situation, however signals by the power holder and changes in the impression manager' situation can dramatically alter the outcome of rational bias. Research int the effect has shown that one of the most powerful switches is contained in the power holder's own behavior. A power holder who has written a bool on good management practices is assumed by default to prefer stereotypi discrimination. Presumably good management says nothing about discrimi nation, and thus the prevailing norms stand. Rational impression manager react to the power holders by discriminating in their own choices. In contrast a power holder who has written a book against discrimination causes quite different reaction among impression managers: They engage in statisticall significant reverse discrimination in making their own decisions. In sum, the activities constituting rational bias can each be diminished or reversed Nonetheless, effort and care are required in the process.

Are Concerns Only Between Superiors and Subordinates?

The term *power holder* was used above. Is it identical with the term *superior*? In fact, superiors may not be power holders, in the sense that the may not be of concern to the impression manager wrestling with the decisio of whether or not to discriminate. A vice president of another division seem less likely to be a relevant power holder. Similarly, as the relationship with the superior becomes more solid, the impression manager's moment-to-mo ment concern with the superior's impression seems sure to diminish (se point 3c in the list above). In contrast, there may be many other power holder who are not direct superiors. These could range from the leaders of importan informal groups within the firm to important customers who will observe an be affected by the performance of the third party. Much of the research o second-order effects examines customers as power holders, resulting i impression management by suppliers.

Second-Order Effects Outside the Organization

One of the interesting aspects of second-order effects is their paralle outside the organization. Family and friends have an interest (howeve legitimate) in seeing that those in the organization "do the right thing." Henc it is not unusual either for the outsiders to pressure those making insid decisions, or for those inside to take the potential reactions of outsiders into consideration. It may be for this reason that the U.S. Congress dismissed the likelihood of women combat officers by decreeing that women naval officers could not serve in combat zones.

Everyone, or Just Some?
A Brief Note on Individual Differences

The research on second-order impression management is relatively new, and it is premature to attempt to determine how broadly it can be generalized. The reader is pardoned for thinking, "But I'm not like that." Perhaps not. Extending the research that does exist suggests that some people are more likely to be concerned by gender-related impression management—or to be subject to it—than others. The thoughts here are offered as a starting point and are subject to verification.

The work of Larwood et al. (1984) offers the suggestion that those in particularly weak power positions are more likely to engage in impression management than are those who are secure. This might be taken a step further—those who feel they are relatively weak or that success in the situation is unusually important, for whatever reason, would seem most likely to become active impression managers. Similarly, those who are actively engaging in self-monitoring are no doubt more likely to engage in impression management than are others who are less self-involved. At a different end of the scale, those who are more Machiavellian seem likely to find impression management an engaging way to manipulate others.

Of course, the need for impression management can be made more or less salient by the circumstances. We know from role theory that sex and work roles become more salient in the presence of someone who emphasizes important differences (someone appealing of the opposite sex or a tyrannical boss, for instance). These circumstances more than others seem likely to result in impression management involving them. This is why the sex of the intermediary or the supervisor (above) is seen as important. Similarly, one might suppose that an employer who customarily made an effort to break down barriers with his or her subordinates would be seen by them as less obviously a boss—and thereby less evocative in them of the need to manage impressions.

Interpreting Some Everyday Events

Before concluding, it is of interest to look at some additional phenomena in light of the analyses above. Other related events have already been discussed.

Typewriters and office equipment. A number of women's success books (e.g., Harrigan, 1977) advise women managers to stay away from secretarial office equipment. Although acknowledging that it is convenient, a first-order rationale is generally provided: By being near the equipment, the woman manager is associating herself with a traditional woman's work role (secretarial work), allowing the inference that she is not a manager. The issue is unlikely to surface with men, and a male secretary must go out of his way to demonstrate his actual work role.

Clothing. Among the difficulties experienced by the women's movement in entering management was the issue of what to wear. Since secretaries wore dresses and male executives wore pants, women impression managers were concerned with how to distinguish themselves acceptably. Formal pantsuits were invented for the occasion, as were an assortment of scarves that could serve in place of a man's tie. Ultimately, executive women learned to adopt a successful executive uniform more subtly. Nonetheless, this may remain a very real issue in second-order impression management in particularly sensitive cases.

Compensation. The concept of equity states that people should be compensated in proportion to their inputs. One of the difficulties with the theory is that the evaluation of perceived inputs can often instead be adjusted to equal the relative proportion of pay. As noted previously, most occupations pay men more. But this is not sufficient to prove discrimination, since it may be that the women are actually worth less. In terms of impression management, it is important that women establish an *independent and objective* measure of their work or performance. If they can establish the impression of high performance, employers concerned with equity are likely to pay them well. If they instead can establish only that they are paid less, the desire for equity is most readily solved by an employer's belief that their work is inadequate—hence worth what is being paid. In other words, there is a two-way impression management inference possible between pay and performance at the level of first-order effects.

With second-order effects, something similar might be expected: The power holder seems most likely to be impressed with someone known to command a higher salary, since performance cannot be directly established in the three-party relationship. Although men would generally be paid more than women, the woman who can unexpectedly command more than men might be assumed to be unusually good. Put most simply, it is exceptionally important for women impression managers to establish their worth because the normative assumption is that they are paid and worth little. As a side note, the same justification is frequently given for hiring the most expensive management consultant available—he or she must be good to command that outrageous figure.

Reverse discrimination. This phenomenon, in which men rather than women are poorly received and poorly paid, is understandable through both of the mechanisms examined in this chapter. The event of reverse discrimination is relatively rare because men's work is more highly paid in Western society, suggesting that it is better. This provides men with the opportunity of either selecting a preferred field or trading it for higher pay in a less desirable field. The presumed less desirable women workers are paid less and have fewer career choices.

Nonetheless, reverse discrimination may occur along first-order lines. Men who accept traditional women's work are considered suspect—the impression is that they either cannot or should not do the task. Like women in management, these men must carefully prove themselves. At the same time, women who are in work roles traditionally reserved for women may be in the position of attempting to show that the men are actually better at something else. This may explain why male nurses appear to move toward nursing administration much more rapidly than women. Second-order reverse discrimination has already been described above for situations in which the impression manager is sensitive to a power holder's counternormative signals. It seems plausible as well that government pressure toward affirmative action can force overreaction such that the impression managers will avoid appearing to be risk takers as seen by their employers (and avoid seeming combative to the government). Thus reverse discrimination may appear to be the "safe" alternative—though it has sometimes been successfully challenged in court when applied incautiously (see Wallace, 1982).

Reality

This chapter began with the request to start with a rational group of people. As with other concepts that are based in attribution theory, impression management as described here is a cognitive phenomenon requiring commonsense inferences to decipher. Rational bias, although seemingly an oxymoron, similarly makes sense in the context of impression management.

Gender effects, however, are based on something more. They assume that individuals have genuinely different capacities (which has been disproven by research), different interests and motivations (which on close inspection also seems not to be true—see Miner & Smith, 1982), or an inborn need to distinguish between groups as like and unlike themselves. Some 50 years of evidence has accumulated to support this last assumption.

In other words, a totally rational group of people will be conscious of sex (as well as race, age, and other) differences, and will tend to accept that they exist despite only stereotypic or flimsy supportive statistical evidence. Since we define our own group and ourselves in terms of these differences, one might question whether most people, however rational they may otherwise seem, really want to avoid these distinctions. In that light, we can design systems for diminishing gender-related impression management and the need for it, but it seems unlikely that the tendency toward making the distinctions—and consequently toward impression management based on them—will disappear anytime soon.

Notes

1. *Impression management* is defined here as behaving or speaking in a manner so as to alter the impression of an observer without necessarily altering the facts that the observer believes (perhaps incorrectly) are his or her primary bases of judgment. An observer who believes that someone who smiles at him likes him might be given a mistaken impression by an insurance salesman who has been trained to smile when talking with potential clients. Although the purpose of an insurance salesman engaging in this type of impression management is obvious, the intention of the impression manager may sometimes be veiled if it is to be most effective, as described later in this chapter.

2. There are, of course, other reasons the same man may or may not want the woman to join him. She may have needed skills or talents that greatly improve the unit's effectiveness, for instance. Alternatively, she may represent a competitive threat. However, such talents are not gender related and are outside the scope of this chapter.

3. The reader should bear in mind that statements of stereotypic notions such as this are reflections of broad consensual belief and are unrelated to individual abilities or interests. They certainly do not represent my own opinion.

4. There are, of course, many other ways in which subordinates might react toward superiors in creating particular impressions. For example, one might lie to a superior and fail actually to do anything, or one might even threaten the superior with exposure if discrimination is really demanded. The discussion of second-order effects centers on two forms of behavior: association and ingratiation. It takes what seems most likely to be the usual case: an individual who is concerned to an extent that the superior like and trust him or her, and who believes that rewards are more likely to be received from the superior contingent on behavior consistent with liking

and trust. Liars, after all, run a long-term risk of being caught, while whistle-blowers often have an even shorter and less pleasant tenure (Parmerlee, Near, & Jensen, 1982).

References

Adams, J. S., & Freedman, S. (1976). Equity theory revisited: Comments and annotated bibliography. In L. Berkowitz & E. Walster (Eds.), *Advances in experimental social psychology* (Vol. 9, pp. 43-90). New York: Academic Press.

Bianchi, S., & Rytina, N. (1984). *Occupational change, 1970-1980.* Paper presented at the annual meetings of the Population Association of America.

Brenner, O. C., Tomkiewicz, J., & Schein, V. E. (1989). The relationship between sex role stereotypes and requisite management characteristics revisited. *Academy of Management Journal, 32,* 662-669.

Case, S. S. (1988). Cultural differences, not deficiencies: An analysis of managerial women's language. In S. Rose & L. Larwood (Eds.), *Women's careers: Pathways and pitfalls.* New York: Praeger.

Colwill, N. L. (1987). Men and women in organizations: Roles and status, stereotypes and power. In K. S. Koziara, M. H. Moskow, & L. D. Tanner (Eds.), *Working women: Past, present, future* (pp. 97-117). Washington, DC: Bureau of National Affairs.

Culbert, S. A., & McDonough, J. J. (1980). *The invisible war.* New York: John Wiley.

Davidson, M. J., & Cooper, C. L. (1984). *Working women: An international survey.* Chichester: John Wiley.

Fagenson, E. A. (1990). Perceived masculine and feminine attributes examined as a function of individuals' sex and level in the organizational power hierarchy: A test of four theoretical perspectives. *Journal of Applied Psychology, 75,* 204-211.

Greenberg, J. (1989). Cognitive reevaluation of outcomes in response to underpayment inequity. *Academy of Management Journal, 32,* 174-184.

Harrigan, B. L. (1977). *Games mother never taught you.* New York: Rawson, Wade.

Hedges, J. N., & Bemis, S. E. (1974). Sex stereotyping: Its decline in skilled trades. *Monthly Labor Review, 97*(5), 15.

Heider, F. (1944). Social perception and phenomenal causality. *Psychological Review, 51,* 358-374.

Horrigan, M. W., & Markey, J. P. (1990). Recent gains in women's earnings: Better pay or longer hours? *Monthly Labor Review, 113*(7), 11-17.

Larwood, L. (1984). *Organizational behavior and management.* Boston: Kent.

Larwood, L., & Blackmore, J. (1977). Fair pay: Field investigations of the fair economic exchange. *Academy of Management Proceedings,* pp. 81-85.

Larwood, L., & Gattiker, U. E. (1985). Rational bias and interorganizational power in the employment of management consultants. *Group & Organization Studies, 10,* 3-17.

Larwood, L., Gutek, B. A., & Gattiker, U. E. (1984). Perspectives on institutional discrimination and resistance to change. *Group & Organization Studies, 9,* 333-352.

Larwood, L., Kavanagh, M., & Levine, R. (1978). Perceptions of fairness with three different economic exchanges. *Academy of Management Journal, 21,* 69-83.

Larwood, L., Szwajkowski, E., & Rose, S. (1988a). Sex and race discrimination resulting from manager-client relationships: Applying the rational bias theory of managerial discrimination. *Sex Roles, 18,* 9-29.

Larwood, L., Szwajkowski, E., & Rose, S. (1988b). When discrimination makes "sense": The rational bias theory. In B. A. Gutek, A. H. Stromberg, & L. Larwood (Eds.), *Women and work* (Vol. 3, pp. 265-288). Newbury Park, CA: Sage.

Larwood, L., & Wood, M. M. (1977). *Women in management.* Lexington, MA: Lexington.

Ledvinka, J. (1982). *Federal regulation of personnel and human resource management.* Boston: Kent.

Matsui, T., Kagawa, M., Nagamatsu, J., & Ohtsuka, Y. (1977). Validity of expectancy theory as a within-person behavioral choice model for sales activities. *Journal of Applied Psychology, 62*, 764-767.

Miner, J. B., & Smith, N. R. (1982). Decline and stabilization of managerial motivation over a 20-year period. *Journal of Applied Psychology, 67*, 297-305.

Olson, J. E., & Frieze, I. H. (1987). Income determinants for women in business. In A. H. Stromberg, L. Larwood, & B. A. Gutek (Eds.), *Women and work* (Vol. 2, pp. 173-206). Newbury Park, CA: Sage.

Parmerlee, M. A., Near, J. P., & Jensen, T. C. (1982). Correlates of whistleblowers' perceptions of organizational retaliation. *Administrative Science Quarterly, 27*, 17-34.

Reskin, B. F., & Roos, P. A. (1987). Status hierarchies and sex segregation. In C. Bose & G. Spitze (Eds.), *Ingredients for women's employment policy* (pp. 3-21). Albany: State University of New York Press.

Schlenker, B. R. (1980). *Impression management: The self-concept, social identity, and interpersonal relations.* Monterey, CA: Brooks/Cole.

Sommers, D. (1974). Occupational rankings for men and women by earnings. *Monthly Labor Review, 97*(8), 34-51.

Szwajkowski, E., & Larwood, L. (in press). Rational decision processes and sex discrimination: Testing "rational" bias theory. *Journal of Organizational Behavior.*

Tienda, M., & Ortiz, V. (1987). Intraindustry occupational recomposition and gender inequality in earnings. In C. Bose & G. Spitze (Eds.), *Ingredients for women's employment policy* (pp. 23-51). Albany: State University of New York Press.

Vroom, V. H. (1964). *Work and motivation.* New York: John Wiley.

Wallace, P. A. (1982). Increased labor force participation of women and affirmative action. In P. A. Wallace (Ed.), *Women in the workplace* (pp. 1-24). Boston: Auburn House.

11

Cultural Influences on
Modes of Impression Management

Implications for the
Culturally Diverse Organization

MICHAEL HARRIS BOND

Before entering a country, learn its customs.
(*The Book of Rites*, second and third centuries B.C.)

My brief in this chapter is to consider cultural and intercultural aspects of
impression management—the process by which individuals influence the
beliefs and feelings others hold about them. In a nutshell, my argument is
that cultural norms constrain how people from a given cultural group behave
in order to win basic approval from their peers. These overlearned styles of
embodying the culturally ideal person often do not "translate" across cultural
lines. People from different cultures misunderstand the intentions of those
with other heritages, and impressions are thereby mismanaged. The consequences are usually unhappy. Let me begin with an example from my own
experience.

A Case in Point

I am Canadian by birth and often mistaken for an American in the Orient, where I have worked for the last 20 years. Recently I was asked to address the monthly "communication meeting" of a large utility company in Hong Kong. The top 160 executives, both Chinese and British, have gathered under the chairmanship of their CEO, an Englishman who is sitting on a raised dais. He presents a five-minute update on recent financial developments and calls for questions.

A bespectacled Chinese pops up to the microphone placed in the audience and in rapid-fire, fluent English thanks the chairman at length for a lucid presentation. Placing hands on hips, he then launches into a lengthy piece providing considerable background information before asking a short question about the corporation's present loan position.

The chairman answers his query and the Chinese questioner, Frank Leung, resumes his seat amid chuckles from the Westerners present and downcast glances from the other Chinese. Something is amiss. Six months later Frank resigns.

The above episode is taken from life and can be used to illustrate the complexities in the management of impressions across cultural lines. In many ways Frank Leung (a pseudonym) is an ideal member of a culturally diverse organization: He is linguistically skilled, forthright, and adventurous. Somehow, though, he manages to offend both his Chinese conationals and his British bosses. From the Chinese perspective, Frank is too assertive and self-promoting, too much the British lackey; from the Westerners' perspective, Frank is too wordy, too obsequious, and often inappropriate in his utterances. Instead of pleasing each cultural group, Frank Leung alienates both.

Let us, then, examine the dynamics of impression management cross-culturally. The discussion begins with the topic of cultural values and how they influence the way people typically present themselves to one another. Next, consideration is given to the implications of these cultural differences when people interact across cultural lines. The role of language will be given special attention in this process of identity negotiation. As my hope is to shed some light where there is often merely heat, I will conclude with some suggestions for improving cross-cultural encounters.

Cultures, Values, and Self-Presentation

There are truths on this side of the Pyrenees which are falsehoods on the other. (Blaise Pascal, *Pensees*)

As Baumeister (1982) has argued, the two prime goals of impression management are audience pleasing and constructing the ideal self. That is, we play both to others and to ourselves. Audiences vary, of course, but within a given culture certain modes of self-presentation will be preferred. So, for example, in a culture placing a high endorsement on humility, a flamboyant, verbally assertive style of self-presentation will be generally disparaged regardless of the social context. Individual members of a cultural group will depart more or less from their culture's mean, but will be constrained by this mean to discipline their self-presentations within a latitude of acceptance. Their ideal self-constructions will be anchored, as it were, by this cultural benchmark. Normative pressure and continuous reinforcement of "correct" behavior leave us largely unconscious of our culture's pervasive shaping of the ways we act.

One practical approach to examining cross-cultural variation in self-presentation is to examine differences in values around the world. To quote Kluckhohn (1951), "A value is a conception, explicit or implicit, distinctive of an individual or characteristic of a group, *of the desirable* which influences the selection from available modes, means and ends of actions" (p. 395; emphasis added). What is important in this definition is (a) that values are transsituational, with the same value capable of informing a variety of different situations, and (b) that values guide action. Given that values are desirable and can be characteristic of a whole cultural group, considerable influence can be exerted on individual acts of self-presentation within that cultural group. The ideal value profile for the culture can be regarded as a target impression to be managed toward.

With this structure as background, what can be said about the empirical differences in the cultural profiles of values around the world?

The Schwartz Values Project

There have been many cross-cultural studies of value. The most useful for purposes of this discussion is that currently being orchestrated by Shalom Schwartz of the Hebrew University of Jerusalem. A listing of its advantages over other such projects would include the following considerations:

(1) It is theoretically driven and carefully grounded in previous conceptualizations of value (Schwartz & Bilsky, 1987).

(2) The instrument has been administered in more than 25 countries, so that a reliable and extensive mapping of cultures can result.

(3) The content of the survey is culturally unbiased and comprehensive, so that important values from all cultural traditions are represented.

(4) The values are broadly phrased and not confined to a specific domain of activity, such as work. This breadth gives the results a wide range of application.

At present Schwartz maintains that data collected from 15 countries allow him to confirm the existence of 10 distinct and meaningful domains of value. Their labels, broad characteristics, and defining values are listed in Table 11.1.

Value endorsements within a domain can be summed and averaged for each cultural group and that culture's position can be compared with others. For example, the power domain yields the following rank order for samples of teachers:

(1) Hebei (northern China)
(2) Guangzhou (southern China)
(3) Shanghai (central China)
(4) Poland
(5) Hong Kong
(6) Japan
(7) Finland
(8) New Zealand
(9) Spain

The higher the rank, the more a given person from that location is oriented toward satisfying that motivational goal, in this case the accumulation of social and material resources.

Relationships among domains. Schwartz maintains theoretically (Schwartz & Bilsky, 1987) and has discovered empirically that the 10 value domains are psychologically interrelated. Some domains, such as universalism and benevolence, are close in their implications for their holder's orientation toward the world and other people. Thus a respondent may endorse them both at the same levels and show behavioral consistency. Other domains, such as self-direction and restrictive conformity, stand in mutual

Table 11.1 Verbal Domain Labels, Definitions, and Defining Values (in parentheses)

Power: social status and prestige, control or dominance over people and resources (social power, wealth, authority, social recognition preserving public image)

Achievement: Personal success through demonstrating competence according to social standards (successful, capable, ambitious, intelligent, influential)

Hedonism: pleasure or sensuous gratification for oneself (pleasure, enjoying life)

Stimulation: excitement, novelty, and challenge in life (daring, a varied life, an exciting life)

Self-direction: independent thought and action — choosing, creating, exploring (creativity, freedom, curiosity, independence, choosing own goals)

Universalism: understanding, appreciation, tolerance and protection to the welfare of all people and for nature (social justice, broad-minded, world at peace, wisdom, a world of beauty, unity with nature, protecting the environment, equality)

Benevolence: preservation and enhancement of the welfare of people with whom one is in frequent personal contact (helpful, forgiving, honest, mature love, spiritual life, loyal)

Tradition: respect, commitment and acceptance of the customs and ideas that traditional culture or religion impose on the self (accept, my portion in life, devout, respect for tradition, humble, moderate)

Security: safety, harmony, and stability of society, of relationships, and of self (family security, national security, social order, clean, reciprocation of favors, sense of belonging)

Restrictive conformity: restraint of actions, inclinations, and impulses likely to upset or harm others and violate social expectations or norms (obedience, self-discipline, politeness, honoring parents and elders)

opposition to one another, in that a respondent who endorses one cannot sensibly also endorse the other. Their expressions in action contradict one another, so that someone high in one must, if sane, be low in the other, and vice versa.

Schwartz has integrated these relations among the domains to produce a circumplex (see Figure 11.1). Domains adjacent to one another are compatible and similar; those facing one another across the ellipse stand in opposition to one another; those at right angles are unrelated.

Schwartz has used this circumplex to group his domains into four composites having even wider range and generality. The domains of restrictive conformity and security, for example, unite to form a broad composite labeled by Schwartz as "conservation." A ranking of the teacher samples used before produces the following order:

(1) Shanghai

(2) Hong Kong

(3) Hebei

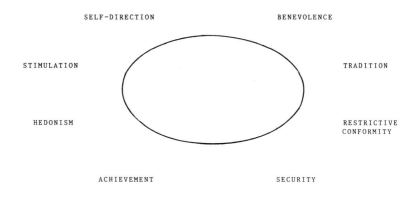

Figure 11.1. A Circumplex Model Indicating the Relative Position of Schwartz's 10 Value Domains

(4) Poland
(5) Finland
(6) Japan
(7) New Zealand
(8) Guangzhou
(9) Spain

As before, a higher rank indicates that a given person from that location is more likely to be motivated by concerns for social order and harmony.

These composites align themselves in polar opposition to one another and can be summed to yield a single score on a broad dimension. There are two dimensions, self-transcendence (universalism and benevolence) versus self-enhancement (power and achievement) and change (self-direction and stimulation) versus conservation (restrictive conformity and security). Scores on these two dimensions can be graphed to yield a visual representation of the value distance between any two cultural groups. The teacher groups yield the display in Figure 11.2, for example.

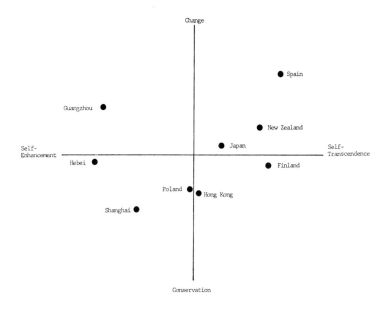

Figure 11.2. Location of Nine Samples of Teachers on Schwartz's Two Basic Value Dimensions

Implications for Self-Presentation

The Schwartz project is in its early stages, but we can use its present lines of development for speculation about goals of impression management and attendant strategies. These speculations involve both the content and the manner of self-presentations, both verbal and nonverbal aspects. For the purposes of this discussion, we will confine ourselves to the 10 domains listed in Table 11.1.

The basic position I adopt is to assume that, if a cultural group endorses a domain strongly, then members of that culture will be relatively more oriented toward achieving that broad motivational goal. Their being so oriented will be generally more acceptable to others in that culture, so that their verbal presentations and nonverbal manifestations are free to embody those themes, thereby inviting approval. Of course, some domains, such as power, achievement, and hedonism, are more self-serving and must be universally tempered to avoid threatening others. Even so, in cultural groups where these domains are relatively more strongly valued, their open expression will generate relatively fewer sanctions.

Let us look at the domains separately and generate ideas about probable consequences for largely unconscious modes of self-presentation. As the discussion proceeds, the reader is encouraged to recall Schwartz's circumplex model of the domain interrelationships. The modes of self-presentation advanced as likely in a given domain will rarely be found in people espousing an opposing domain, and vice versa. In many cases the exact opposite form of behavior will be normative and effective in pleasing most audiences from the opposing cultural group. What I say below about power, then, need not be reversed and repeated when I discuss universalism. Instead, I would ask the reader to make the appropriate recalibrations as we go around the circumplex.

Power. I believe that high endorsements of this domain reflect the hierarchical structuring of society with the attendant desire of people to access status and material resources by obtaining power. Conceptually, this cluster of values overlaps closely with Hofstede's (1980) dimension of power distance.

In such societies people will talk openly about power-related topics, acknowledge others' authority, and avoid remarks that may incur the wrath of superiors. For instance, individuals will discuss the prices of personal items and the merits of their educational backgrounds; they will use titles, praise superiors, and question those superiors' pronouncements indirectly, if at all; they will have ready excuses for any criticism from a boss, interrupt and dominate the air space when with subordinates, insult subordinates with relative impunity, and ignore subordinates' input in meetings if it suits their purposes. Talk about the importance of authority in daily life and the inherent differences among people will rarely be challenged.

In terms of *how* one behaves in such cultures, the relevant question becomes, What is one's status? If one has rank and authority, there is less need to mask it. Expensive clothes, fancy cars, elegant watches, all the visible accoutrements of status may be enjoyed. "Face" is given to those of higher status. Great offense will be taken if miscalculations are made and the appropriate displays of deference, respect, and submission not accorded. Such displays include not challenging a superior who is late, rude, or otherwise indifferent to one's "rights" as a human being.

By the same token, great appreciation will be felt for someone of higher status who does treat subordinates with benevolence and consideration. As such displays are unnecessary and rare, their bestowal will be salient, and strong attributions about the actor's kindliness will be made. Bonds of loyalty can be quickly established through such approaches from superiors to subordinates.

Achievement. Worldly accomplishments are of course one way to establish power, and for this reason the power and achievement domains are closely related in people's minds (and adjacent on the circumplex). Achievement emphases represent a focus on getting ahead and may serve both individual and group goals.

How achievement-related activities are presented to others will depend in part on the political and social climate. One talks about making effort for the group, be it family, company, nation, or humanity, depending on one's commitment to a collective or one's need not to appear self-serving.

The "cult of effort" is important to understand in such cultures, where people will often talk about themselves as hardworking and dedicated. It is, after all, the necessary ingredient for achievement, once abilities have been distributed by the laws of genetics and hereditary position by birth. Motivation is sustained, therefore, in such achievement-oriented cultures by attributing success to effort and by reinforcing effortful displays. This pattern begins with schoolchildren at home, as the work of Stevenson on Oriental accomplishments in primary school has shown. It continues into working life, where employers are expected to honor employees for working hard as much as for "working smart."

Of course, actual achievements must be rewarded and appreciated as mattering if energy is to be focused on such accomplishments. One needs to feel the need to achieve and then to know that one's efforts will materialize to promote this value endorsement. The success of the "self-responsibility system"[1] in China was sustained by these twin pillars of felt need and palpable gain for effort. Where either element is lacking, people will direct their energies toward different goals.

Hedonism. Here, one's goal is enjoyment. In cultures valuing this domain, one may be more open about self-indulgent pursuits and work will play a less central role in people's lives. Taking it easy is less likely to be sanctioned, and work time will be traded for leisure.

Stimulation. People in cultural groups endorsing this domain seek out novelty and change. There will be widely held beliefs in the importance of variety and the usefulness of trying things out differently. In such cultures communications can be couched in such language both to justify one's actions and to persuade audiences to adopt one's viewpoint.

Self-direction. "Doing your own thing" is a powerful motivator in cultures where self-direction is highly endorsed. It is this kind of goal that fuels political revolutions and reflects the desire to exercise one's own wishes in guiding one's life. People in such cultures want to have what Rotter (1966) refers to as "internal locus of control," and will make sacrifices to achieve it. People will be vocal in general, as this is an important aspect of self-expression, and skilled in rhetoric, as this is a tool for bending others to one's will. In discussions people will use the language of self-development to justify their actions and generate group support. They will feel freer to experiment and explore in their dress, their relationships, and their work.

One important aspect of self-direction involves the freedom to express emotions publicly. In cultures that endorse this domain strongly, emotional relations are regarded as a part of one's "true" self, one's inner reality. Sincerity in such cultures involves disclosing one's emotional responses to events. Indeed, these responses are important building blocks in forming honest relationships with other people. If the others likewise disclose their feelings, then participants believe that they are in a position to negotiate a relationship grounded in both parties' phenomenal reality.

Thus persons high in self-direction will show a wider range of emotions at greater levels of intensity. Their postures, movements, speech volume, glances, laughter, and facial expressiveness will all be more "readable," especially in public settings such as meetings, speeches, and classes. They are perceived as expressive, open, and emotional by those lower in self-direction.

Universalism. As can be gathered from its defining values, this cluster encompasses those having a broad concern for the welfare of the planet and its people. Its focus is ecumenical and its concern the well-being of all. This is a broadly integrative emphasis that undercuts any narrow familial, national, or racial boundaries and endorses many values common to the world's religious traditions.

There is a strong egalitarian push to this cluster, the exact opposite of that underlying the power dimension. There is an expectation of noblesse oblige here, allied with a wish to defend and promote the underdog. Its proximity to self-direction is understandable, as these values foster the social climate necessary for the exercise of individual freedoms. This domain is a component of Hofstede's (1980) individualism, and its endorsement is closely connected to a culture's adoption of the International Government on Civil and Political Rights (Bond, 1990).

It stands in opposition to the power and achievement domains, so that comments made there about verbal and nonverbal strategies of self-presentation need merely be turned on their head. In cultures high on universalism, the rhetoric of fairness, equality of opportunity, and human rights will prove a powerful rallying call. Companies will promote their products by appealing to these values in their advertising policy and public statements. Strategies geared to winning approval for one's integrity and compassion will be high in such cultures, activities labeled "exemplification" by Jones and Pittman (1982). So, for example, corruption, nepotism, and empire building will be vigorously decried and rooted out. Bosses will strive to be perceived as unbiased and objective in their decisions about hiring, firing, and promotion.

Benevolence. Those scoring high in this domain are the maintenance specialists, as Bales (1950) calls them—those members of a group who are ready to help, make sacrifices for others, overlook mistakes, avoid abrasive comments, offer jokes, smooth over criticisms, praise others, and so forth. This nurturance role is, of course, the typical female role in society, and for this reason Hofstede (1980) labels this part of the value spectrum "femininity." Some cultures, most notably the Scandinavian, are high on this domain and generally emphasize compassion and harmony over competition and task accomplishment.

This emphasis has obvious implications for any verbal presentations, be they aimed at persuasion or justification. In general, such presentations will be peppered with references to the core values of relationship, love, responsibility, and helpfulness. Behaviorally, the implications for organizational life are far-reaching. Personnel decisions will attach greater weight to these criteria in evaluating employees. Conflict will be resolved by harmony-enhancing strategies such as mediation and bargaining rather than threatening or accusing. Office and workplace design will be geared toward promoting face-to-face contact and friendly interactions.

Tradition. Some cultural groups give considerable weight to time-honored approaches and endow tradition with an almost religious significance. Valued personal attributes such as detachment, devotion, and humility are associated with this other-worldly quality.

Moderation is the keynote here for behavioral acts. Nothing flamboyant, extreme, or modern in speech, dress, or gesture. Mature age is a virtue in such cultures, and business leaders will generally be older. A long-range perspective will be taken in making business decisions, and companies' reputations will be accorded great weight. Appeals to precedent will be potent verbal ploys.

Restrictive conformity. In cultures endorsing this domain strongly, social expectations assume considerable moment in guiding people's behavior. Individuals' actions are informed by concern about their impact on others and their possible reactions assume an important role in guiding all behavior. Such people are "other-directed," to use Riesman's (1950) terminology, or "socially oriented," as Kuo-shu Yang (1986) terms it.

Care and circumspection characterize individuals' acts in such cultural settings. Great consideration is shown to others, even if it is not felt. Tokens of respect are freely exchanged irrespective of rank and there is a guarded quality to all relationships involving strangers or acquaintances. Restraint is cherished and sexuality in particular is deemphasized in dress, speech, and movement.

There is less talk in general, and this talk is marked by indirection and heavy use of moderating adverbs such as *slightly, mildly, a little bit, occasionally,* and *perhaps.* A response of yes generally means maybe, and a response of maybe or "I'll try my best" generally means no. Strong positions are anathema and insults sedulously avoided.

Security. In cultures marked by political and social turmoil, considerable importance is attached to social order and the safety it brings in its wake for self, family, and nation. There is a close connection here with Maslow's (1954) survival needs, and it is probable that endorsement of this domain diminishes as society stabilizes itself over time. In societies where such order has not been achieved, as in China, this domain continues to be critically important. "Stability and prosperity" then become a useful shibboleth in political discourse. Such discourse is often marked by themes of external threat, a strategy that effectively mobilizes unity, a sense of belonging, and group effort. The conjunction of the security and power domains becomes understandable, since the accumulation of power is a tool for ensuring the safety of the people one values.

Cultures high in security endorsement tend to have a collectivist mentality (Hofstede, 1980). There is a strong sense of "we-ness," and considerable energy is spent in preserving the harmony and integrity of in-groups (Triandis, 1989). Open conflict is avoided within the collectivity, although there is indifference, sometimes hostility, directed toward outsiders. Relationships are built through exchanges of favors, gifts, and other tokens of goodwill. A trustworthy person honors his or her indebtedness to others by reciprocating whenever possible.

Speech is peppered with references to "my good friend," "my old class-mate," "my former employee," and other forms of self-enhancement (Jones & Pittman, 1982) through name-dropping. Business cards are liberally exchanged to establish early one's position within a supportive social nexus. People join many groups that extend their interpersonal reach and sense of social identity (Tajfel, 1978). People have considerable affective involvement with their groups and often wear group insignia or decorate their possessions with such markers.

Summary

For each of the value domains, I have speculated about modal behavioral patterns in cultural groups endorsing those domains strongly. I believe that these modal patterns constrain the range of acceptable self-presentations within that culture and must be honored if a viable impression is to be managed. Knowledge about these patterns is essential if one wants to work effectively across cultural lines. In such settings one must be prepared to act differently and to understand differently in order to succeed. Such flexibility may of course be hampered by one's "ideal self," as Baumeister (1982) labels our view of the person we strive to be. This confrontation, however, makes the cross-cultural experience an exciting stage for self-discovery. Let us now turn to the challenges of intercultural management.

Struggling Across Cultural Lines

"What kind of a bird are you if you can't fly?" chirped the bird.

"What kind of a bird are you if you can't swim?" replied the duck. (Serge Pro-kofiev, *Peter and the Wolf*)

Much of our shrinking into a global village arises out of the comparative advantages that derive from international trade. Technology for communication and infrastructure for transport follow in the wake of trade development, bringing personnel from different cultural backgrounds into increasing contact. The growth of knowledge via the cultural borrowing and stimulation that result is enormous, as are the interpersonal problems. Confusion, conflict, and withdrawal are the bridesmaids at intercultural weddings.

Figure 11.3. A Case of Bicultural Misattribution Involving an American and a Hong Kong Chinese

Cartoon copyright Larry Feign. Used by permission.

Impression Management and Misattribution

One way to conceive of culture is as a system of rules for making sense of behavior. An important aspect of assigning meaning is of course to decide what a behavior emitted by an actor indicates about that actor's character. Technically this process of translating behavior into information about personality is called *attribution*.

When persons from different cultures interact, they tread a mine field of potential misattributions. Person A behaves in a certain way that communicates an attitude, intention, or relationship in Culture A. Person B comes from Culture B, which translates the same behavior differently. Depending on the nature of their relationship, confusion, conflict, or chuckles result. An example of this process in Chinese-American interaction, borrowed from the amusing pen of Larry Feign, is presented here as Figure 11.3.

In this cartoon an American gentleman interprets queue-jumping as rudeness, since barging ahead violates the fairness principle underlying the "first come, first served" rule. Given that our defender of law and order is escorting a lady, his challenging the queue-barger could be construed as an act of intimidation (Jones & Pittman, 1982) designed to establish him as a chivalrous stalwart in the eyes of his date. Not so! In a culture where any confrontation is sedulously avoided, public rebukes are impolitic and dangerous. Indeed, her date's "rudeness" is also inconsiderate in that she could easily be embarrassed further should the queue-jumper retaliate and the situation further degenerate. "Curiouser and curiouser," said Alice as she descended deeper into the cross-cultural rabbit hole.

What has this cartoon to do with organizational life? Take any two cultures, one high on the power domain, the other high on the universalism domain, and the answer is plenty. The reluctance to be involved in open confrontation is common in cultures where power is unequally distributed, for the consequences if one chooses the wrong opponent can be disastrous. So, generally, children are socialized from an early age to be sensitive to relative status and to avoid fighting in any form, physical or verbal. To a lesser extent this dynamic also applies in cultures high on the neighboring domain, security.

In work settings this aversion to conflict extends to such diverse activities as enforcing the rules, giving performance evaluations, asking questions in public settings, and negotiating directly with peers for desired cooperation. In their place are a variety of indirect substitutes, such as using middlemen to communicate needs, anonymous letters, and reliance on outside trainers.

Needless to say, these forms of influence are rare in cultural groups endorsing universalism. It will be recalled that this domain is directly opposite to the power domain but adjacent to the self-direction domain. As discussed earlier, the behavioral expectations for persons from these cultures are quite different. Such persons tend to be explicit, open, and legalistic. They regard the previously discussed strategies for conflict avoidance as devious and craven. Of course, the obverse is true for those from the "power cultures" observing those from the "universalism cultures." They perceive their opposite numbers as behaving in blunt, emotional, even explosive ways—"rude," as Larry Feign would put it.

Now, this contrast between conflict avoidance and assertiveness is only one aspect of the complex polarity between universalism and power. It affects how bosses direct subordinates (Triandis, 1967), how one undertakes organizational development (Quill & Rigby, n.d.), how company representatives negotiate (Glenn, 1981), how organizations are structured (Smith & Tayeb, 1988)—indeed, how we think about management itself (Hofstede, 1980).

Obviously the potential for misunderstanding the behavior of someone from an opposite culture is enormous. And we have been focusing here on only *one* of the possible value contrasts. The plot thickens further when we add the starch of language.

The Trap of Second-Language Fluency

In many cross-cultural exchanges, some persons will be using their first language while others use their second. In multinationals this state of affairs is especially likely, with the "head office" language being the first language of the senior executive but the second language of the locals who generally occupy lower ranks.

Whatever the lingua franca, there are a number of problems in impression management to be faced. First, those who speak a second language well are often believed to enjoy an unfair advantage by their conationals who speak the language of senior management less well. Promotions may be regarded by locals as being unduly influenced by language rather than by other skills. In a hostile intergroup climate a fluent person may in addition be treated as a cultural quisling by fellow countrymen.

These were some of the issues at play in the opening case example when Frank Leung was speaking. His fluency in English was resented by the other Chinese, who considered that he had risen above his fair placement in the organization by virtue of his linguistic skills. Furthermore, he did not speak like a proper Chinese. With hands on his hips and a steely gaze to all in the room, he was every bit the Western parliamentarian—assertive, brash, commanding. These are not endearing traits in a cultural system endorsing the domain of restrictive conformity.

But Frank has an additional problem. His English is so good that the British people present can easily overlook the fact that he is using his second language. In this case the listener's attribution system easily switches to "native-speaker mode" and Frank is then evaluated across the whole range of his presentation by British standards (see Bond, 1985). Now, verbally and nonverbally, Frank is superb. However, his pragmatics are all wrong. *Speech pragmatics* refers to the cultural appropriateness of the content in people's utterances (Loveday, 1982). In this area of speech competence, one is assessed on whether what one discusses, questions, and presents is typical of the speech community whose language one is using. And here Frank makes (at least) two mistakes. First, his praise of the chairman is too fulsome. Second, the introduction to his question is too pedestrian and indirect. In these regards Frank is behaving "Chinese" even though he is speaking English (Bond & Hwang, 1986). As the Westerners' chuckles indicate, however, he is judged using the full yardstick of British standards.

It is worth noting in passing that the problem of speech pragmatics can arise even when people from different societies are using the same first language. Dwight Eisenhower once quipped that "England and America are two cultures divided by a common language." In part he was acknowledging the difficulties posed by differences in accent, vocabulary, and slang. He was probably also referring to normative differences in what are appropriate topics of conversation in these two cultural systems. Especially important is the issue of how much self-disclosure is acceptable and in what areas of life—work, marriage, family background, economic activities, and so forth. When one party breaks the conventions of the other party's culture, negative evaluations result. This may be especially true when both persons speak the same language and hence are less forgiving than they may be of a "foreigner."

Working Better With Cultural Diversity

> The people of this world have been brought together technologically, but have not yet begun to understand what that means in a spiritual sense. We have to learn to live as brothers or we will perish as fools. (Martin Luther King)

Advance or Retreat?

As Edward Hall (1977) asserts in *Beyond Culture*, "Most cultural exploration begins with the annoyance of being lost." Confusions arising from cultural differences and language use provide lots of opportunity for the annoyance of being lost in ethnically diverse organizations. Although exploration is one possible response, withdrawal and cultural scapegoating are others. If we wish to influence the direction of our response, it is first necessary to acknowledge the pitfalls and decide whether or not we are willing to span the gaps. Such bridging will not happen without effort. There are two basic issues and a small note about language to consider.

The Role of Cultural Knowledge

Misattributions are rife cross-culturally, and managing impressions effectively requires a conscious, concentrated effort. What can be done to improve our success rate, so that we do not mistranslate the meaning of behavior and make culturally biased judgments?

Information about the cultural dynamics of a group one is encountering is useful in the decoding process and also in the sending process. If one does not wish to misconstrue another's behavior or send the wrong impression one must know how the other's attribution codes are keyed. With that knowledge one can better understand how to manage the impression one creates and how to interpret others' actions.

Many sources are available. One can read about the culture in various media, from newspaper articles to scholarly tomes. Indeed, there are many texts that attempt to accelerate this acquisition process by using programmed learning based on critical incidents in cross-cultural interactions (e.g. Brislin, Cushner, Cherrie, & Yong, 1986). Conversations with experienced conationals where the agenda is "What's going on here?" is another approach. These discussions must be carefully monitored, however, or they can easily degenerate into a game of what Eric Berne (1985) calls "Ain't awful," reinforcing negative stereotypes. Where one has developed a trusting relationship with a "local," even deeper insights can be gained. In such exchanges one can also learn from the process of the interchange as well as from its content. If one is skilled, it is possible to acquire understanding from themes and patterns in cultural productions, such as movies, music, painting, proverbs, novels, and sports.

Knowledge Is Not Enough

Cross-cultural interaction is stressful. Often it occurs in a context where one of the parties involved has been dislocated from his or her home country. In addition to the ecological, bacteriological, and technological adaptation required, there is a supportive social network to replace. As if these changes were not enough, members of the host culture often present a puzzling and unsettling variety of behaviors.

People often respond to such a stressful package in ways that isolate them further from the host culture, thereby short-circuiting the adaptation process. This withdrawal may be cognitively supported by the development of negative stereotypes from misattributions. If their work requires them to interact with host nationals, sojourners may well confine interactions to the task alone and minimize their affective involvement.

The characteristic of interpersonal warmth appears to offset this withdrawal process (Ruben & Kealey, 1979). Ruben (1977) labels this component of communication competence "display of respect." It can be manifested in a variety of ways:

The ability to express respect and positive regard for another person has been suggested as an important component in effective interpersonal relations (Ca khuff, 1969). The expression of respect can confer status on the recipient, contribute to self-esteem, and foster positive regard for the source of the communicated respect.

> People like to feel that others respect them, their accomplishments, their beliefs, and what they have to say. If one is able, through gestures, eye contact, smiles, and words of encouragement, to indicate that he or she is sincerely interested in the other person, then that person is much more likely to respond positively. (p.476)

Such basic interpersonal orientation helps a person draw delight from his or her cross-cultural exchanges and makes them more approachable for the host nationals. This interpersonal "glue" of warmth sustains and deepens cross-cultural exchanges so that the necessary learning can occur. This culture learning then acts as a prophylactic against misattributions and injudicious self-presentations.

Talking Oneself Out of the Language Trap

I have mentioned the potential dangers of being *too* good at the lingua franca. Such an individual is likely to be evaluated too harshly by native language speakers. It is probably useful for the fluent speaker in this regard to engage in various strategies to remind the audience that he or she is using a second language. It may be wise to retain an accent, to appear to struggle a bit for the right word, to remind the audience that one has not had much practice recently, and so forth. This "less than perfect" mode generates sympathy and invites people to use cross-cultural, rather than monocultural, standards in forming impressions about one's speech production.

This suggestion should not be taken to imply that individuals should neglect their comprehension ability in the second language. It is extremely useful to be skilled at second-language reception in order to avoid problems in information transmission. Favorable competence judgments are important, especially when dealing with superiors. This statement is true on both sides of the Pyrenees!

Conclusion

> All men can see the tactics whereby I conquer, but what none can see is the strategy out of which victory is evolved. (Sun Tzu, *The Art of War*)

Although this chapter has not been concerned with war, it has been concerned with a kind of battle—the battle to overcome our cultural predispositions to behave, and to judge the behavior of others, in culturally prescribed ways. These patterns are important signposts in negotiating the maze of interpersonal relations within a given cultural setting. In a different cultural setting, however, these same signposts may be misleading and self-destructive because they point in the wrong directions.

This chapter attempts to provide "a strategy out of which victory [may be] evolved." It does so by mapping the major value domains across which cultural groups differ from one another. These value domains are then linked to modal interpersonal behaviors. It is these behaviors that must be correctly understood *and* presented to others if one is to travel across cultural lines and work effectively at one's new destination.

Knowledge, courage, and a generous spirit are all required in this twentieth-century form of exploration. The personal benefits at the end of the journey are cognitive complexity and behavioral flexibility. These gains translate back to our cultural groups of origin because we find the same patterns of value in some of the people there as we do in people from different cultures. A journey across the seas may provide us with the skills needed to work more effectively with our next-door neighbors.

Within the four seas, all men are brothers. (Confucius, *The Analects*)

Note

1. The "self-responsibility system" involves individual family units contracting with their communes to work a piece of land in addition to their regular communal requirements. They then receive a sizable portion of the production from this land to use for their individual benefit.

References

Bales, R. F. (1950). *Interaction process analysis: A method for the study of small groups.* Cambridge, MA: Addison-Wesley.

Baumeister, R. F. (1982). A self-presentational view of social phenomena. *Psychological Bulletin, 91*, 3-26.

Berne, E. (1985). *Games people play.* New York: Ballantine.

Bond, M. H. (1985). Language as a carrier of ethnic stereotypes in Hong Kong. *Journal of Social Psychology, 125*, 53-62.

Bond, M. H. (1990). Chinese values and health: A cross-cultural examination. *Psychology and Health: An International Journal.*

Bond, M. H., & Hwang, K. K. (1986). The social psychology of Chinese people. In M. H. Bond (Ed.), *The psychology of Chinese people*. Hong Kong: Oxford University Press.

Brislin, R. W., Cushner, K., Cherrie, C., & Yong, M. (1986). *Intercultural interactions: A practical guide*. Beverly Hills, CA: Sage.

Carkhuff, R. R. (1969). *Helping and human relations*. New York: Holt, Rinehart and Winston.

Glenn, E. (1981). *Man and mankind*. Norwood, NJ: Ablex.

Hall, E. T. (1977). *Beyond culture*. Garden City, NY: Doubleday.

Hofstede, G. (1980). *Culture's consequences: International differences in work-related values*. Beverly Hills, CA: Sage.

Jones, E. E., & Pittman, T. S. (1982). Toward a general theory of strategic self-presentation. In J. Suls (Ed.), *Psychological perspectives on the self* (pp. 231-262). Hillsdale, NJ: Lawrence Erlbaum.

Kluckhohn, C. (1951). Values and value-orientations in the theory of action: An exploration in definition and classification. In T. Parsons & E. A. Shils (Eds.), *Toward a general theory of action*. Cambridge, MA: Harvard University Press.

Loveday, L. (1982). *The socio-linguistics of learning and using a non-native language*. Oxford: Pergamon.

Maslow, A. H. (1954). *Motivation and personality*. New York: Harper.

Quill, J. H., & Rigby, J. M. (n.d.). *An approach to the effective application of organization development technology across cultures*. Unpublished manuscript.

Riesman, D. (1950). *The lonely crowd: A study of the changing American character*. New Haven, CT: Yale University Press.

Rotter, J. B. (1966). Generalized expectancies for internal vs. external control of reinforcement. *Psychology Monographs, 80*(1, Whole No. 609).

Ruben, B. (1977). Guidelines for cross-cultural communication effectiveness. *Group & Organization Studies, 2*, 470-479.

Ruben, B., & Kealey, D. J. (1979). Behavioral assessment of communication competency and the prediction of cross-cultural adaptation. *International Journal of Intercultural Relations, 3*, 15-47.

Schwartz, S. M., & Bilsky, W. (1987). Toward a universal psychological structure of human values. *Journal of Personality and Social Psychology, 53*, 550-562.

Smith, P. B., & Tayeb, M. (1988). Organizational structure and processes. In M. H. Bond (Ed.), *The cross-cultural challenge to social psychology* (pp. 153-164). Newbury Park, CA: Sage.

Tajfel, H. (Ed.). (1978). *Differentiation between social groups: Studies in intergroup behavior*. London: Academic Press.

Triandis, H. C. (1967). Interpersonal relations in an international organization. *Journal of Organizational Behavior and Human Performance, 2*, 26-55.

Triandis, H. C. (1989). *Cross-cultural studies of individualism and collectivism*. Paper prepared for the Nebraska Symposium on Motivation.

Yang, K. (1986). Chinese personality and its change. In M. H. Bond (Ed.), *The psychology of the Chinese people* (pp. 106-170). Hong Kong: Oxford University Press.

PART V

Communication and Conformity Applications

12

Symbolic Communication and Image Management in Organizations

GAIL S. RUSS

Organizational facades help managers to justify actions, to acquire resources from environments, and to gain discretion.
(Nystrom & Starbuck, 1984, p. 182)

Communication is a fundamental component of our regular interactions in organizations and in everyday life. Few people would disagree with this statement; likewise, few would find it particularly novel or innovative. What is both novel and interesting, however, is the way formal communications in organizations can be used to affect the perceptions and interpretations of receivers of that communication.

Top managers in organizations are accountable to multiple constituencies, both inside (e.g., employees) and outside (e.g., shareholders), and they often are in a position of needing to communicate information to those constituencies. Sometimes the information passed on to constituencies involves positive events, and sometimes it involves negative events. Managerial efforts to rationalize and to legitimate organizational actions (Pfeffer, 1981a) are directed at external constituencies, and successful efforts to legitimate organizational actions must attempt to satisfy the diverse legitimacy criteria of these groups. This chapter presents discussion of the different strategies and tactics used by top management to manage the perceptions, meanings, and interpretations that their constituencies assign to their formal comunictions.

Several trends in the organizational science literature suggest that the issues of stakeholder management, accountability, and organizational justification are seen as increasingly important (Heath & Nelson, 1986; Tetlock, 1985). Murray (1978) suggests that strategic choice is a negotiated outcome, and notes the increasing pressure on organizations for public accountability. Further, organizational scholars are becoming more interested in ways in which firms signal different types of information to the capital market (i.e., present or potential investors) and the effect of those signals (Feldman & March, 1981; Zajac, 1988). This chapter suggests that a firm's formal organizational communications (e.g., annual reports, press releases, newsletters to shareholders, interviews in business publications) can offer insights into an organization's approach to symbolic management of important stakeholders' perceptions of the firm and of the top management team.

First, the chapter contrasts the more traditional, rational approach to corporate communications with the symbolic approach, in which formal organizational communications are seen as one vehicle through which those in management enact their own view of reality and convey that vision to their constituencies. The symbolic management approach suggests that top managers use corporate communications targeted at external constituencies as a mechanism to influence stakeholders' perceptions of the environment and the organization, through offering management's interpretation of the meanings or implications of events and situations. In addition, formal organizational communications are considered as a means through which management attempts to protect managerial discretion by protecting the perceived appropriateness and legitimacy of managerial actions.

The chapter also examines the self-serving aspect of symbolic management, and discusses two separate theoretical literatures that suggest that people in general (i.e., impression management theory) and top managers in particular (i.e., agency theory) may be motivated to present information in ways that protect their own interests or enhance their reputations. The chapter incorporates the view of self-serving influence processes, thus conceptually linking the symbolic management framework with the impression management literature (e.g., Giacalone & Rosenfeld, 1989).

Impression management theory looks at self-presentation tactics and their role in social influence processes, and has been defined as "the conscious or unconscious attempt to control images that are projected in real or imagined social interactions" (Schlenker, 1980, p. 6). The theory has its origins in the sociological work of Goffman (1959, 1981) on self-presentational behavior. Social psychologists have further developed and tested impression management theory, usually in laboratory settings (see Leary & Kowalski, 1990, for a recent review of this literature).

More recently, impression management in organizational settings has been the topic of considerable interest in the organizational behavior literature (e.g., Gardner & Martinko, 1988; Giacalone & Rosenfeld, 1989), and has been linked with political processes in organizations (Ferris, Russ, & Fandt, 1989). In the present chapter, impression management is depicted as one aspect of symbolic management. The final section of the chapter discusses specific research that has examined the impression management and symbolic management aspects of formal organizational communications.

The Rational and the Symbolic Perspectives

A number of different perspectives have been taken in the study of how organizations attempt to manage their environments. Much of the management literature, from early classical management theory to current research in strategic management, has been characterized by a strong assumption of organizational rationality. In the rational approach, organizational actions are seen as intended to bring about specific organizational goals, whether such goals are explicitly or implicitly stated by top management.

Further, the role of organizational communications is seen as central. Organizational communications, in the rational approach, are taken as straightforward transmissions of objective data that are intended to explain, to promote, or to assist in the attainment of organizational goals. Similar assumptions shape the rational perspective on decision making. Early decision-making models were normative and assumed an economic basis for rationality (Miller & Starr, 1976; Simon, 1979). In these frameworks, managers were thought to follow a thorough, logical decision-making process, impartially assessing all information in order to make their decisions based on the corporation's economic best interests. As Feldman and March (1981) note:

> Bureaucratic organizations are edifices built on ideas of rationality. The corner-stones of rationality are values regarding decision making (Weber, 1947). There are no values closer to the core of western ideology than these ideas of intelligent choice, and there is no institution more prototypically committed to the systematic

application of information to decisions than the modern bureaucratic organization. (p. 177)

Although later decision-making models were revised to admit limits to the ability of decision makers to process information (i.e., bounded rationality) and failure to search for the optimal solution (i.e., satisficing) (Simon, 1945), managers were still seen as *intendedly* rational.

> The individual can be rational in terms of the organization's goals only to the extent that he is *able* to pursue a particular course of action, he has a correct conception of the *goal* of the action, and he is correctly *informed* about the conditions surrounding his choice. Within the boundaries laid down by these factors his choices are rational-goal-oriented. (Simon, 1976, p. 241)

The rational orientation is apparent in normative models of strategy formulation presented in current strategic management texts (e.g., Certo & Peter, 1988; Thompson & Strickland, 1990; Wheelen & Hunger, 1989). Managers are depicted as proceeding through strategy formulation and strategy implementation steps in order to maximize corporate performance (Hofer & Schendel, 1978). For instance, selection of an appropriate corporate-level strategy is assumed to be based on the outcome of a programmatic assessment of the opportunities and threats present in the external environment and the strengths and weaknesses of the firm.

In contrast to the rational approach, the symbolic approach focuses on the emerging or unfolding nature of organizational activity (Weick, 1979a, 1979b). Every day, organizational members are faced with new information and events that are equivocal; that is, the meaning or implication of the information or the event is unclear and open to multiple interpretations. For instance, consider the possible interpretations of an announcement by company X's major competitor that it is going to begin diversifying into other industries so as to lessen its dependence on its (and company X's) traditional industry. What conclusions can company X draw from such an event? What are the implications of such an announcement? Does it mean that this is going to be a real opportunity for company X to pick up some of the competitor's market share? Or does it mean that the competitor knows something that company X does not—but should?

The symbolic approach suggests that a major role of top managers is to enact the environment; that is, to create a shared understanding—a unitary view—of the events that occur and the environment in which the organization operates. This approach has led to an increase in the last decade in studying the symbolic nature of organizational life. In the symbolic management approach, the organization is seen not only as enacting the environment for organizational members, but also as conveying the enactment through symbols to its relevant constituencies. Examples of organizational symbols include company logos, annual reports, organization charts, corporate anniversary celebrations, and organizational stories, "often about [the] organizational founder to explain start up, history and purpose of the organization" (Daft, 1983, p. 201).

This perspective on organizations is very different from the rational view. Rather than being characterized as centers of production efficiency, organizations are seen as systems of shared meanings. "Rationality cannot guide action in this view, because rationality, goals, and preferences are viewed as emerging from the action rather than guiding action" (Pfeffer, 1982, p. 9). Rather than achieving cohesion through the pursuit of mutually agreed-upon goals, organizational members are seen as continually negotiating the "social construction of reality" (Berger & Luckmann, 1966). Any consensus that arises originates from this shared perception of reality.

Symbolic management is concerned with how people create their environments. Much of the work stemming from the interest in symbolic management has been on organizational culture (Adams & Ingersoll, 1990). *Culture* is typically defined as the values and beliefs of the organizational members (Smircich, 1983). Organizational language, myths, stories, and ceremonies are thought to embody the culture of the firm symbolically, and through such mechanisms the culture is believed to be created, altered, and transmitted.

Daft (1983) has developed a model that essentially incorporates both the rational and the symbolic approaches, in that it asserts that symbolic communications can serve a dual purpose. Daft suggests that organizational symbols can be placed on an expressive-instrumental continuum. Instrumental symbols (e.g., receipts) "convey information to meet rules and requirements within the organization" and "help the organization do its work" (p. 202). Expressive symbols (e.g., organizational stories) serve some underlying feelings or emotional needs of organizational members. They also clarify and structure perceptions of managerial and organizational actions. "Expressive symbols are hypothesized to appeal to the deeper needs of organization participants, perhaps by removing uncertainty or providing an object for the individual to identify with" (p. 202).

Daft (1983) also notes that some symbols can serve both instrumental and expressive purposes. For instance, Daft suggests that "organizational health symbols" (e.g., annual reports and public relations statements) serve both instrumental and expressive purposes. The expressive aspects serve to reassure "various publics about the organization and to help people understand the status and well-being of the organization" (p. 204), whereas instrumental information is conveyed because government regulations and customer expectations require objective financial information.

Implicit in Daft's model is the idea that there is a close tie between environmental uncertainty and the need for symbolic communications to reduce that uncertainty. In fact, the symbolic management literature suggests that the "sense-making" or "enactment" feature of organizational life is believed to be pervasive, but it is most obvious and most critical under conditions of uncertainty. Frost and Morgan (1983) suggest that "one important aspect of symbolism in organizations is the way people use symbols to make sense of situations which are problematic, ambiguous or unsettling" (p. 207).

In contrast, the strategy literature, while addressing the role of top managers in nonprogrammed decisions characterized by ambiguity and equivocality, has paid little attention to the symbolic nature of these decisions, preferring to emphasize techniques for improving the rationality of the process. Weick (1987), on the other hand, suggests that rational models of decision making are appropriate for stable environments, but "when environments become unstable, then people need first to make meaning in order to see what, if anything, there is to decide" (p. 123).

There is a continuing trend in the organizational science literature to focus on managers' responses under the extreme uncertainty created by environmental and organizational crises (e.g., Heath & Nelson, 1986; Rosen, 1990). No doubt this trend reflects the general public's growing concern and demand for organizational accountability and social responsibility.

Much of the work on organizational responses to environmental threats or crises has focused on internal processes. Organizational structure is affected, usually shifting to a more mechanistic form (Burns & Stalker, 1961). This shift results in a constriction of internal controls as a consequence of increased formalization and centralization of authority (Hermann, 1963; Pfeffer & Leblebici, 1973; Rubin, 1977; Starbuck, Greve, & Hedberg, 1978).

Attention has also been focused on decision making during crises. An emergent-perspective decision-making model has been proposed by Anderson (1983). In an analysis of the minutes of the Executive Committee of the

National Security Council made during the Cuban missile crisis of the Kennedy administration, Anderson found that the decision process was a highly social procedure that led to the discovery of overarching goals. Through an iterative process of argumentation and debate, committee members came to share a common perspective on the situation. Anderson's "decision making by objection" process emphasized the sense-making aspect of decision processes, rather than the rational solution-seeking facet.

After a decision has been made on how to respond to a threat, managers continue to search for information. As Staw, Sandelands, and Dutton (1981) note, however, "the type of information sought is not information on alternatives nor information about the threat, but instead is support information confirming policy choices that have already been made" (p. 513).

Image management is particularly important following a crisis, and highlights the importance of organizational communications targeted at external stakeholders. "Audiences are particularly attentive during times of crisis. This situation offers special opportunities to communicate and demonstrate the corporation's commitment to responsible behavior" (Heath & Nelson, 1986, p. 185).

But from their work on crises in organizations (Nystrom, Hedberg, & Starbuck, 1976; Starbuck et al., 1978), Nystrom and Starbuck (1984) conclude that "managers' pronouncements, ringing with tones of self-assurance, sometimes mask serious doubts, even utter bewilderment" (p. 183). Such a perspective is consonant with Pfeffer's (1981a) conception of the political aspects of symbolic management, which considers symbolic management as the use of political language and symbolic action to rationalize decisions and policies. "The manager is viewed as having a symbolic, legitimating, sense-making role, providing assurance of the controllability of events even in the absence of such control" (Pfeffer, 1982, p. 11).

Pettigrew (1973) notes the use of symbolic management in legitimating the desires of the dominant coalition, and in legitimating past reactions that are now seen as strategies. In line with Pettigrew, Pfeffer (1981b) suggests that the manager's job is to rationalize and to legitimate the important decisions made by top management: "Political activity in organizations involves both labeling and sense-making as well as the development of a social consensus around the labels and definitions of the decisions and actions" (p. 188). What Pfeffer proposes, in fact, is that symbolic management can be seen as a type of deliberate, intentional influence attempt.

The Case for Self-Interested Behavior

The association of political behavior with symbolic management raises a crucial question: Who benefits? That is, are symbolic management influence attempts intended to be in the organization's or the influence agent's best interests? There are different perspectives on political behavior, and one distinction (although not always explicitly stated) is whether the behavior is considered to be political but still in the best interests of the firm, or whether the political behavior is perceived to be primarily self-interested.

As noted earlier, the traditional rational approach, which rarely addressed the issue of political behavior, assumed that managers act in the owners' best interests. Managers were thought to pursue those interests, which were assumed to be maximized by attainment of organizational goals of efficiency and effectiveness, through structural design, and, more recently, through strategy formulation and strategy implementation. Political processes, when recognized, are seen as inimical to proper planning: "We believe . . . that social and political processes should be considered only after all the basic economic, demographic, and technological analyses are completed, even though it is clear that, in practice, social and political considerations are sometimes the first, and on occasion the only, step in the strategy formulation process" (Hofer & Schendel, 1978, p. 56).

Some theorists taking a political perspective have followed the organizational goal orientation of the traditional rational approach in assuming that political behavior primarily occurs as a natural process for resolving differences among organizational interest groups (Vredenburgh & Maurer, 1984). An alternative, and perhaps more prevalent view, however, is that political behavior is primarily self-interested behavior (Gandz & Murray, 1980; Mayes & Allen, 1977).

There are two bodies of literature that are of particular importance to the issue of self-interested behavior: Impression management theory and agency theory. Impression management theory posits that individuals are generally motivated to engage in behaviors that will favorably influence others' assessment of them, whereas agency theory focuses on corporate governance issues that cause top managers in particular to pursue their own interests.

The impression management literature suggests that the self-presentational process is highly complex. Gardner and Martinko (1988) reviewed the social psychological and management research to develop a framework that includes the major variables found to be important in impression management. The framework includes factors related to the individual engaging in impression management (e.g., the person's status, physical attributes, abilities, self-concept, and need for approval). Gardner and Martinko also considered characteristics of the audience to which such behaviors are targeted (e.g., the power and status of the audience). The model also includes situational factors (e.g., favorability and ambiguity of the situation) and environmental factors (e.g., organizational culture).

Impression management as applied to organizational settings suggests it is possible that efforts to rationalize and to legitimate managerial decisions are motivated by very personal concerns. Managers may fear that their careers would be jeopardized if stakeholders perceived their actions as irrational or irresponsible, or if they were blamed for poor corporate performance. On the other hand, enhancing perceptions of managerial abilities, intentions, and efforts would serve to increase their professional reputations, and could possibly increase their compensation.

Therefore, part of stakeholder management may involve trying to manage constituencies' impressions of the personal attributes of top management. Most organizational impression management studies have focused on micro-level influence processes within the corporation, such as personnel selection (Eder & Buckley, 1988; Kacmar, 1990) and performance appraisal (Fandt & Ferris, 1990). However, organizational-level impression management is thought to be pervasive:

> Organizations are pre-eminently involved with the business of impression management, in relation to the general public, other corporations, consumers, employees, government, and other significant actors capable of influencing their well being. (Morgan, Frost, & Pondy, 1983, p. 20)

A straight impression management approach would suggest that managers may be motivated to represent both the environment and their actions so as to increase their own outcomes (e.g., enhancement of personal reputation, avoidance of blame for poor organizational performance). It should be noted, however, that some research has found that the self-serving bias (i.e., avoiding blame for poor outcomes and claiming credit for good outcomes) may actually be a *real* perceptual distortion, and not just impression management alone (e.g., Riess, Rosenfeld, Melburg, & Tedeschi, 1981; Rosenfeld, 1990). "The traditional view is that these self-serving biases result from a person's need to enhance, maintain, or defend self-esteem" (Rosenfeld, 1990, p. 495).

It was first suggested by Weary-Bradley (1978) that the self-serving bias might really reflect a desire to create or maintain a certain public image, rather than to protect one's self-image. Researchers are still trying to distinguish between behaviors that are really the result of self-deception and those that reflect more conscious efforts to create a positive image of oneself in the minds of others (Zerbe & Paulhus, 1987).

A second theoretical approach, agency theory, suggests a rationale for self-interested behavior in top managers specifically. Originating in microeconomics, agency theory directly considers the problem of the divergency between shareholder and managerial interests that arises as a result of the separation of ownership and control (Berle & Means, 1932). As the number of owners increases, thus dispersing ownership, individual owners (stockholders) can no longer be involved in the day-to-day management of the firm. Owners therefore hire managers to act as their agents in running the firm. This arrangement leaves the stockholders with the risk (but also the rights to any profits), and managers with the obligation to perform as well as possible and to be loyal to the stockholders, in the sense of not stealing or mismanaging the firm. As Eisenhardt (1985) states:

> Agency models explicitly recognize . . . the divergence of preferences among organizational members. . . . In this political view of organizations, the role of control is to provide measures and rewards such that individuals pursuing their own self-interest will also pursue the collective interest. (p. 137)

The board of directors is posited as a means of monitoring management (Fama & Jensen, 1983), in that the board assumes decision control (ratification and monitoring) and management assumes management control (initiation of proposed strategy and implementation of that strategy). Fama and Jensen (1983) conclude that the board effectively solves the agency problem, a position supported by Mizruchi's (1983) empirical findings.

However, others have argued that corporate governance is much more complex than that described by Fama and Jensen (e.g., Williamson, 1983), and that the board, by obtaining much of its information from top management, is imperfectly able to detect opportunistic behavior on the part of management. Indeed, the symbolic management perspective would suggest that top management, by being the major information source concerning organizational conditions, is in an ideal position to influence the board's perception of reality. As Nystrom and Starbuck (1984) note:

> Separation of management from ownership creates opportunities for divergent motives. . . . Also, separation creates needs for owners to evaluate managers, so managers have to appear competent. In modernized societies, prevailing ideologies

generally equate managerial competence with rationality, and rationality connotes purposiveness and consistency. (p. 182)

Together, agency theory and impression management theory suggest that managers may be motivated to present information in a self-serving manner. Research has suggested also that managers act to protect managerial discretion, and that managers "gain discretion by appearing to conform to environmentally preferred ideologies" (Nystrom & Starbuck, 1984, p. 182).

From the literature presented thus far, it can be seen that organizational communications are thought to have rational as well as symbolic functions, and, at least under some conditions, to be self-serving. The remainder of the chapter explores efforts to integrate these different perspectives.

Symbolic Management in Annual Reports

Several studies have focused on letters to shareholders from corporate annual reports. Given its high visibility and broad distribution to important stakeholders, the annual report can be considered representative of a firm's broad array of communication channels (e.g., press releases, newsletters to shareholders, interviews in business publications), and may offer insights into an organization's approach to managing symbolically important stakeholders' perceptions of the firm and of the top management team.

Publicly held organizations are required to issue annual reports on the firms' performance. If they so desired, managers could simply issue reports of financial data (e.g., the 10K report). Further, beginning with 1987 annual reports, corporations are required to include considerably less information in the annual report. Interestingly, however, very few firms chose to move to the summary format, despite its considerable cost-savings advantages (Byrne, 1988). Far from delivering information in a terse, "businesslike" manner, many firms have chosen to present shareholders with "a document that looks and reads more like a newsmagazine than like a dull corporate document" (Byrne, 1988, p. 66).

Research by Bowman (1976, 1978, 1984) typifies the rational approach to organizational communications. He has examined annual reports as a reliable source for discerning organizational strategies. A straightforward, rational approach would suggest that annual reports are a mechanism for transferring objective, concrete corporate information to investors in order to facilitate investment decisions. Such an explanation, however, leaves unresolved the question of why top managers choose to expend time and resources in order to offer more information—and information of a different type—than is required.

Evidence of self-presentational techniques has been found in annual reports. Bettman and Weitz (1983) and Staw, McKechnie, and Puffer (1983) have found that unfavorable performance outcomes tend to be attributed to external, uncontrollable causes (i.e., self-protective attributions), but that favorable outcomes are attributed to internal, stable causes (i.e., self-enhancing attributions). These researchers were not able to determine conclusively, however, the extent to which the self-serving tendencies were deliberate impression management ploys or unconscious attempts to protect (or to enhance) self-esteem.

Salancik and Meindl (1984) examined firms characterized by stable and unstable performance, and also looked at explanations of performance. They found that annual reports were used to manage the impression of top management's control over past events and performance. Rather than deny responsibility for poor outcomes, managers of unstable firms seemed more concerned with conveying their ability to control events. This suggests that these managers were trying to improve their reputation by enhancing perceptions of their credibility and legitimacy.

Abrahamson (1988) has argued, however, that managers are constrained in manipulating public statements by stakeholders' expectations that information in annual reports follow institutionalized formats. In a study examining letters to shareholders of firms that faced bankruptcy, Abrahamson concluded that the data supported an institutional-conformity explanation more than a symbolic management explanation.

Abrahamson, however, assumed that symbolic management theory would predict that managers would decrease the number of references to their financial performance as their risk of bankruptcy increased over a five-year period. The study did not examine the nature of those references to negative financial conditions; that is, no attention was paid to whether the comments were merely statements of fact, causal attributions (either self-enhancing or self-defensive), or interpretations.

Russ (1990) has suggested that symbolic management may be more sophisticated than merely avoiding unpleasant topics, as interpreted by Abrahamson. Symbolic management in formal organizational communications has been conceptualized by Russ as an influence process in which different types of information are presented in an effort to shape others' perceptions of reality. Specifically, Russ argues that managers not only give straightforward information in annual reports, they also identify causes of outcomes as well as discuss their own interpretations of those events. This operationalization of symbolic management is in line with Daft's (1983) view of symbolic management, in which mechanisms of symbolic management exist along an instrumental-expressive continuum. Daft suggests that expressive symbols pertain to poorly understood phenomena, whereas instrumental symbols pertain to phenomena that are well understood.

In Russ's model, representations of fact correlate with the instrumental end of Daft's continuum. Such information is typically objective and straightforward. True *symbolic* management, with its goal of getting another person to accept the conveyer's perceptions and interpretations of reality, is seen as being achieved through presentation of causal attributions (i.e., statements that assign responsibility for causing some event or outcome) and interpretations of events and situations.

Causal attributions are seen as serving both instrumental purposes, by presenting causal relationships as facts, and expressive purposes, by reducing (or attempting to reduce) equivocality—that is, multiple interpretations of a particular phenomenon. But identifying the cause of some event or outcome still does not answer all the questions that might arise. Interpretations, which involve discussing the implications or meaning of some event or situation, serve the greatest expressive purpose by reducing equivocality, and thus lead to a shared view of reality.

Further, this view corresponds with Pfeffer's (1981b) conceptualization of legitimating managerial decisions by developing a social consensus through the processes of (a) labeling and (b) sense-making. Asserting facts and making causal attributions serves to label events, outcomes, causal relationships, and so on. Interpreting the meanings and implications of those facts and relationships focuses on the sense-making aspect.

In an analysis of letters to shareholders from corporate annual reports of securities firms, Russ (1990) found that representations of facts (i.e., instrumental statements) accounted for about 61% of the total of the three symbolic management categories, causal attributions for 13%, and interpretations for 26%. These findings suggest that the letter to shareholders is indeed used for both instrumental and expressive purposes.

Finally, the model not only addressed the change in the relative emphasis on causal attributions as a function of environmental uncertainty, but also tested for the self-serving attributions. In line with previous studies of corporate annual reports, Russ (1990) found evidence of self-serving attributions: The overall average ratio of external to internal attributions for negative events was almost 4:1, suggesting a constant trend of self-serving, defensive attributions. The trend for self-enhancing attributions was evident, but not as strong, as the overall average ratio of internal to external attributions for positive events was approximately 3:2.

These findings suggest an overall view of corporate communications that encompasses the disparate paths taken by theorists with rational, impression management, and symbolic orientations, but also put into perspective the relative emphasis on each of the three symbolic management categories. Further, these findings support Daft's (1983) placement of "organizational health symbols" midway along the instrumental-expressive continuum.

Many firms seem to welcome the annual report openly, particularly the letter to shareholders, as a medium to convey the top management view of the world to their constituencies. One securities firm, Discount Corporation of New York, noted in its *Sixty-Ninth Annual Report* in 1987, "As in past reports to the stockholders, we are following the practice of identifying and commenting on broad trends and potential fundamental changes that may affect the marketplace and your Corporation" (p. 4). The letter indeed covers a broad range of topics. Consider, for instance, this excerpt from one paragraph:

> The budget and trade deficits which so concerned the markets in 1987 continue to be critical. The inability of Congress and the Administration to take meaningful action on the budget, even after the October stock market crash, contributed to overseas pessimism about the U.S. economy. Confidence in the strength of leadership in the United States had already been sadly damaged by the Iran-Contra affair and by other evidence of a weakened Presidency, such as the difficulty in selecting an acceptable Supreme Court Justice. (p. 7)

Although these comments have relevance for the firm's past and future performance, it seems highly probable that such statements are intended to influence a broader range of perceptions.

Further, Russ (1990) proposes a dynamic view of symbolic management, and suggests that the relative balance of instrumental and expressive statements shifts within formal organizational communications across different organizations, as well as within the same organization over time, in response to intra- and extraorganizational factors. For instance, Russ (1990) expects that the more expressive aspects of symbolic management would increase in response to environmental uncertainty. This relationship follows from the conceptual literature on the function of symbolic communication, for instance, Weick's (1987) argument that increased uncertainty increases the importance of the sense-making aspect of symbolic management.

As the environment increases in uncertainty or equivocality, then, there should be a corresponding increase in attempts to interpret and to understand the events through symbolic communications. Thus organizational communications, such as annual reports, that normally serve both expressive and instrumental purposes should shift their emphasis to expressive functions. This means that there should be an overall increase in causal attributions and interpretations, relative to the level of assertions. Further, Russ posits that interpretations reduce equivocality to a greater extent than causal attributions, and suggests there should be a greater increase in interpretations than in causal attributions.

To test this idea, letters to shareholders written the year before the 1987 stock market crash (i.e., 1986 letters) were compared to letters written after the crash (i.e., 1987 letters). The findings supported the idea that greater environmental uncertainty leads to a stronger emphasis on interpretations, and that the shift away from instrumental statements (i.e., representations of facts) is greater for interpretations than for causal attributions.

The increase in interpretations relative to representations illustrates the importance placed on the equivocality-reduction capabilities of interpretations, as well as the importance placed on influencing stakeholders' perceptions of the event. That the increase in interpretations was greater than the increase in causal attributions provides support for the idea that interpretations are farther out along the expressive end of the instrumental-expressive continuum than are causal attributions.

Relative to interpretations, causal attributions are more focused: They clarify causal relationships (regardless of whether those attributions are self-serving or not). Causal attributions, however, do not get at the underlying meaning of an event. They cannot clarify the importance of a given organizational outcome. They cannot create a shared understanding of what the future implications are likely to be. In short, causal attributions cannot convey the broader view of reality that can be expressed in interpretations.

There are other implications of these findings. First, they demonstrate the linkage between expressive symbolic communications and uncertainty. Daft (1983) hypothesized that instrumental symbols would be most associated with well-understood phenomena, whereas expressive symbols would be most related to poorly understood phenomena. The postcrash letters indicate that there is an increased focus on expressive symbolic communications in response to an event whose implications for the future are highly equivocal.

Second, these findings support Weick's (1987) view that the importance of the sense-making facet of symbolic management increases in an uncertain environment, particularly during a crisis (Nystrom & Starbuck, 1984). Apparently, after an event that shakes their industry, managers are not content to sit by and let important constituencies develop their own ideas about what has happened and what is *going* to happen as a result. Formal organizational communications are seen as vehicles for influencing those perceptions.

Some brokerages did not wait for the annual report to try to influence stockholders' and customers' perceptions of the crash, but instead mailed out letters to their constituencies in the days immediately following the crisis. Merrill Lynch, one of the largest securities firms, used the letter to shareholders to emphasize its use of *other* organizational communication media in the days following the Black Monday crisis: "We moved aggressively through the news media, advertising and other public contacts to help calm the markets, reassure investors and underscore our confidence in the underlying strength of our financial system" (*1987 Annual Report*, p. 2).

Is there any evidence of self-serving impression management tactics, such as self-enhancing remarks? The Merrill Lynch letter continues, "We worked with industry, government and regulatory leaders on steps to ease the crisis. And we carefully managed our own operation, staying active in all markets on behalf of all investors. *As a result, Merrill Lynch enhanced its reputation* as a financially stable and trustworthy provider of financial services" (p. 2; emphasis added).

Thus annual reports demonstrate impression management tactics that go beyond the specific self-enhancing and self-defensive causal attributions for corporate profitability outcomes previously identified. Self-promotion can take the form of praising the qualities of the firm's management and employees. Such statements as "Our people are our product," "Our greatest strength is our people," and "Everyone is a hero in our company" are common in annual reports.

Many securities firms, perhaps wishing to emphasize their behaviors rather than their performance outcomes, focused on their responses to the crash. "Our operations personnel . . . worked tirelessly after the October crash" (Alex Brown, *1987 Annual Report*, p. 3). "[Our staff] demonstrated that they were able to handle the market shocks and the aftershocks with true professional competence and character" (IFG, *1987 Annual Report*, p. 3). "Our hard work to preserve shareholders' equity saw us through October 1987" (Kinnard Investments, *1987 Annual Report*). "When the phones rang at Shearson Lehman Brothers on October 19, as every day, they were answered as promptly as possible" (Shearson Lehman Hutton, *1987 Annual Report*, p. 2). Some even mentioned others' assessments of their efforts: "In a survey of top investment officers, Merrill Lynch was named the most helpful firm following the October market decline" (*1987 Annual Report*, p. 5).

Of course, corporate financial performance cannot be completely ignored in an annual report. Comparison of one's own outcomes to those of others, however, may also be an effective way to manage impressions. "IFG survived these sharp market downturns intact. This is a mark of no small significance in a year when so many did not. [Although earnings were down from 1986,] we posted no losses in the millions like some firms, nor were we pushed to lay off platoons of employees" (IFG, *1987 Annual Report*, p. 2). Merrill Lynch noted, "Our profits, while below target, were still the best in the industry by a significant margin" (*1987 Annual Report*, p. 2).

Firms compare themselves favorably to their competition on other dimensions, as well. "We also reaffirmed our commitment to leadership in the municipal and money markets businesses after some competitors decided to cease operations in those areas" (Merrill Lynch, *1987 Annual Report*, p. 2). "One of our greatest points of differentiation from the competition resides in our devotion to the concept of superior client service" (IFG, *1987 Annual Report*, p. 4).

There are times, of course, when even behaviors can be viewed with suspicion. One firm, under investigation for underwriting practices in the municipal bond business and the target of considerable adverse publicity, used the letter to shareholders to elaborate on its *intentions*: "We continue to affirm that . . . we acted at all times in good faith . . . in the sincere belief that we were serving the best interests of our clients and shareholders" (Matthews & Wright, *1987 Annual Report*, p. 5).

Clearly, annual reports are not the only medium used by organizations to manage impressions or to convey their enactment of the environment. Work on media richness (Daft & Lengel, 1984, 1986; Russ, Daft, & Lengel, 1990) suggests that managers tend to use richer media (e.g., face-to-face contact) for highly equivocal communications and written media for clearer, more objective messages. Much of the media richness research, however, has focused on intraorganizational communication patterns, where face-to-face communications are more possible. However, the letters to shareholders indicate that richer media are used for highly sensitive (and, presumably, more equivocal) communications. One firm, having to deal with the scandal caused by its founder's resignation and guilty plea to two felony violations of federal securities laws, reported that "our key people . . . went out into the field en masse to update the Jefferies' story. Because of the enthusiasm and credibility of our sales team, most of our clients were extremely supportive" (Jefferies Group, *1987 Annual Report*, p. 2).

Clearly, the role of the different communication media in symbolic management warrants further investigation. That evidence has been found of substantial impression management and symbolic management influence attempts in annual reports suggests, however, that this formal medium of organizational communications is considered important in dealing with equivocal or ambiguous situations.

On another note, the political aspects of formal organizational communications may be even more pervasive than indicated so far in this chapter. It has been assumed here that the influence attempts (both those that are self-serving and those that benignly enact the environment) are primarily externally oriented—the top management team's influence attempts targeted at external constituencies. This view rests on the assumption that the chief executive, or at least the top management team, actually writes the "president's" letter to shareholders. If, in fact, the letter is really a product of one or more departments in the firm, the letter may really be more of an internal organizational influence mechanism used by one department to manage the impressions of another department.

In a survey of top managers in the securities industry, Russ (1990) found that although various individuals usually had input into the letter, overall the primary author was the chief executive. But even these findings suggest further political implications. Four respondents from one firm seemed to have very different ideas about who actually wrote the letter. The CEO (who is also president) ranked himself as the major author, followed (in descending rank of contribution) by (a) top managers not on the board, (b) a public relations firm, and (c) the chairman of the board. The chairman, however, considered his contribution equal to that of the CEO, followed by the corporate information department and, least of all, by top managers not on the board. The chief financial officer said that the CEO was the major author, assisted by top managers not on the board. Finally, a vice president completely omitted both the CEO and the chairman from his rankings, and instead identified the director of corporate development as the major author, followed by top managers not on the board!

In closing, the symbolic aspects of organizational communications are clearly important and have been for some time, but, perhaps because of their elusive nature, have remained in the background until recently. We have only just begun to develop a more informed understanding of managing images, and to understand the various roles played by formal organizational communications.

What does all this mean for the practicing manager? Increased public scrutiny means increased pressure on managers to be able to communicate effectively with their various stakeholders. As a result of the dramatic increase in the public's interest in business news, "the chances of an executive getting through his or her career without facing the press are growing slim indeed" (Deutsch, 1990). As reported in the *New York Times*, top business schools have begun offering courses in media relations: "The courses . . . are aimed at getting students to view the media as a tool that, if properly used, can enhance their companies' image and their own careers, but if improperly used, can destroy them" (Deutsch, 1990).

Whether facing the public following a major organizational crisis or simply presenting the firm's annual performance data, managers are increasingly called upon to communicate with important elements outside of the organization. As Pfeffer (1981b) notes:

> The task of those who wish to exercise power in organizations is to present the advocated decisions and activities in a meaningful and sensible way to the organizational participants, so that a social consensus and social definitions around these activities and decisions may be developed. (p. 188)

References

Abrahamson, E. (1988). *Public statements during financial crises: Symbolic manipulation or institutional conformity?* Paper presented at the national meeting of the Academy of Management, Anaheim, CA.

Adams, G. B., & Ingersoll, V. H. (1990). Painting over old works: The culture of organization in an age of technical rationality. In B. Turner (Ed.), *Organizational symbolism* (pp. 15-31). Berlin: Walter de Gruyter.

Anderson, P. A. (1983). Decision making by objection and the Cuban missile crisis. *Administrative Science Quarterly, 28*, 201-222.

Berger, P. L., & Luckmann, T. (1966). *The social construction of reality: A treatise in the sociology of knowledge.* Garden City, NY: Doubleday.

Berle, A. A., & Means, G. C. (1932). *The modern corporation and private property.* New York: Macmillan.

Bettman, J. R., & Weitz, B. A. (1983). Attributions in the boardroom: Causal reasoning in corporate annual reports. *Administrative Science Quarterly, 28*, 165-183.

Bowman, E. H. (1976). Strategy and the weather. *Sloan Management Review, 17*, 49-62.

Bowman, E. H. (1978). Strategy, annual reports, and alchemy. *California Management Review, 20*, 64-71.

Bowman, E. H. (1984). Content analysis of annual reports for corporate strategy and risk. *Interfaces, 14*, 61-71.

Burns, T., & Stalker, G. M. (1961). *The management of innovation*. London: Tavistock.

Byrne, J. A. (1988, April 11). Curious about the crash? Don't read your annual report. *Business Week*, p. 66.

Certo, S. C., & Peter, J. P. (1988). *Strategic management: Concepts and applications*. New York: Random House.

Daft, R. L. (1983). Symbols in organizations: A dual-context framework for analysis. In L. R. Pondy, P. J. Frost, G. Morgan, & T. C. Dandridge (Eds.), *Organizational symbolism* (pp. 199-206). Greenwich, CT: JAI.

Daft, R. L., & Lengel, R. H. (1984). Information richness: A new approach to managerial information processing and organization design. In B. Staw & L. L. Cummings (Eds.), *Research in organizational behavior* (Vol. 6, pp. 191-233). Greenwich, CT: JAI.

Daft, R. L., & Lengel, R. H. (1986). Organizational information requirements, media richness and structural design. *Management Science, 32*, 554-571.

Deutsch, C. H. (1990, January 21). Media manipulation 101. *New York Times*, p. F29.

Eder, R. W., & Buckley, M. R. (1988). The employment interview: An interactionist perspective. In G. R. Ferris & K. M. Rowland (Eds.), *Research in personnel and human resources management* (Vol. 6, pp. 75-107). Greenwich, CT: JAI.

Eisenhardt, K. M. (1985). Control: Organizational and economic approaches. *Management Science, 31*, 134-149.

Fama, E. F., & Jensen, M. C. (1983). Separation of ownership and control. *Journal of Law and Economics, 26*, 301-325.

Fandt, P. M., & Ferris, G. R. (1990). The management of information and impressions: When employees behave opportunistically. *Organizational Behavior and Human Decision Processes, 45*, 140-158.

Feldman, M. S., & March, J. G. (1981). Information in organizations as signal and symbol. *Administrative Science Quarterly, 26*, 171-186.

Ferris, G. R., Russ, G. S., & Fandt, P. M. (1989). Politics in organizations. In R. A. Giacalone & P. Rosenfeld (Eds.), *Impression management in the organization* (pp. 143-170). Hillsdale, NJ: Lawrence Erlbaum.

Frost, P. J., & Morgan, G. (1983). Symbols and sensemaking: The realization of a framework. In L. R. Pondy, P. J. Frost, G. Morgan, & T. C. Dandridge (Eds.), *Organizational symbolism* (pp. 207-236). Greenwich, CT: JAI.

Gandz, J., & Murray, V. V. (1980). Experience of workplace politics. *Academy of Management Journal, 23*, 237-251.

Gardner, W. L., & Martinko, M. J. (1988). Impression management in organizations. *Journal of Management, 14*, 321-338.

Giacalone, R. A., & Rosenfeld, P. (Eds.). (1989). *Impression management in the organization*. Hillsdale, NJ: Lawrence Erlbaum.

Goffman, E. (1959). *The presentation of self in everyday life*. Garden City, NY: Doubleday.

Goffman, E. (1981). *Forms of talk*. Philadelphia: University of Pennsylvania Press.

Heath, R. L., & Nelson, R. A. (1986). *Issues management*. Beverly Hills, CA: Sage.

Hermann, C. F. (1963). Some consequences of crisis which limit the viability of organizations. *Administrative Science Quarterly, 8*, 343-358.

Hofer, C. W., & Schendel, D. (1978). *Strategy formulation: Analytical concepts*. St. Paul, MN: West.

Kacmar, K. M. (1990). *Relational communication and mutual influence in the employment interview*. Unpublished doctoral dissertation, Texas A&M University.

Leary, M. R., & Kowalski, R. M. (1990). Impression management: A literature review and two-component model. *Psychological Bulletin, 107*, 34-47.

Mayes, B. T., & Allen, R. W. (1977). Toward a definition of organizational politics. *Academy of Management Review, 2*, 672-678.

Miller, D. W., & Starr, M. K. (1976). *The structure of human decisions.* Englewood Cliffs, NJ: Prentice-Hall.

Mizruchi, M. S. (1983). Who controls whom? An examination of the relationship between management and boards of directors in large American corporations. *Academy of Management Review, 8*, 426-435.

Morgan, G., Frost, P. J., & Pondy, L. R. (1983). Organizational symbolism. In L. R. Pondy, P. J. Frost, G. Morgan, & T. C. Dandridge (Eds.), *Organizational symbolism* (pp. 3-35). Greenwich, CT: JAI.

Murray, E. A., Jr. (1978). Strategic choice as a negotiated outcome. *Management Science, 24*, 960-972.

Nystrom, P. C., Hedberg, B. L. T., & Starbuck, W. H. (1976). Interacting processes as organization designs. In R. H. Kilmann, L. R. Pondy, & D. P. Slevin (Eds.), *The management of organization design* (Vol. 1, pp. 209-230). New York: North-Holland.

Nystrom, P. C., & Starbuck, W. H. (1984). Organizational facades. In J. A. Pearce II & R. B. Robinson, Jr. (Eds.), *Proceedings of the 44th Annual Meeting of the Academy of Management* (pp. 182-185). Boston: Academy of Management.

Pettigrew, A. M. (1973). *The politics of organizational decision-making.* London: Tavistock.

Pfeffer, J. (1981a). Management as symbolic action: The creation and maintenance of organizational paradigms. In L. L. Cummings & B. M. Staw (Eds.), *Research in organizational behavior* (Vol. 3, pp. 1-52). Greenwich, CT: JAI.

Pfeffer, J. (1981b). *Power in organizations.* Boston: Pitman.

Pfeffer, J. (1982). *Organizations and organization theory.* Boston: Pitman.

Pfeffer, J., & Leblebici, H. (1973). Executive recruitment and the development of interfirm organizations. *Administrative Science Quarterly, 18*, 449-461.

Riess, M., Rosenfeld, P., Melburg, V., & Tedeschi, J. D. (1981). Self-serving attributions: Biased private perceptions and distorted public descriptions. *Journal of Personality and Social Psychology, 41*, 224-231.

Rosen, M. (1990). Crashing in '87: Power and symbolism in the Dow. In B. Turner (Ed.), *Organizational symbolism* (pp. 115-135). Berlin: Walter de Gruyter.

Rosenfeld, P. (1990). Self-esteem and impression management explanations for self-serving biases. *Journal of Social Psychology, 130*, 495-500.

Rubin, I. (1977). Universities in stress: Decision making under conditions of reduced resources. *Social Science Quarterly, 58*, 242-254.

Russ, G. S. (1990). *Shaping reality through organizational communications: Symbolic and control aspects of stakeholder management.* Unpublished doctoral dissertation, Texas A&M University.

Russ, G. S., Daft, R. L., & Lengel, R. H. (1990). Media selection and managerial characteristics in organizational communications. *Management Communication Quarterly, 4*, 151-175.

Salancik, G. R., & Meindl, J. R. (1984). Corporate attributions as strategic illusions of management control. *Administrative Science Quarterly, 29*, 238-254.

Schlenker, B. R. (1980). *Impression management: The self-concept, social identity, and interpersonal relations.* Monterey, CA: Brooks/Cole.

Simon, H. A. (1945). *Administrative behavior.* New York: Free Press.

Simon, H. A. (1976). *Administrative behavior* (3rd ed.). New York: Free Press.

Simon, H. A. (1979). Rational decision making in organizations. *American Economic Review, 69*, 493-513.

Smircich, L. (1983). Concepts of culture and organizational analysis. *Administrative Science Quarterly, 28*, 339-358.

Starbuck, W. H., Greve, A., & Hedberg, B. L. T. (1978). Responding to crises. *Journal of Business Administration, 9*, 111-137.

Staw, B. M., McKechnie, P. I., & Puffer, S. M. (1983). The justification of organizational performance. *Administrative Science Quarterly, 28*, 582-600.

Staw, B. M., Sandelands, L. E., & Dutton, J. E. (1981). Threat-rigidity effects in organizational behavior: A multilevel analysis. *Administrative Science Quarterly, 26*, 501-524.

Tetlock, P. E. (1985). Accountability: The neglected social context of judgment and choice. In L. L. Cummings & B. M. Staw (Eds.), *Research in organizational behavior* (Vol. 7, pp. 297-332). Greenwich, CT: JAI.

Thompson, A. A., Jr., & Strickland, A. J., III. (1990). *Strategic management: Concepts and cases* (5th ed.). Homewood, IL: BPI/Irwin.

Vredenburgh, D. J., & Maurer, J. G. (1984). A process framework of organizational politics. *Human Relations, 37*, 47-66.

Weary-Bradley, G. (1978). Self-serving biases in the attribution process: A reexamination of the fact or fiction question. *Journal of Personality and Social Psychology, 36*, 56-71.

Weber, M. (1947). *The theory of social and economic organization* (A. M. Henderson & T. Parsons, Trans.). New York: Free Press.

Weick, K. E. (1979a). Cognitive processes in organizations. In B. M. Staw (Ed.), *Research in organizational behavior* (Vol. 1, pp. 41-74). Greenwich, CT: JAI.

Weick, K. E. (1979b). *The social psychology of organizing* (2nd ed.). New York: Random House.

Weick, K. E. (1987). Organizational culture as a source of high reliability. *California Management Review, 29*, 112-127.

Wheelen, T. L., & Hunger, J. D. (1989). *Strategic management and business policy* (3rd ed.). Reading, MA: Addison-Wesley.

Williamson, O. E. (1983). Organization form, residual claimants, and corporate control. *Journal of Law and Economics, 26*, 351-366.

Zajac, E. J. (1988). Interlocking directorates as an interorganizational strategy: A test of critical assumptions. *Academy of Management Journal, 31*, 428-438.

Zerbe, W. J., & Paulhus, D. L. (1987). Socially desirable responding in organizational behavior: A reconception. *Academy of Management Review, 12*, 250-264.

13

Conformity

A Subtle Means of Impression Management

DAVID A. RALSTON
PRISCILLA M. ELSASS

In matters of clothing, conservative, class-conscious conformity is absolutely essential to the individual success of the American business and professional man. Executives . . . who understand how to cope rather than fight are much more likely to emerge as leaders than as casualties.

(Molloy, 1978)

When in Rome, do as the Romans do.

One of Allen Funt's simplest, yet still dramatic, *Candid Camera* episodes plays on the tendency of individuals to match their behavior to the behavior of those around them. As the episode opens, we see a man, standing alone, waiting for an elevator. When the elevator arrives, and the doors open, both the audience and the man are surprised to see that the elevator passengers are not facing forward, as we typically would expect to find them, but instead are all facing to one side of the elevator. Looking confused, the man nonetheless enters the elevator and joins the rest of the elevator passengers in facing the side wall; the doors close.

This episode makes fun of our inclination to conform to behaviors exhibited by others. When examined under Funt's comedic lens, conformity behaviors become laughable, in part because we are so familiar with the feelings expressed by the man entering the elevator. Most of us can identify with a sense of discomfort or tension resulting from being different somehow from the prevailing opinions or behaviors of those around us. We may experience a need to "go along with the group" rather than take an uncomfortable or solitary position. Despite an inner voice that tells us we should stand facing forward in elevators, we choose to turn to the side like everyone else.

Impression management theory, which tells us that people will deliberately behave in ways designed to convey a desired impression to others, suggests that these conformity behaviors are a type of impression management. In our work lives, we are often required, like actors, to play many different roles depending upon the situation. In an effort to please our audiences, we may find ourselves behaving in ways that may or may not agree with our inner dispositions. The identities we choose to present may be dictated by organizational pressures to fit in, or they may result from an effort to present ourselves as the kinds of persons we perceive will be rewarded by the organization. This conformity may demand myriad impression management behaviors, such as choice of dress (adopt the organizational uniform), comments at meetings (support the winning side), or voiced opinions (agree with the boss).

Some conformity behaviors may occur simply because people agree with those around them. A person may, for example, like the way the people in his or her group dress, and therefore choose to dress that way also. A person may also agree with the opinions expressed by the majority of the members in his or her group, and therefore express those same opinions. However, sometimes people may choose to conform to group behaviors or opinions even when they do not personally agree with those behaviors or opinions. In other words, they will conform outwardly, but inwardly they do not.

Researchers have made a strong distinction between these two kinds of conformity behaviors. They describe the first kind of conformity, in which individuals conform both outwardly and inwardly, as *informational conformity*, and the second kind, in which individuals conform only outwardly, as *normative conformity* (Deutsch & Gerard, 1955). Laboratory experiments suggest that people will tend toward informational conformity in ambiguous situations. If we find ourselves in situations in which we do not know how to behave, or what to think, we will look to people around us for guidance (Sherif, 1936). Thus we conform to reduce ambiguity.

Normative conformity was displayed in some of the best-known conformity experiments, now commonly referred to as the Asch experiments. Solomon Asch (1956) designed a situation that was clearly unambiguous in order to study the effect of group conformity on individual behaviors. His laboratory situation consisted of a group of six confederates and one subject who were asked to judge whether a standard line matched one of three comparison lines that varied in length. What was not known to the subjects, however, was that the confederates had been told by Asch to give the wrong answer. Thus the subjects were placed in the uncomfortable position of having to give their own judgments regarding the line-matching task after listening to five or six of the confederates agree on the wrong answer. In Asch's experiment the majority of the subjects changed their responses to fit the group responses.

Clearly, the subjects in this experiment were displaying impression management behaviors when they chose to conform their opinions to the group consensus. Although the correct answer was unambiguous and obvious, the subjects chose to present a public image of agreement rather than give an answer that they personally believed to be true.

Is Conformity a Social Disease?

For many people during the 1960s and 1970s, conformity was a dirty word. Those nonconformist individuals who flaunted the rules of society, who did their own thing, were idealized and, in some instances, "heroized" by many youthful members of society. Conformity, on the other hand, was viewed as a negative behavior, often equated with personal weakness.

While conformity may receive less attention in the media today than it did 20 years ago, nonconformity remains an American tradition. Now that we have reached the 1990s, conformity may continue to be equally distasteful to some individuals. As a society, we value individualism and the uniqueness of our personal contributions to our work and home environments. We are taught to voice our opinions and to behave in ways that reflect our own personal values. In the business world, keen competition for organizational rewards suggests that conforming behavior may not be appropriate for employees determined to stand apart from their peers (Maccoby, 1978).

However, despite the generally negative connotations given to conforming behaviors, a second perspective on conformity also has to be considered. That perspective would suggest that since virtually all social interactions are driven by a need for social approval, conformity can be considered to be an acceptable, or at least a common, social behavior. In other words, we want to be liked, we want to feel included within a group social situation, and we will act in ways that make us appear attractive to others (Byrne, 1969). Thus impression management through conforming behaviors is simply a normal part of social intercourse.

Individual Reactions to Norms of Conformity

Researchers in the field of impression management suggest that self-presentations may be either *sincere presentations*, in which the managed public impression is in agreement with internal values and objectives, or *insincere presentations*, in which the public impression is in conflict with privately held values and goals (Leary & Kowalski, 1990). In other words, insincere presentations occur when individuals adopt roles and behaviors that match or conform to those of people around them, but those behaviors are not a reflection of their inner dispositions.

Similarly, the dual characteristic of conformity as both a normal result of social interaction and a carefully considered self-presentation implies that a distinction can be made between conformity motivated by a sincere desire to fit into a group and conformity as an insincere behavior designed to make us appear to fit in, even though our internal values may be in conflict with our conforming behavior, in order for us to accomplish some ulterior goal. Most of us realize subconsciously that fitting in, or being attractive to others, is often the first step we can take toward gaining influence over those other people (Blackburn, 1981; Ralston, 1985). Further, a distinction can also be made between nonconformity resulting from a true inability to meet group behavioral standards (but as a sincere expression of personal values) and nonconformity as a political tactic designed to make us separate and distinct from our colleagues in an attempt to gain social influence power (Moscovici, 1976).

Using the individual's intentions (sincere/insincere) and the individual's level of conformity to organizational values (high/low) in a 2×2 classification scheme of self-presentation behaviors allows us to examine four styles of conformity. These four conformity styles are depicted in Figure 13.1.

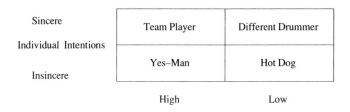

	High	Low
Sincere	Team Player	Different Drummer
Individual Intentions		
Insincere	Yes–Man	Hot Dog

Figure 13.1. Individual Styles of Conformity

Team Player. Some individuals conform to group or organizational standards out of a sincere desire to be part of that group or organization, or out of a strong sense of identification with the group and its goals (Cartwright & Zander, 1968). Thus they dress in the corporate uniform, adopt corporate values, and behave in organizationally encouraged ways because their reason for conforming is not driven by a desire to manipulate the system, but by a desire to be an integral and contributing part of that system. These individuals can be referred to as Team Players because that is how they perceive themselves—as part of the corporate team. The team's successes are their successes, and the team's failures are their failures.

Yes-Man. Insincere conformity, often considered to be a form of ingratiation, includes conforming self-presentation behaviors such as voicing opinions that agree with those of one's superiors, adopting attitudes or values that may be situationally appropriate but inconsistent with personal value systems, or following organizationally prescribed behaviors for personal benefit (Jones, 1964). Yes-Men differ from Team Players in that the conforming behavior of a Yes-Man is perceived to lead to a secondary outcome, some form of personal gain, whereas the Team Player sees identification with the organization as the ultimate outcome of conformity.

The Yes-Man may perceive that organizational success depends upon building strong interpersonal connections with powerful individuals in the organization (Mechanic, 1962), thus this person's self-presentation behavior can be characterized by a conscious, deliberate plan to appear attractive to those powerful individuals by adopting similar traits, attitudes, or behaviors.

Different Drummer. The third conformity mode is characterized by sincere nonconforming behavior. Those who fit this category, as the name suggests, "march to the beat of a different drummer." These individuals deliberately choose not to follow many relevant organizational norms as an expression of their personal value system. While Different Drummers may embrace core organizational values, they do not wish to conform to many of the less critical organizational norms (Schein, 1968). Therefore, Different Drummers may choose to dress or behave in an organizationally nonconformist fashion, but they will still maintain a personal goal orientation that is supportive of organizational values. Different Drummers may be the committee members who consistently act as devil's advocates. They may be the subordinates who question organizational decisions, or who aggressively promote changes in the system for the good of the organization.

Hot Dog. The organizational Hot Dogs also choose to follow a nonconformist path, but their choice is a political decision designed to bring them greater personal rewards than conforming behavior might. By refusing to conform, Hot Dogs try to present a powerful, unique image to those around them. Hot Dogs rely on their expertise as a power base (French & Raven, 1959), or on well-developed interpersonal skills to ingratiate themselves with those around them (Ralston & Elsass, 1989). In fact, without a strong base in some area, the Hot Dog's nonconformist behavior may not be tolerated by organization members.

Individuals who can create a positive impression of themselves based on their past behaviors will accumulate "idiosyncrasy credits" and as such a favorable disposition by others toward themselves (Hollander, 1958). Accumulation of enough of these credits will allow the Hot Dog to deviate from group norms without suffering rejection or negative repercussions. Consequently, for example, the extent to which a Hot Dog is allowed to express nonconforming behaviors publicly may be a function of his or her perceived value to the organization.

Hot Dogs like attention and perceive a direct link between the attention derived from being bold, different, and aggressive and increased social influence. Like Yes-Men, Hot Dogs see their behavior as leading to something they want. While Yes-Men choose to gain influence through conformity, Hot Dogs see nonconformity as the path to that end.

Finally, to be as inclusive as possible, a fifth conformity mode might be labeled Social Outcasts. This relatively small group of individuals may simply not be capable of adopting the requisite conforming behaviors. They may lack the monitoring skills necessary to identify those behaviors. They may be intellectually or emotionally unable to conform to organizational values that do not match their own. They may not have the material ability to adopt the organizational uniform. For any number of reasons, some individuals simply do not fit in. The Social Outcasts differ from the Different

Drummers or the Hot Dogs in that they may feel a need to belong to the group in question, they may want to be an integral part of the group, but they are rejected by the group for their inability to conform to the group norms. In contrast, the Different Drummers and Hot Dogs are quite capable of following group norms, but choose not to do so.

Organizational Implications of Conformity

From the preceding discussion of conformity modes, it is clear that the act of conforming to organizational norms is a means of impression management that may be considered either a social act or a political act. It therefore is important that organizations understand the types of conforming behaviors that occur within their confines, and what they might do to encourage those behaviors they see as preferable. What can an organization do to encourage wanted or desired forms of conformity (for example, a Team Player or a Different Drummer), while at the same time discouraging negative or threatening forms of conformity (such as the Yes-Man or the Hot Dog)?

Since the nature of the conforming behavior of organization members may be the deciding factor as to which types of conformity are beneficial or detrimental to organizational effectiveness, we first need to examine how conformity is learned and rewarded. In other words, where does conformity come from? Once we know how conformity is learned, we can then begin to understand why people choose the types of conformity they do.

National Culture, Organizational Culture, and Organizational Conformity

National Culture

Conformity behaviors to a large degree are shaped by the culture of a country. Since all cultures will try to perpetuate themselves by teaching and maintaining behavioral standards, valued behaviors will be rewarded by society and by entities within society, such as business organizations. Very simply, conformity behaviors are learned and rewarded much as any other culturally dictated behaviors are. In Western cultures, such as the United States, individualism is an accepted, and even cherished, value. The result is that individual nonconformity is considered acceptable to a much greater degree in U.S. companies than in Japanese companies, where collectivism rather than individualism is the norm. In effect, the national culture defines the parameters in which most corporate cultures reside.

Corporate Culture

Organizational researchers tell us that conforming behaviors are intricately tied in with the rituals and experiences that define organizational cultures. Sometimes referred to as the "soul" of an organization, organizational culture can be described as being all those beliefs, expectations, philosophies, and unwritten rules and regulations that make up the underlying structure of organizational life (Deal & Kennedy, 1982). When organizational newcomers "learn the ropes," they are learning the dimensions of organizational culture, from informal pecking order to corporate jargon. When individuals who deviate beyond the culturally acceptable lines of conformity are punished, organization members quickly learn the boundaries of deviation that they may not cross without repercussions.

Like national cultures, corporate cultures been shown to be relatively stable, unchanging phenomena (Kilmann, Saxton, & Serpa, 1986). Individual players may come and go, but the culture tends to live on. Further, the degree to which cultures remain stable is linked directly to the existence of conforming impression management on the part of the organizational members. Those conforming behaviors can be considered both a requirement and a result of organizational culture (Pascale, 1985). A high level of conformity may be a requirement of an organizational culture where acceptance and practice of organizational values and culturally prescribed behavior are required for membership (Schein, 1968). However, being a nonconformist also may be acceptable to or may conform to the culture of some other organization. The point is that different organizations have different needs, and that organizations need to look at their own specific needs before determining what appropriate levels of conformity are for them.

Positive and Negative Consequences of Conformity

To determine the appropriate level of conformity for a given organization, it may be helpful to view conformity behavior as a continuum, running from low levels of conformity to high levels of conformity. Analyzing the polar ends of the continuum should provide a better picture of the positive and negative aspects of conformity behavior.

Low Levels of Conformity

Both positive and negative consequences occur at the low end of the conformity continuum. Low levels of conformity may lead to increased creativity within the organization (Schein, 1968). Different perspectives can be brought to bear on decisional issues, and lack of prescribed approaches and responses to problems can result in enhanced problem-solving capabilities. In fact, some managers, such as Jack Welch of General Electric, encourage aggressive and argumentative communication styles among organizational members. Meetings at General Electric are loud and confrontational (Mitchell, 1987). Peters and Waterman (1982), in their best-selling book, *In Search of Excellence*, also underline a blunt and aggressive approach to management. They note that excellent companies are marked by an intense form of communication in which organizational members are encouraged to voice their own opinions and make their marks on organizational decisions.

However, low levels of conformity may also be linked to low levels of cohesiveness and increased levels of interpersonal conflict (Moscovici, 1976). While such conflict may also encourage creativity and innovation, it may have very strong negative consequences for the individuals in an organization who are caught in the emotional web of interpersonal conflict, or who may not be able to disassociate ideological conflict from personal conflict. In addition, the low levels of cohesiveness linked to low levels of conformity may have a strong effect on general employee job satisfaction. Low morale, absenteeism, tardiness, and low levels of efficiency may be an indirect result of low levels of cohesiveness and the lack of a general sense of organizational community binding members together.

High Levels of Conformity

The positive and negative effects of high levels of conformity lie in direct opposition to those cited for low levels of conformity. Top-level managers may feel it is better able to rely on managers who exhibit attitudes, values, attire, and behavior similar to their own (Beer, Spector, Lawrence, Mills, & Walton, 1984).

Conformity may also lead to enhanced interpersonal relationships, a sense of cohesiveness or team spirit, and increased potential for communication (Peters & Waterman, 1982). In other words, a high level of conformity may yield a kind of camaraderie binding organizational members together when true compatibility or cohesiveness does not exist.

However, if individuals cease conforming, that camaraderie may fall apart rapidly. For example, Baumeister (1989) describes the "Boss's Illusion" (p. 65), which occurs when the boss perceives of employees as being similar to him or her when the subordinates are actually simply mimicking the boss. They may, for instance, deliberately try to present themselves as athletic individuals if the boss is an athlete. If they should stop mimicking the boss, however, he or she may feel betrayed by the perceived hypocrisy of the subordinates.

As noted, organizational innovation and creativity may suffer from excessive conformity. Groupthink, a decision-making phenomenon that occurs as a result of group members' obeying group dictates to agree rather than to consider and evaluate problem dimensions adequately, leads to a lack of consideration of all available information and alternatives and consequent poor decisions (Janis, 1972). Further, when conformity is rewarded, risk taking may be discouraged. Therefore, innovative ideas, new solutions to old problems, or changes in organizational direction may be routinely squelched by dictates of conformity.

Determining the Optimal Level of Conformity

Clearly, for every organization there may be an optimum level of conformity, a balance between the advantages of low conformity, which allows individuals to take risks and encourages innovation, and the advantages of high conformity, which allows the organization to control and maintain organizational policies, processes, and structures. It is, essentially, a balance between the need to be creative and adaptive in order to meet the needs of a dynamic environment and the need to keep the status quo in order to provide stability and group survival. Therefore, we can look at organizations in terms of this balance. The optimum balance between the need to be creative and flexible and the need to maintain behavioral consistency will be influenced by the environmental forces facing the organization.

Research by organizational theorists suggests that effective organizational structures reflect the environments in which they operate (e.g., Burns & Stalker, 1961). For example, stable environments, in which market demands are fairly unchanging and consistent, products firmly established, and distribution channels well developed, should call for mechanistic, or bureaucratic, organizational structures (Burns & Stalker, 1961). Organizations operating in stable environments will find that the need to maintain a consistent and effective organizational response to market demands will override the need for innovation or entrepreneurial activities. Consequently, high levels of conformity may be required in these organizations. Organizational conformity is necessary for maintaining a consistency of output as well as a smoothly run, functionally interdependent operation in which conflict is minimized and efficiency is maximized.

Conversely, organic organizations exist when the market forces are dynamic and turbulent (Burns & Stalker, 1961). Due to the instability of their environments, these organizations must place a heavy emphasis on maintaining flexibility and encouraging innovation and creativity. Seeking out new niches in ever-changing markets, pushing the boundaries of new technologies, and developing and selling products with short life cycles are necessary activities in dynamic environments. Therefore, organic organizations can benefit from the presence of nonconformists who bring new perspectives to organizational problems and are willing to take risks, as well as think and act independently.

Organizational theorists also suggest that the inability of organizations to match their structures to their environments can lead to ineffective management practices and possible organizational failure (Burns & Stalker, 1961; Lawrence & Lorsch, 1967). Organic organizations operating in stable environments may suffer from inefficient and costly excesses of communication and managerial interactions. Similarly, a mechanistic organization operating in a dynamic environment may also suffer due to the inability of the organization to respond to environmental changes in an effective and timely manner.

Therefore, a high level of individual conformity in a dynamic environment may be fatal to an organization. Organizations in which consensual decision making is the rule and conformity to the majority of opinions is required for personal survival may have organizationwide experiences of groupthink and the rejection of unfamiliar or untried ideas (Janis, 1972). Creative or innovative ideas may find it impossible to flourish in a high-conforming environment. Conversely, low levels of conformity in a stable environment may be equally threatening. Lack of a unified approach to organizational tasks may lead to costly excesses and general inefficiencies.

Matching Conformity Styles to Organizational Needs

Once an organization has determined the level of conformity most appropriate to its situation, the question of how to encourage beneficial conformity behaviors while discouraging detrimental ones can be addressed. The following discussion focuses on two critical aspects of that question. First, how do mechanistic organizations encourage high-conforming behaviors and organic organizations encourage low-conforming behaviors? Second, how can organizations discourage individuals from insincerely trying to fit the conformity needs of the organization?

Attaining and Institutionalizing the Desired Conformity Level

Attaining the desired level. Selecting the right people is extremely important in matching individual conformity levels to organizational needs. It is the process of selection that leads to the choice of organizational players. More often than not, organizational selection processes deliberately seek out those individuals perceived as being best able to "fit" the needs of the organization, a process that includes matching prospective employees to desired values, behaviors, or backgrounds (Sathe, 1983). Mechanistic organizations may deliberately try to seek out high-conforming individuals, for example, while organic organizations may seek out nonconformists.

Further, research clearly suggests that selection (and promotion) decisions are often made for political reasons, and managers are often likely to promote individuals whom they perceive to be similar to themselves (Beer et al., 1984). If the managers are politically cognizant, they may feel that by selecting similar individuals, or individuals in their own image, they are, in essence, stacking the deck in their own favor. For instance, conservative managers in mechanistic organizations may shy away from hiring individuals who do not fit the organizational mold, or who may threaten the status quo.

At the same time, prospective employees will self-select those organizations with which they feel most comfortable. For example, Team Players and Yes-Men may self-select the mechanistic organization as being the kind of environment in which they are, respectively, most comfortable or best able to manipulate to their own advantage. Different Drummers or Hot Dogs may self-select more organic organizations, on the assumption that the mechanistic structures either would not allow them to express their independence or might not reward (or tolerate) their nonconforming behaviors.

Institutionalizing the desired level. The different levels of desired conformity can be reinforced through formal and informal organizational processes that define acceptable behaviors. For example, within stable environments, the primary organizational challenge becomes one of production efficiency, minimization of overhead expenses, and the streamlining of internal processes and procedures. Not surprisingly, mechanistic organizations rely heavily on conformity to attack those organizational challenges. Consistent conforming behavior is achieved through a heavy emphasis on standard operating procedures, lack of ambiguity in task requirements, and a functional orientation in job structure. Lines of communication are hierarchical and strongly defined. Risk taking is not encouraged, and often it is discouraged. Reward systems, promotional systems, and performance measures are based on the ability of individuals to conform to organizational expectations as defined and communicated by detailed organizational manuals and hierarchical directives as well as the informal cultural pressures.

In contrast, decision making in organic organizations, which tends to take place at lower organizational levels than in mechanistic organizations, must be aimed at solving the unique problems caused by the turbulence of the environment. Therefore, a high level of organizational conformity is not desirable in the organic organization. Instead, conflict, or decision-making processes ruled by dissension and debate, is encouraged. As such, the organic organization structure is marked by interdependence among organizational members, a shared community of interest and task responsibility, vertical and horizontal lines of communication, and a strong cultural emphasis on commitment to the organizational task as well as development of individual expertise.

Encouraging Sincere Conformity

Discouraging insincere conformity behavior is a more difficult task than acquiring the appropriate level of conformity. Individuals embrace a particular style of conformity that may or may not be sincere from the perspective of the organization, and when these individuals are interpersonally skillful, it can be difficult to differentiate between sincere and insincere behavior. However, organizations do have means to influence which style of conformity (e.g., Team Player or Yes-Man) succeeds within their boundaries. For many organizations, the critical issue may be the amount of political, self-serving behaviors they allow to occur.

Political behaviors will have negative impact on the organization primarily through their influence over the types of decisions made in the organization.

When decisions are made based upon subjective criteria (for example, when individuals are promoted due to their conforming behavior), formal control systems and organizational effectiveness can be seriously compromised. Similarly, when the decisions themselves are part of the conforming behavior (such as when improper recommendations are made simply to "go along with the boss"), organizational functioning is impaired. It has been suggested by many researchers that if organizational members see political behavior expressed by their peers, or their superiors, and if that behavior is rewarded, they will assume a perceived legitimacy for their own political behavior (e.g., Jones, 1964). In other words, we learn vicariously from those around us, and if we see our colleagues getting some desired reward as a result of their "fitting in" with members of the organization who control those rewards, then conformity, be it insincere, is learned (Bandura, 1977). Therefore, if conformity itself is perceived as a political activity, and political activities are seen as a legitimate form of social influence, then a norm of conformity for the sake of self-serving goals is encouraged.

Clearly, the organizational reward system will also influence the degree to which cultures demand compliance to behavioral norms as well as the kinds of behavior, political or social, that are encouraged. For example, are promotions and salary-increase decisions made on the basis of objective, performance-related measures? Or are they based on subjective measures of hierarchical standing? Further, what are the standards for performance based upon? Do we measure the ability of organizational members to conform to the narrowly defined contexts of their job descriptions, or do we measure performance against a more ambitious, entrepreneurial model? Does the organizational system allow members to make mistakes, to take risks? Or are they punished for such activities? It does not take long for word of one episode of punished risk taking to spread through the organizational grapevine and for employees to learn vicariously not to make waves.

Summary

Conformity is a subtle yet important approach to impression management. Within the workplace, we need to understand how individuals use conformity to influence the views of others. Specifically, we need to learn more about what causes individuals to adopt different approaches to conformity. We need to know when conformity is good and when it is bad.

As for now, it is important to recognize that high or low conformity can be either good or bad. Situational variables such as market characteristics can indicate whether we should encourage or discourage high conformity or low conformity in behavior. We need to recognize that individuals will differ in their conforming behaviors, and that some styles of conformity are self-serving behaviors that can be detrimental to an organization. Organizations need to be aware of the possible detrimental effects of insincere conformity behavior. And, finally, we need to acknowledge that different conforming behaviors may be organizationally encouraged as much as are individual traits.

References

Asch, S. E. (1956). Studies of independence and conformity: A minority of one against a unanimous majority. *Psychological Monographs, 70*(9, Whole No. 416).

Bandura, A. (1977). *Social learning theory.* Englewood Cliffs, NJ: Prentice-Hall.

Baumeister, R. F. (1989). Motives and costs of self-presentation in organizations. In R. A. Giacalone & P. Rosenfeld (Eds.), *Impression management in the organization* (pp. 57-72). Hillsdale, NJ: Lawrence Erlbaum.

Beer, M., Spector, B., Lawrence, P. R., Mills, D. Q., & Walton, R. E. (1984). *Managing human assets.* New York: Free Press.

Blackburn, R. S. (1981). Lower participant power: Toward a conceptual integration. *Academy of Management Review, 6,* 127-131.

Burns, T., & Stalker, G. M. (1961). *The management of innovation.* London: Tavistock.

Byrne, D. (1969). Attitudes and attraction. In L. Berkowitz (Ed.), *Advances in experimental psychology* (Vol. 4). New York: Academic Press.

Cartwright, D. P., & Zander, A. F. (1968). *Group dynamics, research and theory.* New York: Harper & Row.

Deal, T. E., & Kennedy, A. A. (1982). *Corporate cultures: The rites and rituals of corporate life.* Reading, MA: Addison-Wesley.

Deutsch, M., & Gerard, H. G. (1955). A study of normative and informational social influence on individual judgment. *Journal of Abnormal and Social Psychology, 51,* 629-636.

French, J., & Raven, B. (1959). The bases of social power. In D. Cartwright (Ed.), *Studies in social power.* Ann Arbor: University of Michigan Press.

Hollander, E. P. (1958). Conformity, status, and idiosyncrasy credit. *Psychological Review, 65,* 117-127.

Janis, I. L. (1972). *Victims of groupthink.* Boston: Houghton Mifflin.

Jones, E. E. (1964). *Ingratiation.* New York: Appleton-Century-Crofts.

Kilmann, R., Saxton, M., & Serpa, R. (1986). Issues in understanding and changing culture. *California Management Review, 28*(2), 87-94.

Lawrence, P., & Lorsch, J. W. (1967). *Organization and environment: Managing differentiation and integration.* Homewood, IL: Irwin.

Leary, M. R., & Kowalski, R. M. (1990). Impression management: A literature review and two-component model. *Psychological Bulletin, 107,* 34-48.

Maccoby, M. (1978). *The gamesman.* New York: Simon & Schuster.

Mechanic, D. (1962). Sources of power of lower participants in complex organizations. *Administrative Sciences Quarterly, 7*, 349-364.

Mitchell, R. (1987, December 14). Jack Welch: How good a manager? *Business Week*, pp. 92-98.

Molloy, J. T. (1978). *Dress for success*. New York: Warner.

Moscovici, S. (1976). *Social influence and social change*. London: Academic Press.

Pascale, R. (1985). The paradox of "corporate culture": Reconciling ourselves to socialization. *California Management Review, 27*(2), 26-41.

Peters, T. J., & Waterman, R. H., Jr. (1982). *In search of excellence: Lessons from America's best run companies*. New York: Harper & Row.

Ralston, D. A. (1985). Employee ingratiation: The role of management. *Academy of Management Review, 10*, 477-487.

Ralston, D. A., & Elsass, P. M. (1989). Ingratiation and impression management. In R. A. Giacalone & P. Rosenfeld (Eds.), *Impression management in the organization*. Hillsdale, NJ: Lawrence Erlbaum.

Sathe, V. (1983). Implications of corporate culture: A manager's guide to action. *Organizational Dynamics, 12*(2), 5-23.

Schein, E. H. (1968). Organizational socialization and the profession of management. *Sloan Management Review, 9*(2), 1-16.

Sherif, M. (1936). *The psychology of social norms*. New York: Harper & Row.

PART VI

Impression Management: Looking to the Future

14

Future Directions

Toward a Model for
Applying Impression Management Strategies
in the Workplace

MARK J. MARTINKO

The prior chapters have provided excellent suggestions for the use and application of impression management in a wide range of organizational contexts including the exit interview, career management, gender effects, the management of conflict, productive negotiations, maintenance of organizational justice, the performance appraisal process, corporate communications, and the development and management of organizational culture. The purpose of this chapter is to consider future directions for impression management by focusing on practical issues surrounding the implementation of impression management in work settings. In order to achieve this objective, an overall model for applying impression management in work settings is proposed and key questions and issues regarding the application of the model are explored. The chapter ends with a summary of issues critical to both the further development and application of impression management strategies in organizations.

A Model for Application

The recent attention afforded to the impression management process has resulted in a number of theoretical models designed to help researchers explain, interpret, and understand the impression management process (e.g., Gardner & Martinko, 1988b). However, the current literature does not appear to provide a model to guide practitioners in the process by which they select and implement impression management strategies in everyday work situations. In view of this need, the model presented in Figure 14.1 is proposed.

The model draws upon the literature from impression management and, in particular, the Gardner and Martinko (1988b) model, but also on the literature from the areas of behavior management (e.g., Luthans & Kreitner, 1985; Luthans & Martinko, 1982, 1987) and behavior self-management (Mans, 1986; Mans & Sims, 1980, 1986). While it is recognized that many IM behaviors may be unconscious and unintentional, the proposed model views IM as a systematic and purposive process of behavior self-management that is both conscious and intentional. The first step in the process is a systematic assessment of situational, audience, and individual characteristics. The information from this assessment is then used to inform the selection of appropriate impression management goals. After goals are identified, the most appropriate tactics for achieving the impression management objectives are selected. These tactics are then executed and the reactions of the audience are evaluated. If the goals have not been successfully achieved, the situation is reassessed and goals and tactics are altered. At the outset it is recognized that although the model depicts a linear and sequential decision process, the actual process is typically more interactive. Thus, for example, one may have already formed preliminary goals before assessing the situation. In order to represent the interactive nature of the typical impression management process, feedback loops depicting the major interactions have been included throughout the model. In the following sections, the details of implementing each of the various steps in the IM model are discussed.

Step 1: Assess the IM Situation

The assessment of the impression management situation includes the evaluation of three major components of the impression management setting: (a) the organizational environment, including its physical, cultural, and task characteristics; (b) the audience; and (c) the individual. While most managers conduct such assessments informally and unconsciously, the following information should help managers in developing more purposeful and accurate assessments of their situations.

The Organizational Environment

In general, managers need to consider the major components of their organizational environments before deciding on their specific impression management goals. These three components and the major considerations regarding these components are as follows.

The physical setting. Physical settings provide many of the props for impression management performances and determine, to some extent, which types of performances may be considered legitimate. A behavior such as slapping a person on the back is differentially acceptable depending on whether the setting is the person's office, the back-slapper's office, the company cafeteria, a company softball game, the factory floor, or a bar after work. Thus each impression management attempt should be considered within its physical context and managers must evaluate the effects different settings may have on their own behavior. As suggested by Ornstein (1989), managers may alter the decor in their offices to create conditions conducive to specific impressions and should be aware of the IM implications and attempts suggested by the decor of other people's offices.

The importance of the physical setting is illustrated by the practice of most athletic team coaches of taking their players to the field the day before or on the afternoon of a game. Similarly, it may be beneficial for a manager to view the site of an important meeting or speech prior to the event, particularly if he or she is unfamiliar with the setting.

Culture. Thorough knowledge of an organization's culture is a prerequisite of effective IM behaviors. As suggested by the work of Schein (1985), culture may be manifested at three levels: overt behaviors and artifacts, values, and implicit assumptions. Effective impression managers should become familiar with the norms for behavior within an organization as well as the meaning of the various symbols and artifacts. Thus, for example, white shirts and ties are a reputedly critical part of the culture of IBM, making the norms for dress at IBM different from those of other electronic firms. Similarly, norms for dress differ in educational, manufacturing, and service industries. More important, these norms are related to the different types of behavior considered acceptable in these different types of organizations. Clearly, impression management goals, efforts, and successes will differ depending on the different natures of these types of organizations. Thus knowledge of an organization's culture is an important prerequisite of IM

Step 1: Assess the IM Situation
    Consider:
        The Organizational Environment
- Physical Setting (e.g., office, playing field)
- Culture
    — observable behaviors and artifacts
    — underlying values, norms, and assumptions
    — information suggested by symbols, stories, history, myths, heroes, dress, and nationality
- Nature of the task (e.g., ambiguity, product vs. service, etc.)

    The Audience
- Novelty versus familiarity
- Appropriateness as an IM target
- Experience/knowledge
- Power
- Attractiveness

    The Individual
- High versus low self-monitor
- Self-esteem
- Self-efficacy
- Attractiveness
- Status

Information Sources: annual reports, public relations information, direct observation, participant information, financial directories, managerial and psychological assessments.

Outcome: An explicit statement of the major organizational, audience, and personal characteristics related to credible and successful IM attempts.

Step 2: Identify and Prioritize IM Goals
    Consider :
- The Pareto principle
- Perceptual Mapping
- Satisficing

Outcome: A written set of the specific outcomes desired, specifying the corresponding target impressions.

Figure 14.1. A Practitioner's Guide to the Impression Management Process

Step 3: Select the Appropriate IM Tactics
Consider :

- Self-promotion, intimidation, supplication, ingratiation, and exemplification
- Verbal self-presentational behaviors of self-description, organizational description, opinion conformity, accounts, apologies, acclaiming, other enhancement, and rendering favors
- Nonverbal behaviors such as eye movement and posture, artifactual displays such as dress, and office decor
- Third-party tactics such as a trusted friend or a public relations firm
- Other tactics including setting and announcing high goals and the indirect tactics of blurring, blaring, burying relations, and establishing connections
- Issues of validity and credibility

Outcome: A written plan detailing the specific tactics to be used to achieve the desired impressions. The plan should include specific cues for key performances as well as scheduled times for rehearsal.

Step 4: Produce of Specific IM Behaviors
Consider:

- Scheduling, strength, and appropriateness of each performance
- Cues for IM performances
- Rehearsal and practice, both physical and mental
- Modelling outstanding performers

Outcome: Production of specific IM behaviors.

Step 5: Assess Audience Reactions and Personal Outcomes
Consider:

- Feedback systems such as performance appraisals, sales reaction forms, TV ratings, and teacher evaluation forms
- Incentive modification
- Feedback from mentors, coaches, and counselors

Outcome: A written assessment of audience impressions and the personal outcomes of these impressions.

Step 6: Maintain or Modify Goals and/or Tactics
Consider:

- Continuous adjustments
- Assistance by mentors, bosses, or others

Outcome: Successively approximate goals and impressions.

success and will likely differentiate successful job applicants and managers who receive promotions from their less successful counterparts.

Underlying the observable aspects of organizational environments are the values and assumptions of the cultures. Identifying these values and assumptions and incorporating them into the development of impression management goals and tactics should lead to higher levels of success. As suggested by Gardner and Martinko (1988b), organizational policies, symbols, history, myths, stories, dress, and communication patterns often provide information regarding an organization's culture. Failure to recognize or consider culture will undoubtedly lead to unsuccessful IM attempts that lack credibility. Thus, for example, a "tough guy" image may be appropriate in a law enforcement agency but detrimental in a social service organization.

From a broader perspective, in Chapter 11 of this volume Bond suggests that differences in regional, ethnic, and national cultures impose important parameters on IM behaviors, particularly for individuals in multinational business situations. Noting cultural differences and their meanings is a prerequisite of effective IM in unfamiliar settings.

Nature of the task. The nature of the task is often closely interwoven with the culture of the organization. Thus, for example, police organizations, social service organizations, educational institutions, and manufacturing organizations all have substantially different missions and operations for achieving their goals. Consequently, they have very different cultures and norms. Task knowledge and familiarity are critical in assessing IM situations and defining IM goals.

As suggested by Ferris, King, Judge, and Kacmar in Chapter 3 of this volume, ambiguous tasks and situations are often the breeding ground for political behavior. Recognizing ambiguous environments and the opportunities they create can be an important step toward more effective impression management.

The audience. Several aspects of audiences, such as novelty, are particularly relevant in determining IM goals and strategies. Novel audiences are more often the target for self-descriptions than are familiar audiences (Gardner & Martinko, 1988a). Thus it would appear that novel audiences may be somewhat more impressionable than familiar audiences. Examples of novel audiences include interviewers, classmates on the first day in a freshman dorm, and the meeting of unfamiliar people at cocktail parties. These types of audiences and situations are breeding grounds for both successful and unsuccessful impression management incidents.

Another crucial issue is the identification of the appropriate target audience. Too often, individuals fail to identify the proper targets for their IM attempts. For example, all too frequently in university systems young assistant professors identify their deans and department chairs as the targets for their IM attempts, and ignore their colleagues both within and outside of their institutions. These assistant professors realize far too late that it is a vote of their peers rather than their department chair's evaluation that determines both their promotion and tenure. As another example, in Chapter 8 Wall indicates that negotiators often have to manage the impressions of three different audiences: their competitors, their competitors' organizations, and their own organizations. These different audiences all suggest different IM goals and tactics. Thus the proper identification and assessment of the targets for IM attempts can be crucial determinants of organizational success.

Other relevant characteristics of audiences that should be considered in a thorough assessment of the impression management environment include the audience's experience, power, status, and attractiveness. All of these variables are related to the types of impressions that may be considered legitimate and viable.

While the majority of the information regarding target audiences is generally gathered by direct observation, managers should not overlook other sources of information such as formal surveys, annual reports, stories from the media, and the observations of their peers.

The individual. Characteristics of individuals not only influence the types of goals that are attractive but also place constraints on the types of performances that are possible and credible. Self-monitoring abilities appear to be critical. As suggested by the literature, high as opposed to low self-monitors appear to be more aware and capable of manipulating their performances to achieve specific IM goals (Snyder & Copeland, 1989). Other personal characteristics such as self-esteem, self-efficacy (belief in one's ability to accomplish specific IM goals), personal attractiveness, and relative status all appear to be related to IM goals and behaviors. Knowledge of these characteristics is thus important in concluding which types of IM tactics can be produced with credibility.

Mans and Sims (1986) discuss a variety of self-observation techniques such as developing observation forms and personal checklists to monitor behavior. In addition, there are a variety of psychometric scales measuring attributes such as self-esteem and self-monitoring.

The end result of the situational assessment should be an explicit, preferably written, account of the major organizational, audience, and personal characteristics that are related to effective IM performances.

Step 2: Identify and Prioritize Goals

The literature on goal setting clearly indicates that individuals with specific and challenging goals outperform those with no goals or goals that are general and easy to achieve. Goals differ depending upon one's assessment and evaluation of the situation. As Ferris et al. note in their chapter, impression management goals differ in selection and performance evaluation processes. Similarly, Wall notes that goals may differ depending upon the targets for impression management behaviors. There are two major objectives for this second step of the IM process: the identification of relevant goals and the prioritization of key goals.

Goal Identification

Typical IM goals suggested by the literature include the needs to be seen as desirable, attractive, competent, powerful, knowledgeable, pitiful, conforming, nonconforming, and a team player. Knowledge of the organizational setting, audience, and personal characteristics should suggest goals that are personally relevant. Several popular books on time management and management by objectives provide guidelines for establishing goals (e.g., LeBoeuf, 1979). Most important, the initial goals should be specific, challenging, and defined in terms of observable outcomes. After defining outcomes, it is important to identify the exact impression that will be necessary to achieve the designated outcomes. Thus, for example, a negotiator may decide on a particular level of settlement that she believes will be reasonable and will create a solid, long-term relationship between her company and its work force. This goal might require that she be perceived by the union negotiating team as tough but fair. Thus the end product of this part of the process should be a list of desired outcomes with the corresponding impressions that will be required.

Prioritization of Key Goals

The Pareto principle suggests that 20% of our goals account for 80% of our effectiveness. The objective of this phase of the process is to prioritize goals and focus only on the 20% that will achieve maximum effectiveness.

As suggested above, there are frequently multiple audiences, settings, and situations that result in conflicting goals. There are several techniques for prioritizing goals. The first is a simple priority list. Goals are evaluated in terms of their importance in achieving the objective and their congruence with the individual's personality. Eighty percent of the goals are culled until only the key goals remain.

Another potential technique for analyzing goals is called *perceptual mapping*. Borrowed from the area of marketing, this is a statistical technique that places perceptions for two or more products on a two-dimensional space in order to compare their similarities, differences, and position of a new product. Perceptions of different cultures or audiences could be compared in a similar fashion to determine appropriate positioning for managerial impresions.

A final useful concept for prioritizing goals is Herb Simon's (1945) notion of "satisficing," which recognizes multiple and often conflicting goals. Thus the objective of the goal-setting process is to develop a path that provides reasonable attainment of all goals by sacrificing the maximization of specific goals. Politicians often use this strategy, failing to develop optimal solutions for any specific constituency but succeeding in not offending anyone. Obviously, this approach is most necessary when impressions are consumed by multiple audiences. In cases where there is a clear definition of the audience and the motives of the audience are relatively uniform, specific goals designed to optimize impressions will be most appropriate.

Regardless of whether one selects IM goals that will maximize specific objectives or satisfice multiple objectives, the end result of this stage should be an explicit statement of the desired end results and the corresponding impressions required to achieve the results. These clear and specific goals set the stage and provide the direction for specific tactics.

Step 3: Select Appropriate IM Tactics

There has been considerable attention devoted in the literature to identifying and describing specific IM tactics. Jones and Pittman (1982), for example, identify the tactics of self-promotion, intimidation, supplication, ingratiation, and exemplification, which correspond to objectives to be perceived as competent, dangerous, pitiful, attractive, and morally worthy, respectively. Similarly, Gardner and Martinko (1988a) describe the verbal self-presentational behaviors of self-description, organizational description, opinion conformity, accounts, apologies, acclaiming, other enhancement, and rendering favors, all of which can be used to accomplish a variety of IM goals and objectives. Other IM behaviors described by Gardner and Martinko (1988a) include nonverbal behaviors such as eye movement and posture, artifactual displays such as dress and office decor (i.e., purposely modifying the stage for performances), and alternative tactics such as using a third party (e.g., a trusted friend or a public relations firm) to communicate the desired image. Still other tactics suggested by the chapters in the current text include setting and announcing high goals (Ferris et al.) and the indirect tactics of blurring, blaring, burying relations, and establishing connections as described by Cialdini (1989).

The key to this third step of the IM process is matching the IM goals from the second step with the appropriate IM tactics. The two major considerations in this process are credibility and effectiveness. Credibility is concerned with whether or not IM attempts are perceived by the target audience as believable and valid. Effectiveness is concerned with the issue of whether or not an IM attempt creates the desired image. Thus, for example, an apology may be believable and credible but still be ineffective because it underscores and accentuates a poor image rather than resulting in the target's attributing the actor's behavior to external circumstances. Rosencrantz and Guildenstern from Shakespeare's *Hamlet* provide haunting images of ingratiation attempts that are neither credible nor effective. While the research gives some guidance regarding standards for effective and credible IM attempts, it would appear that audience feedback and the monitoring of that feedback are the best assurance regarding the appropriateness of specific tactics. Often, such feedback will be almost immediate and spontaneous. While high self-monitors may be somewhat more astute in reading and reacting to feedback than low self-monitors, conscious awareness of goals and audience feedback should increase the IM effectiveness of all managers.

Step 4: Production of Specific IM Behaviors

Once IM goals and tactics have been selected, the fourth step in the process is implementation of the tactics. As suggested above, primary guidance for the scheduling, strength, and appropriateness of the various tactics will come from audience feedback. The current research literature is somewhat limited in the amount of direct guidance that can be provided at this stage, although several good guidelines for implementation emerge from the behavioral self-management literature (Mans, 1986; Mans & Sims, 1980, 1986), including the notions of cuing, rehearsal, and incentive modification. Taken from the behavior modification literature, cues are antecedent conditions that set the stage for behavior. The process of implementing IM tactics can be facilitated and managed by developing a specific repertoire of cues for IM performances. Thus, for example, if one consciously identifies Monday-morning meetings as cues for IM tactics, it will facilitate both the planning and delivery of IM tactics. Thus managers should identify specific observable and measurable cues to alert themselves that they are "on stage." Other typical cues for IM performances could be the morning ride in the elevator, an airplane ride with the boss, and the company picnic. Thinking through such situations further may generate even more specific cues. Thus the appearance of the waiter at an important dinner may cue a specific performance if one has identified it as a cue beforehand and planned a specific tactic. Without planning and cue recognition, the appearance of the waiter might result in a very disorganized and poor impression.

Another important aid to implementation is rehearsal. Just as stage performances are rehearsed, important IM attempts should be rehearsed, at least mentally. Mental rehearsal of performance appraisal interviews, entry and exit interviews, and other types of verbal self-presentations will undoubtedly enhance potential for success, particularly if one is cognizant of the specific goals and impressions desired.

A final suggested aid to implementation is modeling. Robbins (1986) suggests that the most efficient way to become an expert in any field is to identify the peak performer and systematically model that person's behavior. Thus if one wants to become an excellent golfer, one models the best player available. A thorough approach would include learning about and imitating the model's mental approach to the game, practice habits, swing, game preparation procedures, and equipment. Within an organizational context, if one wants to be perceived as competent, one finds and models the star performer in terms of behavior, dress, personal habits, hobbies, life-style, education, and so forth. Thus one can literally become what one imitates.

The end result of this step is a written plan detailing the specific tactics to be used to achieve the desired impressions. The plan should include specific cues for key performances as well as scheduled times for rehearsal.

Step 5: Assess Audience Reactions and Personal Outcomes

Successful IM attempts require constant assessment of audience reactions and feedback. Some examples of feedback systems that have been designed to evaluate IM attempts include television ratings, customer sales reaction forms, and teacher reaction forms. In jobs where feedback is not easily accessible, the actor may have to design his or her own incentive modification program. In Chapter 2 of this volume, Dov Eden suggests the use of mentors as accurate sources of feedback. One may also solicit the aid of trusted colleagues, counselors, and bosses as additional sources of feedback. Moreover, since the outcomes of IM attempts are often experienced long after the attempts themselves, incentive modification plans may be particularly beneficial. Thus contriving one's own reward system, provided that it accurately rewards appropriate IM behavior, may be critical in the management of both self and others.

Step 6: Maintain or Modify Goals and/or Tactics

The last step is dependent on the assessment of outcomes and audience reactions from the prior step and is the maintenance or modification of IM goals and/or tactics. This process is represented by both the last step in the model and the feedback loops in Figure 14.1. Several aspects of this part of the process are worth noting. First, as suggested by the feedback loops, the process is often ongoing and interactive. Thus one may be modifying goals and tactics during the course of a specific IM attempt. However, it may also be a fairly formal and systematic process, as in the case of modifying the strategies of a candidate running for office. Second, this process may be conducted by an individual or assisted by other persons such as mentors, drama coaches, or campaign managers. Finally, the process should be viewed in terms of successive approximation. The process of image-making is always in a state of flux, requiring constant participation and adjustments by both the actor and the audience. It is only through the process of constant refinement and adjustment that one develops the ability consistently to convey credible impressions that result in effective outcomes.

Future Directions

This chapter and this book are initial attempts to provide more specific guidance to practitioners for IM applications within organizational settings. Given that significant interest in IM within organizational contexts has emerged only within the last 10 years, there is a relative paucity of systematic IM research as well as reliable guidance for practitioners. Thus the recommendations that have been provided are tentative. However, recognizing the lack of systematic IM research in organizations should not lead to the inference that we know very little about IM. As the chapters in this volume demonstrate, the IM process is an integral part of organizational life, and many successful practitioners execute effective IM strategies and tactics every day. Given the pervasiveness, frequency, and observability of IM processes, it would seem that our ability to understand IM from an organizational perspective can advance rapidly if we pursue several different but related directions.

Qualitative Research

IM research appears to offer an unusual opportunity to bridge the often-lamented theory/practice gap. If ever a topic was amenable to qualitative field research, impression management is. More specifically, it would appear that practitioners can provide a rich source of data for understanding the IM process. Direct observation, in-depth interviews, and self-observation studies (Martinko, 1988) all have the potential for yielding information and suggesting hypotheses that might take years to tease out in laboratory situations. It should be noted that this call for a more ethnographic and qualitative approach to fieldwork does not ignore or discount the need for controlled testing of hypotheses in laboratory and field settings. Much work is needed under controlled conditions in order to validate the many hypotheses that have already been suggested. On the other hand, it is suggested that progress may be much more rapid if qualitative approaches are used.

Archival Data

Many impression management attempts in organizations are formally recorded. Thus, for example, there are usually written records of board meetings and important speeches. Annual reports, which are often systematic impression management attempts, are often available to the public and contain a wealth of systematic information intended to convey specific impressions of organizations. In addition, with the recent increased availability of audiovisual equipment, many fairly routine communications in organizations are documented and readily available. Security systems record a considerable number of typical communication transactions in organizations. These data sources offer a tremendous opportunity for research on impression management tactics and strategies. Some interesting questions amenable to archival research include the following: How do IM tactics differ in annual reports when companies have had particularly profitable versus unprofitable years? Do IM tactics used by individuals during board meetings differ as a function of position, status, or gender? How do individuals' IM tactics differ when they are addressing employees versus the general public? Are status and dress related to the IM tactics employed by salespersons? Clearly, the wealth of archival data available in organizations offers a rich opportunity for field research on impression management.

Multidisciplinary Research

It would also seem that other fields have much to contribute to the study of IM in organizations. Practitioner-oriented fields such as public relations, drama, communication, marketing, political science, and speech are all concerned with purposeful attempts to impress particular types of audiences. One particularly interesting area in the field of communications is that of neurolinguistic programming (Robbins, 1986), which is concerned with the relationship between mental processes and physical behaviors. For example, there appears to be some evidence that eye positions relate to cognitive functioning. Thus eye positions may differ depending upon whether a person is trying to recall information or experiencing an emotional reaction. Similarly, information about emotional states may be provided by posture. Depressed individuals are typified by downcast eyes, slumped shoulders, and slow movement. Systematic training in reading such audience cues would obviously enable better IM tactics. Moreover, it may be that purposeful cue production can result in more credible and effective performances by managers.

As Goffman (1959) originally suggested, there are many parallels between the drama of real life and the disciplines of theater and drama. Just as there are producers, set directors, and casting directors for theatrical performances, these same roles and functions are often present in real-life performances. Likewise, the elements of effective and credible IM attempts in work settings are undoubtedly similar to the elements of effective and credible theatrical performances. Thus, given the relative longevity of the disciplines and practices of theater and drama, it would seem that both the theory and practice that have evolved in these disciplines have potential for enriching IM theory and practice.

No doubt a closer examination of all of the above disciplines would yield information that would assist in both understanding the IM process and training managers to become more effective in this process.

Specific Issues

There are also numerous specific issues related to the IM process that, if addressed, could lead to more effective IM tactics and strategies. Some of the more salient issues, along with some suggestions for pursuing their resolutions, are discussed below.

Plasticity. The issue of plasticity is concerned with the malleability of behavior. Those favoring a trait approach would argue that behavior is not very changeable and malleable. They would suggest that effective IM performances are the result of natural talent and that it is naive to believe that managers can be trained to become better IM managers through aids such as the present book and the model suggested above. Those arguing that IM behavior is plastic, malleable, and changeable would support the notion that managers can be trained to become better IM managers and would support the development of theory and models of the IM process. Most people's experience and intuition would suggest that there is merit to both positions.

A more subtle reflection of the above distinction is concerned with the degree to which IM attempts are purposeful, conscious, and goal oriented versus naturally occurring. A corollary issue is concerned with the degree to which one may change from unconsciously staged to consciously staged impressions. Clearly, the answers to these questions are critical to the future of IM as a discipline and suggest a challenging agenda for research. As indicated above, it would seem that qualitative field research could provide many preliminary answers to these questions and suggest fruitful hypotheses that will result in expanding the knowledge base rapidly. More controlled experimentation for validation should follow.

Perception versus behavior. Another issue that needs attention is the basic nature and definition of impression management. From a scientific perspective, data need to be observable and measurable. Since impressions are perceptions, they are not directly observable and measurable and thus offer many challenges for research. Impressions are most often measured by questionnaires or by subjects' behavioral reactions to some specific stimuli. Again, it would seem that more qualitative approaches to research would offer the most rapid guidance in understanding the situational cues associated with IM and the processes of creating and managing impressions. The fact that impressions are not directly observable and measurable suggests that more traditional research methods may not be as fruitful, at least at the initial stages of inquiry. A more qualitative and phenomenological approach such as suggested by Morgan and Smircich (1980) may be more amenable to describing the process by which we create the socially constructed realities referred to as impressions.

Credibility. The credibility of IM attempts should also be addressed. As suggested by Feldman and Klich in Chapter 4 of this volume, inappropriate and self-interested use of IM behavior may result in inauthentic behavior and interpersonal relations, ultimately compromising the standards of excellence in organizations. Some key questions with regard to credibility are concerned with the recognition of credible versus phony impressions by audiences, the specific cues and behaviors associated with credible IM, and the mechanisms by which individuals monitor the credibility of their performances. Again, it is anticipated that qualitative fieldwork may be the most efficient way to generate preliminary answers to these types of questions.

Ethics. The question of ethics is suggested by several of the contributors to this volume. Feldman and Klich suggest that some individuals are more concerned with the impressions they create than with their overall effectiveness. Bond implies that the different values and environments of different cultures affect the norms for effective, credible, and ethical IM behaviors. Where does one draw the line in terms of the ethical use of IM strategies and techniques? Should researchers adopt any particular guidelines regarding the dissemination of the information on IM? To what extent is there a danger that research in this area may result in encouraging IM that is counterproductive for both organizations and society? While Velasquez, Moberg, and Cavanagh (1983) suggest ethical guidelines for organizational politics, and Moberg (1989) has discussed the application of these guidelines to IM, there is no consensus regarding the ethical uses of IM. Obviously, the ethical implications of IM research and applications need additional attention.

Training. The above model and research suggest that, at least to some degree, impressions can be consciously managed. At this point, however, theories of IM do not appear to have had a direct contribution to the training and development of intentional impressions. While there are a number of popular books suggesting IM tactics (e.g., Gray, 1982; Molloy, 1978; Ringer, 1976), the information in these books is often unsystematic and atheoretical, providing no framework for either theory or training. On the other hand, there are a variety of programs that train people to make specific impressions in areas such as speech, drama, interviewing, and career planning. Yet, for the most part, these programs do not incorporate explicit theories of the IM process.

It is anticipated that as the area of IM develops, there will be more interchange between IM theory and training practices. Certainly, current theory may benefit from the study of contemporary training practices. Likewise, it is anticipated that insights developed through IM theory can make substantial contributions toward more effective IM training.

Self-monitoring. The notion of self-monitoring is related to many of the above issues and deserves additional attention. Of particular interest are questions concerning the ethics, purposiveness, plasticity, and effectiveness of high versus low self-monitors. Snyder and Copeland's (1989) review of the self-monitoring research suggests that self-monitoring is related to job preferences, job search processes, career knowledge, success in boundary-spanning roles, and leader emergence. These authors conclude, however, that neither the high nor the low self-monitoring style is unilaterally superior in terms of occupational success. Situational conditions influence and determine the relative efficacy of the different styles. As Snyder and Copeland suggest, much more remains to be done if we are to comprehend fully the relationships among self-monitoring, IM behaviors, and organizational prcesses.

Demographics. There are also a number of interesting IM research issues relating to demographics. For example, are males versus females more or less susceptible to IM or more likely to engage in IM behaviors? Are there differences in the types of IM behaviors that are considered credible for males versus females or blacks versus whites? Are there differences in the credibility of excuses and accounts related to gender or cultural origin? In the area of age, several interesting questions relate to whether IM strategies change over time. Are IM strategies related to organizational level, and do the criteria for credible IM behaviors differ depending on the status and organizational level of the actor? The answers to all of the above should lead to both better theory and better practice, enabling more credible and effective impressions.

Conclusions

As suggested above, the area of IM is fertile ground for the development of both theory and applications that should result in more effective manager and leader behavior. The concept is readily observable and well grounded in everyday practitioner behaviors. It is anticipated that both theory and practice can and will advance rapidly, particularly if researchers move toward more qualitative research orientations and more systematically observe the IM process in its natural setting. The knowledge and experience of effective practitioners offers a rich source of data for enhancing both theory and practice.

A view of the future suggests both theory and models that provide more explicit guidance for selecting and implementing IM strategies and tactics. It is hoped that the chapters presented in this volume provide the beginnings of a foundation enabling managers to convey more candid, direct, and credible impressions of their true intentions resulting in enhanced individual and organizational effectiveness.

References

Cialdini, R. (1989). Indirect tactics of image management: Beyond basking. In R. A. Giacalone & P. Rosenfeld (Eds.), *Impression management in the organization* (pp. 45-56). Hillsdale, NJ: Lawrence Erlbaum.

Gardner, W. L., & Martinko, M. J. (1988a). Impression management: An observational study linking audience characteristics with verbal self-presentations. *Academy of Management Journal, 31*(1), 42-65.

Gardner, W. L., & Martinko, M. J. (1988b). Impression management in organizations. *Journal of Management, 14*, 321-338.

Goffman, E. (1959). *The presentation of self in everyday life*. Garden City, NY: Doubleday.

Gray, J., Jr. (1982). *The winning image*. New York: AMACOM.

Jones, E. E., & Pittman, T. S. (1982). Toward a general theory of self-presentation. In J. Suls (Ed.), *Psychological perspectives on the self* (pp. 231-262). Hillsdale, NJ: Lawrence Erlbaum.

LeBoeuf, M. (1979). *Working smart*. New York: McGraw-Hill.

Luthans, F., & Kreitner, R. (1985). *Organizational behavior modification and beyond*. Glenview, IL: Scott, Foresman.

Luthans, F., & Martinko, M. J. (1982). Organization behavior modification: A comparison between academician and practitioner perspectives. *Journal of Organizational Behavior Management, 3*(3), 33-50.

Luthans, F., & Martinko, M. J. (1987). Behavioral approaches to organizations. In C. L. Cooper & I. T. Robertson (Eds.), *International review of industrial and organizational psychology* (pp. 35-60). Englewood Cliffs, NJ: Prentice-Hall.

Mans, C. C. (1986). Self-leadership: Toward an expanded theory of self-influence processes in organizations. *Academy of Management Review, 11*, 585-600.

Mans, C. C., & Sims, H. P., Jr. (1980). Self-management as a substitute for leadership: A social learning theory perspective. *Academy of Management Review, 5*, 361-367.

Mans, C. C., & Sims, H. P., Jr. (1986). Leading self-managed groups: A conceptual analysis of a paradox. *Economic and Industrial Democracy, 7*, 141-165.

Martinko, M. J. (1988). Observation methods. In S. Gael (Ed.), *Job analysis handbook for business and industry* (pp. 419-431). New York: John Wiley.

Moberg, D. J. (1989). The ethics of impression management. In R. A. Giacalone & P. Rosenfeld (Eds.), *Impression management in the organization* (pp. 171-187). Hillsdale, NJ: Lawrence Erlbaum.

Molloy, J. T. (1978). *Dress for success*. New York: Warner.

Morgan, G., & Smircich, L. (1980). The case for qualitative research. *Academy of Management Review, 5*, 491-500.

Ornstein, S. (1989). Impression management through office design. In R. A. Giacalone & P. Rosenfeld (Eds.), *Impression management in the organization* (pp. 411-426). Hillsdale, NJ: Lawrence Erlbaum.

Ringer, R. J. (1976). *Winning through intimidation.* Greenwich, CT: Fawcett.

Robbins, A. (1986). *Unlimited power.* New York: Ballantine.

Schein, E. (1985). *Organizational culture and leadership: A dynamic view.* San Francisco: Jossey-Bass.

Simon, H. A. (1945). *Administrative behavior.* New York: Free Press.

Snyder, M., & Copeland, J. (1989). Self-monitoring processes in organizational settings. In R.A. Giacalone & P. Rosenfeld (Eds.), *Impression management in the organization* (pp. 7-19). Hillsdale, NJ: Lawrence Erlbaum.

Velasquez, M., Moberg, D. J., & Cavanagh, G. F. (1983, Autumn). Organizational statesmanship and dirty politics: Ethical guidelines for the organizational politician. *Organizational Dynamics*, pp. 65-80.

Name Index

Subject Index

About the Authors

D. Neil Ashworth (Ph.D., University of South Carolina) is a Professor of Management Systems and currently serves as Associate Dean of the E. Claiborne Robins School of Business, University of Richmond. Prior to joining the UR faculty, he held teaching appointments at the University of Mississippi and the University of South Carolina. He has also served as a Visiting Professor in the Graduate School of Management, University of Queensland, Australia. His primary areas of interest are organizational behavior and human resources management.

H. John Bernardin is University Professor of Research in the College of Business at Florida Atlantic University. He received his doctorate in industrial-organizational psychology from Bowling Green State University in 1976. He is coauthor, with R. W. Beatty, of *Performance Appraisal: Assessing Human Behavior at Work* (Kent, 1984) as well as more than 50 empirical articles on the subject of performance appraisal. His consulting experience is extensive and includes such areas as performance appraisal, turnover, personnel selection, and compensation systems.

Robert J. Bies (Ph.D., Stanford University) is Associate Professor of Management, School of Business Administration, Georgetown University. His research focuses on the delivery of bad news, account giving, procedural justice, and legalistic influences in organizations. His research has appeared in *Communication Research, Academy of Management Journal, Academy of Management Review, Research in Organizational Behavior,* and *Research on Negotiations in Organizations.*

Michael Harris Bond was born in Toronto, Canada, where he received a transplanted public school education from teachers with British accents. His cultural confusion was reinforced by trips to Quebec, where he heard a euphonic language and saw people drinking wine at lunch. His fate was sealed when he was enchanted by another foreigner, Edwin Hollander, whose television programs on social psychology were beamed across the border from Buffalo. Subsequent travels took him to exotic cultures, like California, where he received his Ph.D. from Stanford University in 1970. His appetite for the extraordinary thus whetted, he continued going West as a young man until he arrived in the Far East, where he has now reached middle age teaching psychology at the Chinese University of Hong Kong. His most recent act of cultural hubris was writing *Understanding the Chinese People* for Oxford University Press.

Gabriel F. Buntzman (Ph.D., University of North Carolina) has been associated with the Management Department of Western Kentucky University since 1983. His publications include articles in the *International Journal of Conflict Management, Journal of Psychology,* and *Psychological Reports,* as well as contributions to three books: *Managing Conflict: An Interdisciplinary Approach* (1989), *Theory and Research in Conflict Management* (1990), and *Effective Management in Nursing* (3rd edition, in press). His current research interests focus on relationships among ethics, strategies, and conflict management.

Dov Eden is Associate Professor of Management at Tel Aviv University's Leon Recanati Graduate School of Business Administration, and Director of the Israel Institute of Business Research. A member of the Academy of Management, the American Psychological Association, the Israel Psychological Association, and the Israel Association for Labor Relations, he has authored many articles on management and organizational behavior and consulted on executive development with some of Israel's leading industrial and public sector organizations.

Priscilla M. Elsass is finishing her Ph.D. in organizational behavior at the University of Connecticut. She teaches at Clark University in Worcester, Massachusetts. Her areas of research interest include occupational stress, careers, and the role of affect in organizational processes.

Don E. Eskew (M.A., psychology, Kansas University, 1986) is a doctoral candidate in human resources management/organizational behavior at the Ohio State University. His research interests include organizational justice, recruitment/selection, and performance appraisal.

Daniel C. Feldman (Ph.D., Yale) is Professor of Management and Business Partnership Foundation Fellow at the University of South Carolina College of Business Administration.

Gerald R. Ferris (Ph.D., business administration, University of Illinois, Urbana-Champaign) is Professor of Labor and Industrial Relations and of Business Administration at the University of Illinois at Urbana-Champaign. He has also served on the Department of Management Faculty at Texas A&M University. His research interests are in the areas of interpersonal and political influence in organizations, performance evaluation, and strategic human resources management. He has published in such journals as *Journal of Applied Psychology, Organizational Behavior and Human Decision Processes, Personnel Psychology, Academy of Management Journal*, and *Academy of Management Review*. He is author or editor of *Strategy and Human Resources Management*; *The Employment Interview: Theory, Research, and Practice*; *Method and Analysis in Organizational Research*; *Personnel Management*; and *Human Resources Management: Perspectives and Issues*. He serves as editor of the annual series *Research in Personnel and Human Resources Management* and is consulting editor for the *South-Western Series in Human Resources Management*. He has consulted on a variety of human resources topics with companies including ARCO, Borg-Warner, and PPG, and he has taught in numerous management development programs in both the United States and Greece.

Robert A. Giacalone is Associate Professor of Management Systems at the E. Claiborne Robins School of Business, University of Richmond. He was named one of the Outstanding Young Men in America in 1985, and was named in *Who's Who in the South and Southwest* in 1990. He has been a consultant to both the private and public sectors and has been actively involved as an academic consultant to the publishing industry. He is coeditor (with Paul Rosenfeld) of *Impression Management in the Organization* (Lawrence Erlbaum, 1989) and has authored papers on the role of impression management in organizational life. His work has appeared in *Human Relations, Business and Society Review, Journal of Business Ethics, Group & Organization Studies,* and *Journal of Social Psychology,* as well as a variety of other journals. In addition to his work on impression management, he has actively researched the areas of business ethics, organizational sabotage, and exit interviewing.

Jerald Greenberg (Ph.D., I/O psychology, Wayne State University, 1975) is Professor of Management and Human Resources, and Director of the Doctoral Program in Organizational Behavior at the Ohio State University. He is a Fellow of both the American Psychological Association (Division 14, SIOP) and the American Psychological Society, as well as a member of the Society for Organizational Behavior. Professional honors he has received include a Fulbright Senior Research Fellowship (1980), the OB Division's New Concept Award (1986), and the Pace Setter's Research Award from OSU's College of Business (1989). He has been an active member of several professional editorial review boards, including the *Journal of Applied Psychology* and *Organizational Behavior and Human Decision Processes.* He is the author of more than 80 publications, including *Behavior in Organizations* (3rd edition), with Baron, and *Controversial Issues in Social Research Methods,* with Folger. He has been on the faculties of Case Western Reserve University and Tulane University, and was a Visiting Professor at the University of California, Berkeley.

Timothy A. Judge is Assistant Professor, Department of Personnel and Human Resource Studies, and Center for Advanced Human Resource Studies, New York State School of Industrial and Labor Relations, Cornell University. He received his Ph.D. from the Institute of Labor and Industrial Relations, University of Illinois at Urbana-Champaign. He also holds an M.A. degree from the University of Illinois and a B.B.A. from the University of Iowa. His research interests include the role of disposition in human resources management, fit in the staffing process, antecedents and consequences of withdrawal and adaptive behaviors, and influence behavior in organizations.

K. Michele Kacmar is Assistant Professor of Management in the School of Management at Rensselaer Polytechnic Institute. She received her Ph.D. in management from Texas A&M University. Her current research interests include organizational staffing and the use of impression management by job applicants and organizational decision makers in the employment process.

Thomas R. King is an Instructor in the Department of Management and Quantitative Methods, Illinois State University. He is currently completing requirements for his Ph.D. from the University of Illinois, Urbana-Champaign. His dissertation title is "The Reestablishment of Organizational Legitimacy in Cases of Corporate Misconduct." His research interests focus on the macro areas of organizational politics: legitimacy and the management of meaning. He has received honors in undergraduate teaching and is active in the Organizational Behavior Teaching Society. He has also taught management development classes at companies such as State Farm Insurance.

Nancy R. Klich (Ph.D., University of Florida) is Assistant Professor of Organizational Behavior at the University of North Carolina at Charlotte.

Stephen B. Knouse (Ph.D., Ohio State) is Professor of Management at the University of Southwestern Louisiana. He has published in a number of journals, including *Personnel Psychology, Personnel,* and the *Journal of Business Ethics.* His current research interests are in impression management in human resources management activities, equal opportunity issues, and business ethics. He is coediting a book, *Hispanics and Work,* to be published by Sage Publications.

Laurie Larwood is Dean of the College of Business Administration at the University of Nevada, Reno. She is coeditor of the Sage Publications series *Women and Work* and the author or editor of 10 books in the fields of women in management, technology, career development, and organizational behavior. She has chaired the Academy of Management's Women in Management Division, as well as two other divisions, and is former editor of *Group & Organization Studies.* Prior to obtaining her Ph.D. in psychology at Tulane, she was president of a manufacturing firm in California.

Mark J. Martinko is a Professor of Management at Florida State University. His research has focused on the observation of leader behaviors, impression management, learned helplessness, and performance management. He is the coauthor of two books and more than 40 research articles. He has conducted numerous workshops in the United States and abroad, and is a regular presenter for the Walton Institute and trains Wal-Mart store managers in the areas of leadership and performance management. He served two consecutive terms on the editorial board of the *Academy of Management Review* and is currently a member of the editorial boards of the *Journal of Organizational Behavior Management* and *Organizational Dynamics*. He also serves on the Board of Governors of the Southern Management Association.

M. Afzalur Rahim is Professor of Management at Western Kentucky University. He holds B.Com. and M.Com. (Dacca, Bangladesh), M.B.A. (Miami, Ohio), and Ph.D. (Graduate School of Business, University of Pittsburgh) degrees. He teaches courses on organizational behavior, strategic management, and management of organizational conflict. He is the author of more than 65 articles and book chapters, five cases, and three research instruments on conflict and power. He is the editor of the *International Journal of Conflict Management* and the *International Journal of Organizational Analysis*. He is the founder of the International Association for Conflict Management and President of the International Conference on Advances in Management.

David A. Ralston has been Associate Professor of Management and Organization at the University of Connecticut since 1981. Currently he is serving a two-year appointment as Visiting Lecturer at the Chinese University of Hong Kong. He received his D.B.A. degree in 1981 from Florida State University. His research interests include impression management, international management, and flextime.

Paul Rosenfeld has been a Personnel Research Psychologist at the Navy Personnel Research and Development Center in San Diego, California, since 1986. Previously, he was an Assistant Professor of Psychology for four years at the Pennsylvania State University in Erie. He received his bachelor's and master's degrees in psychology from Queens College of the City University of New York and his Ph.D. in social psychology from the State University of New York at Albany. He is coeditor of *Impression Management in the Organization* (Lawrence Erlbaum, 1989), with Bob Giacalone, and coauthor of *Introduction to Social Psychology* (West Publishing, 1985), with Jim Tedeschi and Svenn Lindskold. He has written nine introductory psychology ancillaries for Random House and McGraw-Hill publishing companies and has published more than 20 scholarly articles/book chapters related to impression management theory in professional journals and edited books. He is also currently editing *Hispanics and Work* (with Steve Knouse and Amy Culbertson), which will be published by Sage in 1992. In addition to his current duties for the U.S. Navy, he is an adjunct faculty member at the

California School of Professional Psychology in San Diego, where he teaches graduate seminars in social psychology and attitude formation and measurement.

Gail S. Russ is an Assistant Professor of Management and Quantitative Methods at Illinois State University. She received her B.A. degree in psychology from the University of North Carolina at Wilmington, her M.A. degree in social psychology from the College of William and Mary, and her Ph.D. in management from Texas A&M University. Her current research interests focus on organizational communications, symbolic management, organizational legitimacy, and influence processes, and her research has been published in such journals as *Management Communication Quarterly* and *Human Resource Planning.*

Peter Villanova is an Assistant Professor of Psychology at Northern Illinois University. He received his Ph.D. in industrial-organizational psychology from Virginia Polytechnic Institute and State University in 1987. He has authored a number of papers on performance appraisal that have appeared in both journals and textbooks, and he has served as a consultant to organizations in the areas of performance appraisal, turnover, and the design of incentive systems.

James A. Wall, Jr., is Professor and Chair of the Department of Management in the College of Business and Public Administration, University of Missouri, Columbia. He received an A.B. from Davidson College and an M.B.A. as well as a Ph.D. from the University of North Carolina. Before assuming his position at Missouri, he was Associate Professor at Indiana University. He is the author of *Negotiation: Theory and Practice* (1985) and *Bosses* (1987). His research articles on negotiation and mediation have appeared in *American Journal of Trial Advocacy, Journal of Applied Psychology, Journal of Conflict Resolution, Journal of Dispute Resolution, Journal of Experimental Social Psychology, Journal of Personality and Social Psychology, Judicature,* and *Organizational Behavior and Human Decision Processes.*